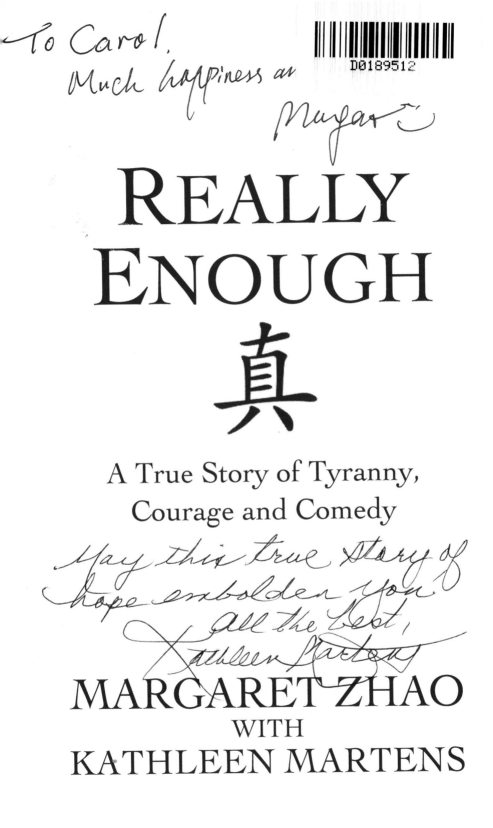

To Carol,
Much happiness an

Margar—

REALLY
ENOUGH

真

A True Story of Tyranny,
Courage and Comedy

May this true story of
hope embolden you
all the best,
Kathleen Martens

MARGARET ZHAO
WITH
KATHLEEN MARTENS

Copyright © 2012, Margaret Q. Zhao and Kathleen L. Martens

All Rights Reserved. No part of this book or the related files may be reproduced or transmitted in any form, by any means, electronic, photocopying, recording, or otherwise, without the prior written permission of the authors.

ISBN: 0985689889
ISBN-13: 9780985689889
Library of Congress Control Number: 2012918457
CreateSpace Independent Publishing Platform
North Charleston, South Carolina

Our special thanks and gratitude to:

Kristen J. Sollee, Editing
Jean K. Aziz, Reader
Marissa Mossberg, Graphic Design

Note to Reader: With the exception of the immediate Zhao family members, the names of the characters have been changed to respect privacy.

TABLE OF CONTENTS

*To avoid revealing information that may give away story outcomes, Margaret Zhao's current biographical information, her blog, and a fascinating gallery of family and historic photographs can be found at www.ReallyEnough.com.

DEDICATIONS

I dedicate my story to all of the people who helped me to ride the undulating back of my life's dragon—the gentle Ogres, my siblings, especially, my daughter, and most importantly, Wang Upright Justice, the tigress who was my Mother. I send my encouragement and hope to you, the reader, in reaching for your unimaginable dreams.

Margaret Q. Zhao

I dedicate this book to Margaret Qin Zhao, the remarkable person whose life story, indomitable spirit, and uplifting sense of humor informed this profound writing process. My heartfelt love and gratitude go to my husband, Steuart, for his patience in listening to chapter after chapter, and for his tears and laughter, which kept me inspired.

Kathleen L. Martens

A LETTER FROM MARGRET ZHAO

Dear Reader:

Without wanting to reveal any details that will spoil this true story for you, I cannot resist sharing the evolution of this book. At a social event in 2010, I casually shared a few of my childhood experiences. My stories drew instant interest from Kathleen Martens, a witty and magnetic woman in the group. I discovered that she was a writer who had lived, worked, and traveled throughout Asia in the seventies and eighties, part of the same period in which my story took place. The immediate connection we made led to the magical collaboration that brought my story to life.

We came from two dramatically different backgrounds, yet she amazed me with her uncanny ability to sweep my feelings directly from my heart into her elegant words and to catch the subtleties of the Chinese culture. Creating Really Enough: A True Story of Tyranny, Courage and Comedy was a profound and spiritual journey that took us from laughing until we lost our speech to crying until we had to stop, opening the blossom of my memories growing up in rural China in the time of Chairman Mao.

Kathleen translated the nuance of every memory, captured the spirit of each character, and helped me fulfill my long-time dream of using my life story to entertain and inspire. Together, we gave voice to those who in their time could not speak and breathed life into the people whom I wished to honor from my past.

The creative process we experienced in writing the book was reward enough, but sharing it with you, the reader, with the hope of inspiring your life, makes it even more rewarding.

With gratitude,

Margaret Q. Zhao

THE TITLE CHARACTER
REALLY

真

The Chinese character that you see in our book title is called Zhen. The "Zh" sound is pronounced like the "ds" in the word "hands," or "Dsen." Zhen means really, truth, authentic, and sincere. It also has a special meaning to me that you will discover only when you read the book. If you study this character, you can see that the top looks like a cross, which is the Chinese word for "ten" The middle rectangular section means "eyes." Look closely and you will see that the square is like an eye with three eyelashes. The bottom section has two legs walking. Together these symbols say:

With ten eyes watching, what one sees is real, true, authentic, and sincere.

Really!

CHAPTER 1
RECALLING THE FALL

"For the people!" they shouted as the men in shoes, like a long line of ants, carried more of our dwindled possessions away. There were too many shoes for me to count, shoes that unthinkably stayed on their feet, walked on our shiny wooden floors, shuffled angrily, moved too fast to be polite—so unlike the slow walk Mother taught us. "You have three days to leave this house." Their unkind words echoed in the high ceilings, calling to Father as though he were a lowly dog. I watched them through the cutouts in Mother's precious blue and white porcelain stool that stood beside her favorite chair. Their rough movements and their harsh voices stopped my playful hiding game, choked my giggles, made me small and silent.

Two feet came dangerously close to my secret place to draw another note upon the wall above me. I pulled deeper under the chair's seat and pressed my hot cheek against the cool blue dragon that danced around the side of Mother's treasure. They spread out rolled-up papers and slashed more characters on the walls that I could not read.

"Tear down this wall," one man muttered. The sudden buzzing with lowered voices and heads together made me quiver even more. I heard them slap and paste the paper mark on our door as they left—the mark that Mother threatened to claw off, the mark that made Mother and Father tilt toward each other in a way I had never seen before, red face to red face.

After the men with dirty shoes came to sadden our carved red door, I hid beneath Mother's favorite chair listening to my parents' voices rising up and growling down.

"Ignorant! Ignorant! Don't they understand we are *not* Landlords? We were only a hard-working business family." Mother looked at Father with squinted eyes. "You tell them this is a mistake! You lost your grandfather's legacy. Now save the only thing we have left—our home," she said.

"I am sorry our days of wealth are long gone," Father said, "but there is no fighting this. At least our losses had some benefit."

"I should be happy you managed to squander our fortune with your foolery long ago?" Mother said.

"It did save our lives, after all," Father said.

"This is how you justify your past?" Mother answered, moving toward the door. "I will strip down this vile mark. They will not evict us from our home. You did everything wrong. Now you have a chance to get one thing right."

Father stepped closer to calm her, the raging red centipede scars twitching on his face and down his neck. Mother gave him a warning look that even I, as a child of barely four, understood.

"We have no grounds to argue," he urged. "We should have left three days ago, the day the mark was first placed. Your defiance may cost us more than our home," he pleaded weakly, enraging her more.

"I will go to the officials to explain this horrible mistake myself, if you have no dragon in you. They gave us the classification themselves over ten years ago. They announced it to us in front of this entire village: 'Under the new laws, your family is classified, Gong Shang Ye Jian Di Zhu, 'Industrial Business Owner with a lesser classification of Landlord.' You heard them! With that classification, they had no right to confiscate our factory. We did not even argue when they asked us to relinquish it to the people to shelter the victims of the flood. We cooperated, and this is our thanks?"

"We were fortunate. Others lost their lives, and—" Father's words were interrupted by Mother's passionate anger.

"Fortunate? Oh yes, I have not forgotten their words: 'Only through the generosity of Chairman Mao may you stay here.' It was so generous to allow us to starve in our own glorious home, left only with antiques and books to eat and no means of earning a living! I should be grateful our children were born into this luxury, heirs to this legacy of loss." Her sarcastic tone stung, and Father stepped back.

Mother turned, slid back the wooden bolt, and pulled open one of the heavy double doors. I saw one-half of the men's rudeness stuck on our beautiful entrance. The pattern of the carving was disgraced by the disrespectful paper mark that stretched from top to bottom, crossed from left to right, right to left.

"This—this is a mistake," she screamed as she scraped desperately with her fingers at the hardening glue that melted the paper into the deeply etched wood. She turned back inside and left the room. I pulled my head back down behind the barrel-shaped stool that, gratefully, was big enough to hide me as she blurred past. While she was gone, Father tried to replace the flaking pieces that Mother had torn off. She returned with a long knife, and he wisely moved away from my raging mother.

"The law clearly states that we should be embraced as friends, as Industrial Business Owners. So ridiculous, we don't even *have* the business anymore!" Starting from one end of the paper, she wildly peeled at the white tape to remove the insult from the door. "We provided the cooking oil to this entire county for generations." Mother's hands strained and wiggled the knife under the paper. "We were always kind to our workers. Generous. Half of my time and your grandfather's were spent in works of charity." Finally, a long strip fell away, leaving irregular bits of white in its path. "What more can they take from us?" she asked, working on the second line of white.

"They can take more," Father said softly so as not to rattle the hornet's nest that was Mother.

"What, our thinning children whose cheeks are hollowing by the day?"

"No, the parents who are their only hope. Remember the fate of our competitor, Li? He protested and earned a shot through his skull in front of his entire family."

"Poor Li's family. I remember their so-called 'Liberation' very well, so sad that they were classified as Landlords and Exploiters of the People."

"We lost many friends to suicide and torture," Father warned.

"Ever since nineteen forty-nine, the law called for acceptance for Industrial Business Owners." Mother raised the knife, then slid the sharp edge under what remained of the mark and flicked off another stubborn piece. "Still, we have always been treated shamefully. I will go to the brigade to protest being treated like Enemies of the People. We are certainly not a family of Exploiters, and we are no Black Elements," she argued.

"We have to accept our fate," Father said.

"We have rights, and I will go to the leaders to educate them," Mother snapped back.

I heard the voices before I saw the shoes the second time. They caught her hand and wrenched the knife away.

"What are you doing still living here? We have work to do in here."

"I want to protest to a higher authority. This is a mistake," Mother said, "We are not to be treated as Enemies of the People. We were not assigned the Landlord classification. We are—"

The man leaned forward, and Mother held his eyes.

"A higher authority, you say?" the man asked, laughing. "A higher authority will do worse than throw you out. Do you prefer prison, your children to be orphans? Perhaps you want to feel the sting of a bullet to your pretty head?"

"There is always torture first for the especially haughty ones," another man suggested.

"Fine, we will send the higher authority to pass down your fate, today. Don't go anywhere." The men left, laughing.

Father called my two sisters and my brother and gathered them into the library with Grandmother, but I, the youngest, could not find my voice to call out and thus was left behind in the confusion. I ran my hand across the smooth golden silk on the back of the chair for comfort and felt the puff of air on my face as Mother dropped herself into the seat above me. Her exhausted hand hung down, her shredded fingers tapping urgently on the carved flowers that ran along the seat's edge. I twisted my hair around my finger and rocked myself, eyes closed, hidden from her unhappy hand. I listened only to the song of a small bird through the window behind me, waiting for how long I did not know, until I opened my eyes and saw the boots.

Mother stood straight and calm as the men with red armbands scattered through the house. I heard those boots thudding on the high ceiling. They were in our bedrooms above, except for one man who stayed behind. I huddled under the seat with hands over my ears, rocking, rocking, telling myself, "Wo bu ting, Wo bu ting—I won't listen, I won't listen."

With his gun raised, he faced my parents. "Stand over there, now." He flicked his gun in the direction of the wall that held the memorial painting of Great Grandfather.

"We are here to officially take over your home. It is needed by the people for another purpose. You have been warned before. I am told that you dared to question the decisions of Chairman Mao."

"This is my point. These are not the rules of Chairman Mao. You have already taken our money, land, and any means of earning food for our children. Why are we being punished in this way? With our classification, we should never have been punished in the first place, according to the law," Mother said.

"So, now you speak for Chairman Mao, The Savior of the People?" He shoved them forward toward the wall. "Chairman Mao has freed the exploited peasant workers from the wealthy likes of you—families of Landlords who have exploited the people for their own gain for generations. The remnants of the feudal past must be destroyed; the people must be liberated from the tyranny of the exploiters and the capitalists. This is the law of the Communist Party."

My parents obediently pressed themselves against the wall under Great Grandfather's portrait. They stood straight-backed under the gaze of the powerful man who had amassed their fortune, built their majestic home, and given so generously to all. The official looked up into Great Grandfather's kind eyes, the eyes I knew could follow him no matter how he tried to move to avoid his shame. Many times I myself had failed to escape those eyes.

"We were assigned Industrial Business Classification," Mother said again with a clear but small voice.

Father added with fear, "Although, it is true my family did own much land, it is long gone." She sent a silent warning to him with wide eyes. They stood waiting.

The official looked up and stared over their heads. His eyes darted to the massive portrait. He paused and dropped his head for a torturous minute, then stepped in closer with his gun raised. I could make myself no smaller in my secret place. I kept my sight fixed on my parents' shoes that stood side by side by the door, two delicate and embroidered silk, two dull and worn leather. Then I turned my eyes to the bare feet of my parents, their toes gripping white on the dark polished floor facing the pair of angry, dirty boots. The man leaned in close enough to breathe in Father's frightened breath and whispered, "I knew your grandfather."

"I...hope your memories are fond," Mother said quietly.

"Do it! Let's go! We have other assignments," another man insisted. He had descended the stairs with the carved wooden box of Mother's special old family papers. It was not to be touched! I wanted to warn him as Mother had done with us so many times before. "Don't touch," I tried to say, but it could not leave my covered mouth.

Leaning closer, the one in charge whispered only for my parents' ears, nodding toward the portrait, "He gave my family food and cooking oil when the flood took our home. He saved our lives," he said, glancing up at the portrait.

Stepping back, he announced in a booming voice for all to hear: "Industrial Business Classification, is it?"

"With a lesser crime of Landlord, for certain," Father added weakly, trying to add some weight to the scales.

Then the words of relief came: "No matter. You have already contributed your exploits to the people. Do not resist. You were not shot during Liberation because you accepted the government's decision. Now you have a second chance to live. Through the generosity of Chairman Mao, you will receive one more gift— you will be spared."

"How are we to support our children? We are a business family with no business to run," Father said.

"You have been given your lives a second time, is that not enough?" the angry man who held Mother's box yelled from across the room.

"What exploits do you keep in this treasure box?"

"None," Mother said.

A small edge of fear was in Mother's controlled voice. She breathed to regain her calm and continued. "There is nothing of value in the box—just my family's history, some notes from my ancestors, no value, no meaning to anyone." Mother restrained her emotions. *Why didn't she cry out "Don't touch!" as she had when my sister tried to pry open the precious find?* I wondered.

"Where is the key?" he asked roughly.

"Lost, long ago." Mother insisted.

"Now you have me curious. An intricately carved box like this?" he taunted. "No problem. Let me help you. You must miss the words of your scholarly bourgeois ancestors." He gently set the box on the floor. Relieved, I breathed out for the first time since he arrived with the treasured box. Then, shockingly, his boot thrust down on the box, crushing its double happiness design, shattering the fine wood again and again, scattering ruddy splinters over the hard floor that stopped just short of my hidden knee.

"Comrade Chang. Stop, enough!" the kinder man with the gun interrupted. "Leave that useless thing and gather the plans."

Whispering, the secret advocate leaned forward and said the words that Mother needed to hear: "According to the law of the Central Government, you are correct. Your status of Industrial Business Owner calls for you to be reunited into society as friends of the people. What is written on paper in Beijing is not in the minds of these local leaders, so beware. Perhaps, in time your rightful place will be restored."

Mother's eyes with liquid edges sent gratitude to the man who acknowledged that she had been right. She whispered back, "Mountain high, Emperor far."

"Indeed," he answered. "You're fortunate that it was I who came to resolve your situation. Now, pick up what you can and run for your life and give thanks to Chairman Mao."

I watched the boots leave, clunk, clunk, clunk, taking with them my voice with which to call my mother.

"Children!" Father called. My confused sisters and brother came out from the library, where they were hiding with Grandmother, and relief washed over my parents' faces.

"Where is your sister?" I heard Mother ask, referring to me. The boots had stolen my words, and only my eyes would work. I tried to signal I was there, curled beneath the chair.

"I didn't see her. We thought she was with you," my brother answered.

I am here. See me, here? I thought.

"Everyone, look for her."

"Zhen? Really?" Mother called.

Father tried. "Zhen'er?"

Still I could not leave the safety of the chair.

"Zhen Zhen!" The fear in Mother's loud voice made me pull in tighter. Still calling my name, she fell to the floor, sweeping her palms in wide circles to collect up the fragments of her past. I watched her bury her hands into the mangled heirloom. Finger by finger, she strained to peel the damaged hinges back to rescue the pages of hand-drawn characters trapped inside.

"These are the thoughts from the fine minds of a thousand years of scholars," she said in a tight voice. She lifted the crudely stitched stack of fragile, yellowed papers from the shattered box like a newborn baby, holding them to her heart. So strange to see her knees upon the floor without the Buddha smiling down upon her prayers. So rare to see Mother cry such tears, holding the book so lovingly. I so wished for her to hold me with such care, and that desire finally coaxed my too-weak words from my silenced mouth.

She tilted her head, thinking she had heard my sound. "Zhen?" she called my shortened birth name, again.

Finally, she called out, "Zhen You Yuan Xi, Really Enough Complete Happiness." The sound of my full name so rarely used shocked me from my frightened state. Again, I called out weakly, "DaDa," my special name for my mother. She stopped and looked around the large room, echoing with the worried calls of my family. "Zheeeeen? Zhen'eeeer?"

"Wait." Mother quieted everyone, and I tried to force another sound from my trembling lips again, "DaDa," I managed. She tilted her head and on hands and knees, spied me motionless in my place and reached under the chair to retrieve me.

"Zhen Zhen," she called my name and lifted me into her safe arms. "This was not a place for you. You should not have heard this, little thing." I could not unfold my frozen self. Her voice held both anger and relief. "Don't cry, don't cry," she said when my silence finally broke into sobbing.

Before the day the shoes first came to mark our door, before the boots came to take our home, I had only known the excitement of hiding behind the heavy carved antique chair waiting to squeal with delight, waiting to be found by my sisters or brother. After they came, hiding in my favorite place was no longer a game. For three days, I took to curling myself up under the elegant chair whenever Mother and Father argued or to hold my stomach in secrecy when there was no rice to cook. Back in the comfort of Mother's chair with my head to her chest, I pulled at the closures on her shirt, desperately seeking the comfort of her empty breast.

Grandmother looked around the room. I had never seen her flattened hair bun in such disarray. She stood fragile, a tiny, wasted woman in her baggy pants, the color of the button knots that lined

9

the side of her jacket worn to white. She wore no reflection of her former royal self except the embroidered special shoes that held her bound feet, the necessary shoes worn to aid in her walking inside the house, where she spent all of her days.

"Maybe we can sell some of our furnishings, the more valuable ones that we can live without," she suggested.

"No amount of worldly wisdom can help us to understand these times, Grandmother. Sadly, these are worthless valuables now," Mother explained.

"Why? These are beautiful things."

"I am sad to say, who would have money with which to buy them, and what would they use them for, these symbols of the Exploiters—firewood, perhaps? Do you understand, Grandmother? Our neighbors seek just a basket of the dwindling grain, a bowl of rice. They have no use for items from a dynasty of the past that exist only for the looking. There is no price put on pleasure now," Mother answered. "These things have little practical use in times of hunger."

Grandmother touched the edge of the finely carved dragon clock and dropped her head down to her withered chest.

Mother and Father worked all day to empty the treasures of our lives onto the street in front of our house. I kept my eye on the open door, still decorated with the scraps of paper that had survived Mother's ire, as Father and my siblings carried our furnishings outside. Father didn't speak. He packed as many of our possessions as possible into the wooden cart: dark red antique furniture; two heirloom quilt covers, the dragon and the phoenix adorned with their glorious peonies; the antique clock whose good-luck dragon eyes watched over our main gathering room; the heavy carved chest; two dining tables, one with a suspicious broken leg, with their four matching benches; two blue and white ceramic stools and two double happiness jars made of the same; the massive gold silk chair—my secret hiding place; our basin nestled in its carved stand; wooden canopy beds; the family's old sewing machine; the baby basket that had held my sister and me after the family's ancient cradle was taken; and Mother's precious Buddha statue and its rightful place, the long and narrow altar table with tiger claw feet and curling edges praying to the sky.

Mother dragged the trunk of her family's books to the door.

"We have no room for useless things," Father warned, "We cannot live by fancy brush strokes on old yellow paper or ancient poetry. After we are unloaded, I will return for all the rest."

He turned to see Mother's face. There was no question that her learned self would leave so much as one of them behind. "These are the books that hold the learning of generations of my Book Fragrance Family. These books are my legacy." Mother ran her hand slowly over the chest. "These books have felt the touch of wise ones' hands, whose blood is in my own," she said, turning over her hands. In these books you call 'old yellow paper' live the voices that can only keep on speaking through the careful strokes that dance upon these fragile, handmade pages." She stood defiantly with her one special book cradled in her arms, the salvaged family heirloom with the details of our family's history.

Mother reviewed the contents of the cart, pulled out the baby basket, and threw it to the ground, hoping that along with it would go any chance of anymore unwanted happiness beyond the six children they already had to raise. Sacrificing sentiment to save the past, she flicked her eyes toward the chest with a look my father understood at once. Books loaded, we left our home.

Grandmother rode along on the cart, while my sisters and I pushed from behind, and Father and Brother guided the front. Mother trailed behind with her head twisted back for one last look at our home. We walked only a few paces in silence before Mother stopped, strutted back to the house, stripped the final sticky paper that marked our criminal status from the still-open front door, and slammed it shut.

Slowly, we helped move the cart along the rough path with outstretched arms, driving legs and groaning mouths, on the way to our new place to live. Mother said it was a "place to live," but it would never be called our home. My parents mumbled about the absurdity that we had become the underlings and those who served us would be served. They were unable to believe that the simple people, their own workers, were made their superiors and the ruling class by the government after the sky turned—after Chairman Mao empowered the poor peasants to revolt against the rich as evil remnants of the feudal past. The family's temple, built by Great Grandfather, stood proudly in the distance, its gold ball top welcoming us from the far side of the village. "I suppose the golden orb that tops the temple itself will be stolen next when the swarming red bees gather in the rest of the county's honey," Mother said.

Soon we stood at the door of the shabby peasant home. Looking up at the low ceiling and down at the dirt floor, she turned to Father.

"We should go to the city. We can be close to our two eldest children's schools. They are there alone in dangerous times. We have four more children to educate, and there is more civility there, I am sure," Mother pleaded with Father. "We have no skills. We cannot work the land. Our children will be laboring donkeys if we are sent to work in a brigade of a commune," she continued.

Father insisted we follow orders to move into the assigned house. "We have already been spared our lives; there will be no third chances."

"So, we are to give in, drag our few salvaged things into this pathetic house? We are to share a few rooms and a useless kitchen with no food to cook until the end?" Mother asked.

"We should be grateful this family of kindly field workers took pity on us when the government asked them to house us," Father said.

She placed her Buddha on the dark red altar and sat in her gold silk chair in silence. The furnishings and belongings filled the walls of the rooms, leaving only space to bed us down at night together. There was no room to fit more treasures in the cramped space, but Father made another trip to our home to see if the remaining things could be stored in some sympathizer's barn, perhaps. When he arrived in front of his family home, little was left of their precious things. Except for a few special family heirlooms, which had no practical use, everything else had been stolen or shattered into pieces on the road by playful children. He gathered the few remaining things and stored them on the side of the dilapidated house that Mother again warned us to never call home.

With no space to keep the realities from our ears, my frightful memories of the men and the boots were fleshed out. Each detail was seared into my mind by the many passionate arguments Mother and Father had while living in the crowded room of the assigned house. What should they have said? What should they have done? They reviewed every word the men had said, with her begging to move to the city and him insisting that we stay. Their constant arguments were choked down into growls through clenched teeth to keep their conflict from the neighbors' ears.

"When they took our land and factory, they called it 'Liberation.' Now they take our ancestral home and call it 'repurposing' for the people. Words, clever words. I call it robbery. But then, perhaps it *is* our liberation," Mother's eyes angered as she looked at Father, "for now we are free, free to starve." I shivered beneath my hiding place. She stood before her Buddha and sighed. "This is far too familiar a change for me. I have known the taking of my rightful place two times too many in my years."

I later learned the meaning of her mysterious words as she told me the stories of her life while hiding me from the jaws of the commune fields. It was not the first time she had fallen from powerful to powerless, from unusual high to unbearable low.

CHAPTER 2
UNDER THE RED VEIL

I t is said that the universal law for women is: Marry a rooster, follow the rooster; marry a dog, follow the dog; submit to your father when in girlhood; submit to your husband when married; submit to your son, if widowed. I don't know if my father was a rooster or a dog, but from the hours of my mother telling me the details of her younger years, I do know that he wasn't her soul mate. She had to follow no matter which, rooster or dog.

When a child was not forthcoming in a family, another wife was added, and then another until a child, hopefully a male heir, was born. In Mother's family, there were three wives before there was a birth. DaMa, the most powerful first wife, was proud to show off her new daughter, Upright Justice. My mother, a perfect reflection of her dignified name, was the firstborn child in this scholarly family called the Book Fragrance Family, due to their emphasis on education. What a lovely tradition, to assign beautiful words like that to describe the work of a learned lineage with generations of teachers, ancient poets, and writers. Her grandfather was a schoolmaster and her father, a well-known teacher and scholar. They called my mother "Puppy," an endearing baby name at the time, animal names having been used to help ensure that the child would survive.

With this strong family tradition of valuing education above all, they even allowed precious Puppy, a mere girl, to go to school. It was so rare to see a little girl sitting in the classroom full of disciplined little boys who studied for their future. The other parents wondered at the foolishness of wasting time to teach a girl, who would only belong to another family after marriage and would have no use for such things. With respect for the service her scholarly family provided to the town, such as writing letters and agreements, teaching, and keeping many ancient books, it was allowed.

DaMa would take lunch to school for her daughter, Puppy, proud to watch her reciting poems in the classroom. Puppy had the life of a princess and a scholar, a rare and unheard-of gift for a female child. She also unknowingly lived the life of a lie, for barren DaMa, the most powerful first wife, was not her true mother. Although Puppy was born to the young third wife, my mother's father and the relieved family, desperate for a child, had elevated her to be the honored firstborn, thus DaMa accepted her at birth as her own. Her birth mother was sworn to secrecy for the benefit of the child. She kept her word until she selfishly could no more. Even though she knew it would change her child's fate forever, lowering her position in the family to be the daughter of the lowly third wife, her jealousy overcame her logic. She wanted to lay claim to her own flesh, to capture the honor that was due to her as the mother of the firstborn child in an heirless family.

Her plan was flawed. When Puppy's true mother revealed the secret to her, DaMa was consumed with anger and humiliation. Even her own servant could not tolerate the cruel woman and left her service. When it came to Puppy, DaMa was both too resentful to love her and too indignant to give her up. Puppy, my indulged mother was no longer her true daughter in DaMa's eyes. Robbed of her chance to continue her beloved studies, little Puppy was diminished from pampered daughter to a life of servitude to the embittered woman. Puppy spent her remaining childhood years carrying DaMa's fetid chamber pot until the woman died of misery and insanity. Only then did Puppy find the arms of her rightful mother, wife number three, whose selfishness had both stolen and restored my mother's world.

真

When Mother was 16 years old, two well-dressed men with hats and long, silk Mandarin robes paid a visit to her family. According to the matchmaker, because Mother was from a family of highly respected scholars, it was expected that a good match to a well-to-do family would be arranged. Upright Justice nervously awaited the visit of her prospective groom. Through the crack of the door, against all sense of the manners of the times, she caught sight of a very handsome, smiling young man during the marriage negotiations. Soon after, a wedding date was set.

It was quite some distance from my mother's home to the groom's home. As the higher class standard dictated, she did not have to walk or ride a horse to the wedding. Instead, a luxurious sedan of gold and red lifted by eight strong men was sent from the groom's family to carry her. Following the sedan was a marching band playing happy folk music for the fête, which was the greatest privilege any lucky bride could enjoy. She arrived demure and joyful at the thought of seeing his wonderfully handsome young face again. Her heart fluttered in anticipation of a lifetime of the warmth she had seen in his smile in that one peek through the anteroom door.

What great fortune, for in the past she had gasped when she had seen so many of her friends matched with an older or unfortunate-faced man. She walked in with joy to be presented to her lifetime love. When her heavy embroidered red silk veil was lifted at that special moment of joining, she faced a man she had never seen before. He was not the handsome man she had seen through the crack of the door. The Groom who stood before her was a different man. The shock blacked out her brain, but just before she fainted, she caught a glimpse of the glowing face she had held in her dreams for months. There, standing in the crowd, was her new husband's young Uncle Cun, "Village," who was on his way to college in London. The young man, she later discovered, had merely accompanied the groom's family to help make the lifetime arrangements months before when she had mistaken him for the prospective groom.

The fainting bride slumped into the arms of my father, the stunned bridegroom, causing him to touch her unthinkably before the vows were finished. This romantic lusty fairy tale of the beauty falling for her new husband and master became a part of the town's lore, making my father the envy of many men and my mother a heavy-hearted wife. Thus began the lifetime commitment of Wang Upright Justice to the man who would be my father, a fatherless young heir to his grandfather's fortune.

My father was expected to be successful with the given name Hui Xian, "Effulgence Advance," with Effulgence meaning radiant and beaming and Advance referring to the direction of his prospects for his future. This was an appropriate name for a son having grown up in a rich family that owned department stores, land, and a cooking-oil factory that supplied the entire county. Unlike his powerful grandfather, who was the creator of the riches, my father possessed neither his ancestor's keen business mind nor his sophistication. Instead, as a young man, he had a quick temper and a few addictions such as smoking, taking opiates, and womanizing. Rumors passed that he had even had an affair with a married woman.

There were many changes that came with her marriage. Mother's thick, long pigtail had to be redesigned into the flat, round bun of a married woman. She had many people to submit to besides her husband, particularly Grandfather, who held the power and the rule over everyone in the household. Neither Mother nor the entire household of servants was allowed to go to sleep until the revered one took to his bed each night, which resulted in her exhaustion.

It is an open secret in the depths of a man's mind that as a father, his son is the best, but as a husband, other men's wives are better. Of course, if a man doesn't generate offspring to carry the family name, the ultimate sign of his manhood, it is the wife who is to blame. With great misfortune, Mother gave birth to a baby girl. When my eldest sister was born, it was amid wealth and abundance when having children was considered such good fortune. My parents named her Double Happiness, although, regretfully she was not a boy. No matter, there was still the glowing future for bringing to life their heir to carry the wisdom of my mother's long line of scholarly ancestors and my father's legacy of wealth. However, Grandfather, the head of the family, was growing old and was disappointed.

"If you don't produce a son with the second child, my grandson will have to marry a second wife," he warned Mother.

By then, the winds had blown away a portion of their fortune. The wind was in the form of my father's weaknesses. He was not his grandfather's heir in wisdom. With no father to guide him in his youth, he had squandered much that had been his birthright to his passions of the flesh. But in the end, it was true that my father's unfortunate face and fortunate failings saved our lives, for when the time came, we no longer had such a Landlord's legacy of wealth with which to lure the ire and the bullets of the communist government officials.

真

A few years later, Mother, a petite young lady, could stand a little taller because her belly listened to her whispers and produced a son. They named him Repeat Happiness. A woman became more valued when a precious son, an heir, was born. As a result, my mother enjoyed royal-like treatment and favor again. She felt she could pursue a little fashion, too. As short hair became popular with the girls in the city after centuries of being burdened with the care of long hair, my mother had her hair cut short, keeping the sentimental memento in her favorite box. She felt happy, energetic, modern, and light with no heavy, flat bun to heap upon the back of her head.

The pleasure was short-lived. When she encountered Grandfather, even though she held her baby boy high to block his view of her new look, he caught sight of the change.

"How dare you imitate the rebellious girls from the city. You had better put back the long hair right now!" he demanded.

Sadly, she retrieved the fallen locks from the box and fastened them to her head until she could regrow her proper hair. The hair incident was nothing compared to the disaster that followed. My father's philandering had ended with his marriage, or so it seemed, until a former impassioned mistress with whom he had severed his ties in order to try to pull himself together for married life lured him into her house. She showed him a newly sharpened butcher knife and asked him to join her in killing her husband, who was returning from business that night, so that she and my father could be together once again. He was in shock. Refusing to be a part of the scheme, he tried to leave, but she didn't let him go. She blew out the light. The darkness blinded his eyes. As he was probing his way out of her house, she chased him, stabbed him, mercilessly slashing him along the way, over and over. Holding his injured face, blood trailing behind him, he dragged himself out-side, crying for help.

The next day, Mother audaciously took off her reattached long hair, boldly went with her servants to the mistress's house, and destroyed the devil woman's family shrine—the ultimate revenge. Not having yet extinguished her anger at my father, she took her two children and her newly bulging belly and returned to her family home.

"Mother, it is impossible for me to live with him now as a humiliated wife. He has no refinement." Mother begged her own true gentle mother to understand, to help release her from this unfortunate match.

"I cannot support such an outrage from my own daughter. What's done is done. He is your husband. It was in the past, this other woman. You have his heir in this very house. Whether dog or rooster, you must follow. I will not tell your father of your request. You visit for a while, then return. There will be no shame in this family. We will have no bad luck from a daughter returning to her parents' home. Married daughter, poured water," her mother said.

"What about *my* happiness, Mother?" my mother asked.

"That you will make on your own, my daughter, if you have the right mind to," she answered.

A note was delivered to my mother from my father: "Please return with my most sincere apologies. You are needed. Grandfather's heart is weakening, and I fear news of this will surely be his undoing. I beg you."

Mother was surprised by his words of contrition, and the word "beg" had quite an effect. To hear those words from a man to a woman was quite astonishing. At that moment, her mother swept Mother's letter from her hand.

"See! Here is the happiness you are seeking, delivered within days of your request. My daughter, this empowers you a great deal, even more than being delivered by an eight-man sedan to your husband's majestic home."

With no options, Mother gathered up her children and returned to my father's home. She thought, *Better to be begged, better return.*

Grandfather's death was a time of great sadness. Very soon after Grandfather took his last breath and left this Earth, it became Mother's unfortunate timing to bring more Happiness into their lives. According to tradition, so as not to disrespect the somber moment of his passing with the unsavory act of childbirth, the servants prepared the stable with the luxurious rising phoenix quilt on a thick bed of straw, and Mother brought another heir for the honorable family into the world. Unlike the other two siblings entitled with the Happiness names, he was named Little Ox, perhaps reflecting the environment in which he was born or perhaps out of Mother's rebelliousness and stubbornness, but definitely with endearment because the oxen had lowed and crooned her through the painful night.

My father needed my scholarly mother to manage the family business. She took over many of Grandfather's roles. Charity was also a big part of the operation. Whenever there was drought or flooding, victims could line up in the factory to receive free food and supplies such as rice and cooking oil. Despite his demanding nature, Grandfather had always been a generous man, admired by all. People would walk hours to come to the door of his estate to tell him they had buried a dead body found by the banks of the Yangtze River, and he would always reward them for their good deed of citizenship. Mother kept the tradition flowing with one difference—she had both a generous and progressive mind when it came to women. After the grandfather's death, she even allowed his young wife to remarry, which was a very rare and unheard-of privilege for a widow.

Mother had a good command of the abacus. As one hand was calculating—click, click, click, sliding the little beads along the rods—the other hand recorded their ever-growing wealth. She treated the workers kindly and ran the business efficiently. She was a rarity indeed, drawing both admiration and shock from everyone in the county as a woman managing a family business while still following the dog. My father, however, scars like centipedes marking his stitched face and his sullied past, continued to find ways to slide the beads in the other direction, squandering what his grandfather had built. She was a rising woman chasing sliding numbers.

In the midst of her burgeoning business activities and dwindling wealth at my father's hands, my mother found she was to give birth once again. With this fourth child, her heart sank. With no way to prevent her ongoing pregnancies, the only solution she could think of was to send a plea to the gods above to stop the chain of babies through the power of the baby's name. Mother named the girl child Complete Happiness to tell the god who ruled such things that four children were sufficient to fulfill their dreams, to tell the powers that controlled such things that she had already had her fill of Happiness.

CHAPTER 3
ENOUGH HAPPINESS

My mother was right. There was no room for more Happiness in their lives, not only because of the burden of extra work for her and my father's poor business sense and squandering, but also because of the country's crushing Liberation. It swept through the country, instantly changing the fate of my family in a way Mother could not correct with even the nimblest of fingers on her abacus. Like all affluent people, my mother and father were stripped of everything for the good of the people, with no concern for the good of our family. My family could no longer afford another mouthful of surprise; they already had Complete Happiness, after all.

Mother prayed daily that the affliction of another child would be someone else's burden to bear. She feared that it would be years that they would continue to suffer with the uncertainty of their fate and their food, years that they would live in their useless luxury with no reliable means of support. In desperation, despite her weakening state, she used her elegant scholar's hands, meant only to hold a book or brush, to learn to sew from a tailor. Father, a lover of animals, chose to study with a veterinarian in hopes of them having two skills that would be desirable wherever they should go. They struggled to feed their growing family in the empty luxury of their family home.

Of course, there was no way Mother could consider ridding herself of a baby, with neither access to a doctor for a prescription of herbs nor money to spend. Therefore, after Sister Complete Happiness was born and Mother became pregnant yet again, she had a mission to end the pregnancy herself.

First, she tried to carry water home from the Yangtze River, up the hill and down the hill with two big unwieldy, heavy buckets full of sloshing water—the labor only a man should do. She was exhausted, but the baby was not disturbed.

Second, she climbed up onto the big square dining table and jumped down to the floor, over and over until one of the legs of the table broke, but the baby stuck to her belly and enjoyed the free fall with no apparent harm.

Third, Mother went around in the fields, collected certain wild weeds that supposedly had agents with the power to meet her goal, and boiled them into juice. She took it daily, bitter like bile, but instead of losing the baby, her body became swollen, growing clusters of huge, weeping hives.

Fourth, it was said that excessive alcohol could help, so she came up with a way to have a friend invite her for dinner so she was able to drink too much of their alcohol, having no such luxury at home. She was dancing, singing, and laughing as she stumbled home, like walking on clouds. Then she retched, losing the precious alcohol to the roadside, but the baby remained sober and secure.

Finally, thanks to her determined research, she found the ultimate, powerful ancient remedy. It required a little courage, yet Mother said it was worth the try. She needed to catch two green lizards with bulging eyes. The tails had to be long, whole, strong, and fast-wiggling. She was told she must let them swim in the bucket of water, changing the water a few times in order to clean them. After that, all she had to do was to get up early in the morning with an empty stomach, open her mouth wide, inhale hard three times with a long "Huuuuh," then pick up the live, kicking lizards and swallow them, one by one. It was believed that the lizard's sharp claws and long tails could scratch the baby off the inside of her belly.

All of the children were motivated to help hunt for the lizards, innocent of their true purpose. It was great fun for them. It was just so exciting to get to keep lizards as pets. The effort paid off; two light-green-colored, bug-eyed lizards were caught. Mother shivered when she took a quick first glance at the angry lizards.

It was almost midnight. Everyone had a different idea about how to keep the lizards contained. The children didn't want to put them into the bucket because they didn't want to drown them. Mother decided to let the children have their way because they were the ones who had caught them with the fish net. So it was agreed that the lizards would be kept under our big, rusty, soot-coated cooking pot lid to foil any attempt at escape.

Mother did not sleep well. She got up very early and double-checked the children, making sure they were still sleeping because she was about to steal their new pets. She filled the bucket with water and sat herself down, wondering how to transport the lizards from the pot cover to the bucket. She didn't want to use her bare hands because they might bite. She decided to use the iron poker. She took a long deep breath and quietly inhaled with mouth wide open, "Huuuuh." Lifting the pot lid slightly, she stabbed randomly through the gap. All she felt was dirt with no reaction from the lizards. After probing for a long time, she finally lifted the pot lid up. There she found nothing but dirt. The lizards, mysteriously, had disappeared. Mother never did find out how they escaped their tightly covered trap.

Thus, the fifth child, a baby girl, was born on a hot summer day, crying and kicking hard with her little fists waving in the air as if claiming victory or protesting having been through such unspeakable things. She was given the name Enough Complete Happiness. For short, my family called her "Enough."

For a family of field workers, children are the future. In my fallen family, without the experience to make the barren fields bear fruit, babies were the only misfortunate crop that seemed to grow.

真

Getting pregnant accidentally was a lot easier than keeping an extra baby alive without food. Unlike the families with too many mouths to feed who searched their brains to find a means of limiting births, there were those with means who ached for just the opposite. There was a couple that belonged to the new ruling class. This peasant couple was blessed with sudden new fortune and power, but not with babies. They tried every way possible to get pregnant but failed.

The wife, named LanZi, "Basket," was a chubby, poor little peasant in her thirties, newly outfitted in beautiful clothes that hung upon her like a stranger. She visited Mother one time during Mother's pregnancy, bringing her rice liquid, the broth that remained after sifting out all of the precious rice for her full meals. She told Mother it was egg rice soup. Mother said she was still very grateful, even though she knew there wasn't a ghost of an egg in it at all.

Basket's visit had a purpose to serve. She wanted to know the little secret about how Mother was able to get pregnant so easily, one after the other. Not without embarrassment and with great effort, she began.

"Your home is beautiful," Basket said, looking around at the lovely carved doors and high windows.

"Yes, but beauty doesn't feed a family. I am sorry I have not even a cup of tea to offer you," Mother said.

"Well, at least you are fortunate. You were allowed to stay in this home to raise your many children," she said.

"What is it I can help you with?" Mother asked, brushing past the sensitive subject.

The peasant woman seemed uncomfortable as she stuttered her request.

"When it comes to your…um? Do you wear anything, uh…special? Special colored underwear, perhaps?" She was scarlet-faced but continued. "Or do you choose some certain good feng shui time for the bedroom thing?"

"Basket! These things I cannot—these things are not to be discussed!" Mother said.

"Yes, so unmentionable, yes, but would you speak with me of this unmentionable thing?" Seeing Mother's surprised reaction, shrinking with embarrassment, Basket flipped her hand and dismissed the idea. "Suan le, suan le—just drop it, just drop it," she said.

"It is OK," said Mother, after she thought for a moment about the power the ruling-class peasant had over her family's fate. "After all, you brought me the soup. As far as the pregnancy," Mother whispered, "it seems that I can even get pregnant by just a brush of the flare of his pants."

"There must be something. Could it be your underwear? Yes, it must be. May I borrow them?" Basket pleaded.

"Oh, you don't want to do that. I have only one pair, and I wash them when there is sun, so I have to wait for them to dry to put them back on. They are quite worn out with layers of patches. No, no, you don't want to wear them, trust me."

"I don't mind if it helps us to have a child. My husband's old father is threatening a second wife, although it is against the law now. I fear he will find a way to break my husband's love for me. Maybe the patches did the trick to catch the baby seeds," she continued. "I told my husband I was coming to seek your help. He is anxious to know what you will do to help us." Basket delivered her thinly veiled threat.

Fear struck Mother. Knowing that the peasant's lawless husband could make up lies and could easily betray her, she relented. When you have the memories of longsuffering at the hands of those who hold your fate, your resistance turns like rice noodles left too long to simmer in the pot, and the only powers you are left with are your wits and cleverness. So Mother gave up her heavy, grey, patched underwear to the peasant who had the power to trigger her deepest fears. When she saw that Basket was thrilled, only then could she take a breath.

As soon as the demanding woman left, Mother began to work to fashion a garment to restore her own dignity. She could not bear that she had to give the woman such a shameful thing. With no money for fabric, she cut the precious quilt that in its day blossomed with beautiful flowers and the rising phoenix, with splashes of gold and the colors of hopeful sunsets. She cut it until its beauty was gone, gone like the revolutionaries who swept through our village wiping clean any memory of the glorious past, gone like any remnant of our former blessings, any sign that we had meaning in a land that sought to strip our souls of hope. She could only hope that the absence of the beloved family quilt that had swaddled Double Happiness, Repeat Happiness, Little Ox, Complete Happiness, and Enough Complete Happiness was the wishful magic that might end her days of endless childbearing.

Months went by, and Mother had the new baby, but Basket still didn't get pregnant. Her flat stomach was a reminder to her daily to make another visit to my mother. She came back and returned the useless underwear. Baby Enough was wrapped in a thin sheet of rags, her only blanket. She was a good baby, lying in the small basket cushioned with the remnant of the beautiful phoenix and flower quilt that shielded her tender body from the rough bamboo. She kicked her little pink feet out from under the ragged sheet while sucking on her thumb.

Basket bent over to look at the baby and suddenly burst into a loud cry, wailing to the sky. Mother was so frightened, knowing that with her bad classification, she couldn't afford to make a ruling-class lady cry. She feared the woman's cries would be heard throughout the village. With the People's Militia nearby, she tried hard to calm her down, but Basket was hysterical. Mother asked Basket why she was crying so hard, although she had an instinct as to why. Basket couldn't speak but simply pointed to the baby. Mother pressed her fists to her racing heart.

Finally, Basket calmed down and took a seat next to the baby, watching her hungrily sucking on her little thumb. After a while, she dried up her tears and started to smile. Like an actor in a Peking Opera, her face changed from sadness to happiness in an instant. Mother was relieved that she was feeling better but could see that Basket had an idea.

"How about I give you ten Jin of rice and you give me the baby? It's a good trade."

Mother was startled. "You are joking. I am sure you don't want a burden like a baby on your hands," she said, trying to bring the reality of caring for a baby to the woman's mind.

"I am serious. You know it is a lot of rice, and it will feed your family for a long time. You know I will feed the baby good food and dress her in good clothes."

"No, please, you don't want to do that!"

"Yes, give me the baby, and your life will be easier with one less mouth to feed. How about your dinner? What is this mother going to feed her hungry children for dinner? You were borrowing rice from my next-door neighbor just yesterday," Basket argued.

Mother realized there was no food for dinner that evening. Father was out of the house the entire day, the cooking pot was empty, and Grandmother was sick in bed upstairs. In fact, the salt had run out, too. She had already gone to borrow salt with a little candle cup from the next-door neighbor. "Older Uncle," she had used the term of respect, "we only wish to borrow a small amount of salt." Mother had humbled herself, a necessary but uncomfortable deed for the scholarly woman.

"Of course you may, as soon as your former debt is paid. It is the custom," he told her. It was a custom she had never needed to follow in her past.

It was as though Basket read my mother's mind. "I will also give you a jar of salt," Basket added. With tears running down her face, Mother looked at Basket. Her offer was so tempting, and it was likely the selfish woman would cause trouble, tell lies, and take her baby anyway, Mother thought.

"I can't sell my daughter for the food...I just can't," Mother managed to squeeze from her narrowed throat.

"No, don't think of it that way. I am just helping you. The baby is going to be happier with a better life. You know that all your children belong to the title "Enemy of the State," but this little thing won't. She will always have food and with our best classification of Poor Peasant. She will be lucky for sure. You can't buy that privilege, even if you had barrels of money. And ten Jin of rice will fill your children's empty bellies for a long time," Basket said convincingly.

Mother's legs became weak; she was giving in. "So, you will give her a new name? She already has a name, you know. Her name is Enough Complete Happiness. We have already started to like the name."

"Oh, we will have a better name than that. My husband will decide it, though."

"You will feed her pure rice porridge without adding wild weeds to it?" Mother begged for reassurance.

"Oh, yes. We have plenty of rice, and we don't eat those rough bitter weeds. Those are for the animals, and they taste awful."

Mother picked up the baby's basket and handed it to her. "Keep the baby. You don't have to give me the rice or the salt. It cannot be a sale. Just treat her well, as you have promised," she said. Ignoring Mother's refusal, Basket dropped the rice and salt on the table and swept the baby away.

It was one of the darkest evenings ever. Father came home, and under the weak light he saw a bag lying on the table with a jar by its side. He touched the bag and examined the jar.

"Where did all this rice come from?" he asked. Mother and all the children were quiet. The kitchen was still empty, as were their stomachs. "I am glad we have rice. Look what I brought home." He had some peas nestled in his handkerchief. "A fortunate night for sure. It will make a good dish with the salt now, eh?"

Mother started to cry. Father looked around, realizing Baby Enough was gone. After he heard the details, he silently grabbed the rice and the salt and charged through the door. She dragged along on his leg as her own legs gave out from under her.

"We can't afford to offend them. They can ruin our lives and make us miserable if we go and take back Baby Enough. You know her husband is powerful. He will take her anyway," Mother said, trying to explain her actions.

"I don't care. I can't let my bone and flesh down. Enough found her way to our home. She wanted us to be her mother and father," he said, choking back tears. "Listen," Father said, helping Mother to stand up, "we can't abandon her. If we have to starve to death, we die together. You shouldn't have done that in the first place. I thought you were the one always wise and kind, loving your children, fighting for what was right. What would we do if we don't have Enough?"

"That is why I gave her away. We do not have enough," Mother cried.

Out in the darkness, Father went for his baby. Mother was helpless, anxious, and fearful. She sat at the table with the mismatched repaired leg, remembering the time she had tried to release her baby from her weary body. At that moment, she wanted Enough Complete Happiness from her deepest heart, but she was worried about Father provoking a fight and the huge disaster that could be bestowed on the whole family. In desperation, she grabbed the failed patched underwear that Basket had returned and dashed into the darkness after Father.

As Father broke through Basket's door with the rice and the salt, she and her husband were rocking the baby in a beautiful infant-rocking cradle. Before they realized what was happening, he had already swept up the baby. Just then, Mother rushed in, holding the underwear.

"Listen, Basket, I have brought you the underwear back. It is yours now."

"It didn't work!" Basket cried.

Mother pulled her to the side, and in an out-of-breath whisper she revealed, "It was because you were not wearing it the right way."

"So, you do have a secret!" Basket said.

"Yes, I am about to tell you, but first, would you let us have Enough back?"

"Enough what?" she asked.

"Our baby girl, Enough Complete Happiness!"

"Yes, if you tell me the secret, of course we would rather have our own baby."

"Very good."

"So?" Basket was eager to know.

Mother finally said, "After the bedroom thing, you put on the underwear inside out. Let the patches touch your skin. Remember? You yourself said the patches might do the trick to catch the baby seeds? It will, if you wear it the right way."

"Ah, finally you tell me the truth!" A smile rose to Basket's face. She spun the underwear in the air and whispered in her husband's ear.

Enough was brought home that night. She stopped sucking her thumb, and her little head, too heavy for her thin neck to hold, rested on Father's shoulder. He had never held his other children so tightly in his arms; he wanted to make sure that no one could ever take Enough away again.

In the end, it seemed it was Mother's old grey, patched underwear that saved us. A few months later, Basket did get pregnant and gratefully delivered a son whom they called Treasure. In this way, Mother's unmentionable underwear that was responsible for the birth of the couple's heir became their treasured family heirloom with a secret all its own.

A short time afterward, Basket's sister, also a Poor Peasant, came to visit, seeking the same help.

"I have been sent by Basket, my sister, to beg for a special garment. Like my sister, I have not been able to have a baby, and my husband is growing impatient. Basket promises there will be no more requests if you will help me," the woman said.

As soon as the woman left, Mother again began to work to fashion a second patched garment from the rising phoenix quilt. She slipped the remaining scrap from under the baby. It was the only diminished remnant of the family heirloom she had risked her life to save when she hid it from the People's Militia, who came so many years before to take the factory and whatever else they pleased. The well-loved heirloom had returned the favor by giving up its glory to save our family from our near demise and to keep our beloved sister, Enough.

Mother turned to the drawer and lifted the only remaining coverlet into her arms, swirled it to settle on her tired shoulders, and held the golden dragon quilt adorned with beautiful sprays of peonies tightly across her chest. Mother's heart so deeply held the love of the old, but the old had come to be meaningless. Our beautiful home only masked our impoverished life. Our family home, the landmark used by travelers to guide their way, the central point of orientation for the entire county, was an empty shell. Sadly, my family lived in hunger in its luxury with no remnants of its former luster in the shadow of the very Buddhist temple that was built by my father's great-grandfather in the days when worship was an option, when my family had their good name.

真

After Mother gave birth to Enough, the monthly red did not appear for several years. She was relieved, but she started to feel sick and gradually feared the worst was near. Even though in her desperation she had wished to die in her sleep many times, she changed her mind upon seeing the dark face of the beyond without her children. Death was far more unwanted than any of her children had been. There was always some hope to live for, and she was good at finding hope like she was good at somehow finding a way to keep us all alive. And besides, after saving Enough from Basket, Mother said she could not bear to leave her youngest daughter without a mother.

Finally, she was able to see an herbal medicine doctor, to find out how much time was left for her to live. After the doctor felt her pulses, he said, "There is something good to tell and something you do not want to hear. Which do you want me to speak of first, the yin or the yang?"

"Oh, the yang first, of course. If I die, I die happy," she answered weakly without even the strength to smile at her own little joke.

"The yang is, you are not going to die."

"Oh, thank your golden words, but the yin?" She was nervous, wondering if it was worth living with whatever horrible affliction he was about to name.

"The yin of my diagnosis is that you are going to have a new mouth to feed."

Born in the wrong place and wrong time, you have to be tough to survive. It was true that Mother didn't know she was pregnant with me. And so, since she was too weak and too sick to jump on any tables, carry water to exhaustion, or swallow a lizard whole, she let her belly grow.

Even the power of the Enough message did not work its magic because a sixth child, an unwelcome daughter, was born in the most humble and abject of times. In desperation they named me Really Enough Complete Happiness, or Zhen, "Really," for short.

As soon as she was able, Mother secretly brought me to the great East Mountain Temple to have my fortune read.

"There is something so powerful about this temple. I feel safe, and my heart is always calm here," she said to the monk.

"Yes, all this splendor you see here was built by this child's great-great-grandfather. For years, he visited the wealthy residents of this Hubei province and traveled by foot as far away as Hunan province to raise the money to build this holy place. So strong was his faith, it impassioned others to contribute as well." The monk looked up at the beautiful temple and was moved. "I fear someday they will destroy our great East Mountain Temple to send a message to the people about the evils of worshipping a god who does not sit in Beijing."

"I cannot imagine a kindly god would allow its destruction," Mother said. "I miss the open days of holy worship, but my prayers are still in my power," she whispered, "and to see you labeled a Ghost Seller and Evil God Worshiper makes my heart even heavier."

He lowered his voice. "I am no longer safe here, myself, as an Enemy of the State. The forbidding of worship makes me a target, as well. There will be a time when I will move to the mountains to be with the great Masters until the sanity returns. We must pray and preserve ourselves for a time when peace comes into our world again. For now, I am here. Let us look at the future of this little girl."

The monk, who had the special sight to tell the future, looked down at my little self and asked my mother, "What did you name her?"

"We decided to follow the pattern of Happiness. We call her Really Enough Complete Happiness, although the messages of our babies' names to our god never seemed to take," she answered.

He touched my little fingers. "A baby born four years after your birthing years have ended has a very strong fate. She had such strength to ride over your body's own nature to enter this world. She will be either at the front of the boat or the back of the boat. She will be the first or the last," he predicted enigmatically.

As for the first, it was yet unclear what he meant. As for the last, he predicted Mother would have no more children. In a way he was wrong, but in a way he was right because my sickly baby brother born after me did not see his third year, for which I took some responsibility to heart. Having been destined to be the last, I thought there was no room for his little heart because of me. I sent him my apologies and my tears for causing his death through my fortune as he lay still in the grain-sifting basket.

"Her unusual fate will be too strong for her to call you 'Ma,'" the monk continued. "She should call you 'DaDa,' our country-side term for Auntie. This one you will never harness with reins; this one will lift off on wings."

真

While living in the family home for nearly four more years after my birth, Mother and Father continued to struggle to keep us all fed. It had been more than ten years since the government had liberated us from our wealth and factory; the home was all we had left that reflected our former life. Few realized how destitute we were when passing by the beautiful home, but gold carvings, hand-carved furniture and silk we could not eat.

CHAPTER 4
INTO THE TIGER'S MOUTH

For more than one year, my family crowded into the small home, sharing the kitchen with a Poor Peasant family. One morning, an announcement was made throughout the village: "There will be food for everyone at the new communal dining hall. There is to be no cooking by anyone. Cooking is now forbidden, wasteful! All meals are to be taken communally." Obeying the new rule, my parents followed the crowd to the assigned location of the new dining hall.

"At least we will feed the children," Father said.

They arrived at the designated spot where a crowd of people stood admiring the finely polished wood exterior of a magnificent building. They were running their fingers over the lavish, intricate carvings adorning the heavy frames of the large windows, and arching their necks up to see the two-story palatial home with the beautiful dark red, carved double door that led to their new dining hall. Sadly, Mother and Father entered their own front door.

My sisters and Brother Little Ox were excited to be back home.

"Mother, look at all the people. They must need rice and cooking oil, but we don't have any, do we?" Brother Ox asked.

"Come, let me show you our bedrooms. Yes, this is our home," my sisters said with excitement.

Before Mother could stop them, Sister Complete and Sister Enough took the hands of several nearby children and ran upstairs through the crowd to show them their recaptured rooms. They entered each room excitedly and found the same thing—people eating at long wooden tables. The excitement of the rightful residents died in the confused eyes of the other children.

"Where are they? What happened to the rooms you spoke about? This is a dining hall! You fooled us; now we lost our place in line." The other children ran downstairs to join the growing line of hungry people.

Dragging our feet through the familiar rooms of the home that had sheltered Father's generations, the beautiful residence from which Grandfather gave oil and rice to the poor, we sat and ate with my parents from the generosity of Chairman Mao. As we walked back across the village to our home, Mother broke the silence.

"We need to find a home in the city now, close to our eldest children's schools. There is more chance for better education and civility there, I am sure," Mother repeated her daily lament, "and Double Happiness and Repeat Happiness will be near us again. We can turn the fortunes of this family. Our only hope is to raise our children to be educated, to have a better future," she said once more to Father.

"No, on this I disagree. The cities are in chaos. Double and Repeat are safe in their schools with roof and food, thanks to the kindness of my uncle, Village. We have no options there, and the countryside will be much gentler on the children. Besides, what will I do in the city when I become a veterinarian?" Father insisted.

"What will a scholar do amidst ignorance?" Mother argued, "And what kind of education will the younger four children get in the simple countryside schools?"

"So, do you not see what is happening here? Are you too blinded by your book learning? So, what, you will sleep under the pagoda with six children, stay in the city street on the banks of the river under a paper umbrella?"

"You will wish them to have teachers who blur their characters in their unskilled hands? You will take us from the tiger's cave into the tiger's mouth," Mother cried.

"Don't be foolish. We have no options there in the city," Father argued with fiery eyes and palms-up pleading. "This insanity cannot last long, and the gangs are forming in the city. You heard it; they are executing people without question. The farther away from the rule, the easier the rule; the more educated, the more despicable you are in their eyes."

"Mountain high, Emperor far," Mother responded in a soft tone, disagreeing but not wanting to further evoke Father's ire.

"There is no more Emperor to keep the rule, my scholar, no matter how close or how far," he said. "It won't be for long. Right now we have no choice. Do you know the trouble we are in? We need to think of survival. No matter, I have good news. I received word from our friend, Old Peng, that we can use his friend's abandoned house in a village only a long walk from here. We will have a home to ourselves again." He settled the argument.

When Mother had no strength to argue but only the strength to go, they left their village and their family temple area for the countryside with Grandmother, four children, our salvaged furniture, and of course, the chest of books. Mother was a city scholar, country doomed. Never had they farmed, so they knew nothing about growing vegetables or crops, nothing about the sharpening or care of tools, nothing about the life they would lead.

真

Burdened with hungry children and my father's aged mother, my parents moved into the abandoned house. My frail grandmother had to be carried the entire distance to our new house. Her feet, bound in the traditional way for a lady of her stature since she was a little child, were deformed; walking was nearly impossible for her.

The village house had not a hint remaining of its former charm. It was built of sorghum stems with patched mud walls on a frame of wooden posts with high ceilings to catch the heat and cooking soot. The dried mud from the walls had peeled off in many places from the beating of the wind and rain. The roof was covered with small, grey, curved tiles, layered in slanting rows but with many tiles missing, making the sky visible here and there.

In summer, I loved to see the sunshine play on our earth floor. In winter, our blue lips smiled when we woke up to find the holes in the old ceiling had delivered a child's gift and a mother's heartache—mounds of fluffy white heaped on top of our suddenly heavy quilts. When it rained in later years, I was in command of our small fleet of buckets, basins, and cooking pots to catch the raindrops from the leaks above. Sister Enough and I took turns wielding a long bamboo pole, reaching up to shuffle the ceiling tiles left and right, nudging them, shifting them, spreading them carefully to cover the many holes.

The most frightening time was when fierce storms happened in the middle of the night. As the lightning flashed up in the sky and the thunder shook the Earth, the entire family had to fumble and crawl under the table or a bed or scurry to find a pot or basin to put over our heads to protect us from the shrapnel of tiles that scattered above. Like black bats, they swooped down, pinging the pots and thudding the wooden bowls on our heads.

Often on these particularly stormy nights, we used our make-shift armor overhead to run to our neighbor's house with the low, rough, sturdy straw roof, which had no openings in the ceiling to welcome in the rain. Uncle and Aunt Liu—we called all adults "Uncle" and "Aunt"—were ruling-class poor peasants under the new Communist rule, with a better life than we Enemies. They took mercy on us, taking us in time and again when we arrived like matted dogs at their door. Without a second thought, my sisters and brother and I, cold and wet, crawled into the neighbor's children's warm, dry bed, like squirming puppies all in a pile of shivers, while Mother and Father sat leaning against the wall or upright in chairs all night, sharing sleepless nightmares in the howling storms.

The abandoned house was located in the Shui Yue, Water Moon, Security Zone next to a man-made high levee built to protect the area from floods and to mark the brigade limits. It also

gave a small child a view across the endless perfect lines of plant-
ings, perfect patches on a quilt—the farming efforts of the people.

There was a small pond nearby, but the water was always yellow-
ish. The entire neighborhood washed its laundry and vegetables
in it, and the cows bathed and relieved themselves in it as well.
The aqueduct nearby was hardly any better, tainted with DDT and
disgraced by animal feces and rotted plants. My parents didn't use
the pond that often because they didn't have enough vegetables
to wash or many clothes to clean. Due to Mother's sense of dignity,
we walked hours to reach the rushing clean curls of the Yangtze
River whenever the weather or our energy permitted.

Every household had an assigned plot in which the family was
to plant vegetables to sustain themselves and to grow feed for the
chickens and pigs. However, my parents' garden plot was always
barren. When they saw the neighbors harvest their produce,
such as cabbages, carrots, and potatoes, they realized they hadn't
planted anything yet. Then, to follow suit, they hurriedly would
dig the dirt and sow whatever seeds they could beg or borrow. The
mystery of the seasons, what to plant and when to plant, continued
to confound my parents. They followed the neighbors' lead, covering the newly planted seeds with straw and leaves to protect what
little hopeful green sprouts might finally appear. When they saw
any fruits of their labor poke up through the uncooperative soil,
they were thrilled. With no understanding of the ways of farming,
it came as a shock when they woke to find that nearly everything
was wiped out and destroyed down to the stub of each stem.

They sat on guard one early morning before the rooster welcomed the sun, only to find it was unexpected visitors who had
squeezed through our shabby fence to peck away all the buds of the
vegetables. We always envied how plump and healthy our neighbors' chickens were, but complaining made no sense because it
was the unworthiness of our fence that was to blame.

My family continued on with only the hope of surviving the
day, but there was no sympathy in the village to be had. Neighbors,
members of the brigades, villagers, even friends, pointed fingers at
my parents, the Enemies of the State who had no sense.

"They deserve to be poor. All they do is to pop out babies like chickens lay eggs."

"They have a teenage girl, the oldest daughter, the best laborer, but they send her off to live at a city school instead," they gossiped.

"Making her work in the fields would earn them points to receive crops and allocations, but no, they educate away their chance for food—foolish!"

"You will see they will end up eating their books!" they chattered back and forth.

We were shunned. More tongues were wagging: "You watch— her daughter may bring home an illegitimate baby, too. Aiyaa! That will be something!"

"Ignorance is a gift for a woman," one peasant said. "What man would want a woman smarter than himself?"

Father heard the gossip, and the words stung.

"It might not be a good idea to let Double Happiness continue on in boarding school for high school after all, even though Uncle Village pays a large portion. She is old enough to work to help the family, and in the end she would belong to another family since she would get married sooner or later. Other people never send their daughters to school. Maybe they are right when they say it's… a waste," he suggested after repeating the village gossip to Mother.

Nothing made Mother more furious than someone hurting or criticizing her children. For a woman who at one time had such dignity and status as the daughter of generations of respected scholars, these admonitions from the ignorant peasants were too much.

"According to the design of Chairman Mao, these people who had never put a pen to paper or passed their eyes over a single word in a book are now my superiors, our advisors? This upside-down world has destroyed our lives, but I won't allow it to destroy hers," she said as she banged the empty iron pot on the table. The loud noise made Father's eyes bulge out like a green lizard, and it shut him up right away.

"Who are you to tell me what to do with *my* daughter? She wobbled in my belly"—Mother patted her stomach—"not in yours.

You were the one who carried me into your life with eight men and a golden sedan," she snapped.

Father knew better than to argue when Mother's passion for her children was on fire. He dropped the discussion. She believed if my sister finished her high school and then college education, she could save us all from the evil dream that was our family's life. The entire family all worked to keep Sister Double Happiness living at her high school and Repeat Happiness at his middle school. Father's Uncle Village, the man of Mother's young, misdirected wedding dreams, was a professor living in Shanghai. Understanding the value of an education and as a childless man, he also helped pay for their education.

Even Grandmother helped. Although unable to stand and pained by her bound and broken-boned feet, she worked in our family patch hoeing the weeds while seated in a chair. As each section within reach was finished, she struggled to shift the flimsy chair to move down the row without complaint. There was no question that she would do this, no matter that she had once been like a royal princess who was delivered as a child bride to my wealthy and powerful grandfather. The innocent child who had watched her tiny feet ceremoniously bound to ensure her beauty, whose dainty feet had never touched the road, now stumbled on bleeding stumps through fields of bitter weeds in hopes that my oldest sister's college education would lift us from our lowly situation and restore our family's name. We were selling suffering and buying dreams.

CHAPTER 5
REALLY ENOUGH

I remember Mother's volumes from my early years, especially her ancient book of writings saved from the boot of the red-banded officials the day we lost our home.

"Don't touch, careful, gently." She turned the yellowed, stitched, handmade pages one at a time to show me the beautiful brush strokes to distract me. Holding my limp body, racked with fever from diphtheria, she boiled loofa soft enough to slide down my narrowing throat while reading the ancient poems of my ancestors aloud one after another in a soothing rhythm.

"Perhaps this is her strong fate," Father whispered to Mother, fearfully.

"She is only a few years in the world, and this gentler life in the countryside you promised may take her now," she answered.

Even the tender loofa gagged me. Mother urged me to eat. I saw her face disappear as she rolled me over onto her lap. My cough was so fierce it tossed up a rotted piece of flesh from deep inside. Father picked up the villain and put it in the drawer to show the vet to help in their decisions for my treatment. With little knowledge of herbs for curing, he ran to find his friend who tended to the animals nearby.

The veterinarian was tall and lean. I saw his calloused fingers approach my face holding a hollowed piece of straw. He opened a square of folded paper that held a white powder. Breathe in, breathe out, he drew it into the straw and puffed the evil-tasting treatment down my throat. Burn.

The next day, I heard his scraping voice speaking with Father outside the door. So I sneaked out behind the house and hid beneath the sorghum pile. When I was found, I locked my mouth to avoid another puff. Father looked about the kitchen in desperation.

"Where is that poker? I will have to pry her teeth open!"

With that, I opened up enough to endure another suffering. Gratefully, the poker remained beside the fire. When you have few tools, they have many uses.

As I stayed inside to become stronger, Mother and I could hear the sobs of women in the distance. She knelt to pray.

"You are a lucky little thing. Others were not so lucky," she said.

Once diphtheria had passed and the less fortunate children had been carried out by weeping families and were safe beneath their mounds of soil, I continued doing my household chores again. Each morning, I grabbed onto our handmade straw broom with two hands to sweep the dirt floor awkwardly. Sometimes I joined Grandmother pulling weeds in our little patch of a garden while waiting for a sunny day to face the most difficult task—the family laundry.

"Zhen Zhen, your brother Ox needs his clothes cleaned. This is something you will need to do. I have to sew for Auntie Tang," Mother said.

Because the sting of nearly losing Baby Enough had long ago subsided and the near tragedy had time to simmer in Mother's heart, I turned the terror to humor, for that was our way. I reenacted the pleading for the underwear as a way to distract her from my assignment. I twirled a pair of underwear from the laundry in the air just like Basket had done.

"What if word spreads in the village about your secret underwear, DaDa?" I asked, feigning fear.

"Zhen'er, that is not a proper subject for a young girl." Mother always had to start with talk of what was proper before she spilled her laughs with me.

"Maybe your secret magic underwear became famous in the village. What if Basket passed them on and your powerful good-luck underwear caused babies to be born as far away as Sand City?"

Mother turned her eyes quickly to me and smiled, her mouth about to erupt with the sweet sound of her laugh.

I pushed on. "And what if we went to Sand City and all along the road the children looked like me or Enough?" I laughed, not understanding anything about how those things worked but delighted at the thought of so many of me.

Mother laughed. "That is where we will end this talk, little thing. Only you will look like you, don't worry," she said, beginning to look off in that strange way that told me the laughter would end soon. I saw her saddened look and quickly changed my story to avoid the laundry task.

"Mother, it is cold today," I whined.

"I know, little thing, but the sun is shining, warm enough to dry the clothes. Your brother's clothes have been on his back too long."

"The last time it was very cold, Father's pants never dried. They stood right here by themselves as though he were still inside them." I pointed to the place in our main room, standing stiffly with my arms locked by my sides, coaxing a smile from her.

"It is not so cold today as it was the winter day your Father's pants stood up in this room without him." Mother started to smile as she packed her sewing basket.

"And Father had to stay in bed for an entire day for the lack of clothes to wear, remember, DaDa?" I continued. I was certain that would change her mind.

"Yes, if not for the sun that melted his pants on the floor from that hole in the crumbling ceiling, he would still be in bed today." She smiled slightly. She was trying to hold back her laugh, but I felt I had a chance.

"And Brother's shirt froze stiff in half over the clothesline as though he were taking a forever bow. You remember, right, DaDa?" I bent in half, stuck in place with stiff arms hanging down. Her frown moved at least to a straight line, but she kept the corners from curling, and I knew I would lose the fight when there was no laughter.

"You need to be as good at laundry as you are at negotiating," she said.

I tried again. "Tomorrow might be warmer."

"There is never tomorrow—there is only today, Zhen'er, there is only today," she said, and that set my fate.

While Mother sewed to earn our salt and Grandmother coaxed something green for our meals from the stubborn plot of land, I dragged the heavy laundry basket to the kitchen stall. With no money for the Foreign Devil soap that our neighbors used, the big yellow bar made by evil foreigners from very far away across the ocean, Mother taught me how to make a kind of soap from the ashes of the kitchen fire.

I went quite early to skim a few buckets of the least yellow water to heat for the washing before the neighbors could stir the murky silt to the pond's surface. Although much colder, the light yellow, lucky water of the morning was so much cleaner than the rust-colored water of the afternoon. It would make my cleaning job easier.

Into the wooden washing basin went Brother Ox's shirt and pants he had worn for days while waiting for a day of drying sun to make the change. I stretched a sheet of cloth worn thin from use across the basin. Scooping a pile of ashes from the kitchen's cooking fire, I piled them onto the sheet and poured the heated pond water over, letting it seep through slowly. Gathering the sheet, I twisted and twisted to squeeze the ashes, and they left their cleaning powers behind. I swirled the clothes until they began to give up their dirt and sweat stains to the ashen water.

It was his great fortune that Mother was finally able to sew a second shirt for Brother Ox to wear while the other was scrubbed. I had just one set of clothes, so the sun was my dearest friend while waiting on the bank in my outer clothes for my inner clothes to dry.

I tried to lift Brother's soaking shirt, but the weight of it was too much for my thin arms to bear. So, I squatted, held on with two tight fists, and cleverly turned my back while driving my legs to pull the heavy cloth over my shoulders from the basin, soaking my own clothes as much as the weeping shirt. Then I twisted and stood up, letting it drop to the scrubbing board. I rubbed in rhythm with my song:

Xi ya xi,
xi ya xi
Ning ya ning,
ning ya ning,
Shui bian zang le,
Yifu cai gan jing.

Rub, rub, rub,
Rub, rub, rub
Wring, wring, wring,
Wring, wring, wring
Water becomes dirty
Clothes become clean.

With one hundred rubs across the worn down rubber ribs, the collar, and the cuffs, I released the oily brown stains from my brother's hard work. Mother was right, although I had to tuck my hands under my arms to warm them for a while. They were only red, not blue, and the stiffness was not nearly as bad as that pants-standing winter day.

When I finished the scrubbing, I walked with the clothes over the levee to the aqueduct, trying to count my steps as Sister Enough had taught me. When I got to ninety-nine, I was distracted by a sparrow swooping and had to start again. I trudged up the ramp to the top of the levee, bent over with the weight of the wet clothes. In the cleaner water of the narrow canal that was stolen from the

Yangtze River for the crops, I rinsed the clothes, dipping, dipping, nine times each. Lifting the heavy bludgeoning stick, I beat the shirt and pants until they gave up even more of their soapy water, then I rinsed again to ready them for drying. I loved the echoing of the sound of the thump as I squeezed the excess water out. I tried to match my timing with others who thumped in concert along the levee. Lift and thump, lift and thump, until the clothes were rinsed and ready to hang on a string or perch on stiff, strong weeds to smile at the sun.

At home, following Mother's requirements, I folded the still-damp pants, running my hand along the pant leg to smooth out all the wrinkles. The last step of the job was my favorite—sitting on the nest of carefully folded pants on the chair to hatch the perfect crease.

Mother always said, "Now, at least your brother can walk proud to the fields in clean pants with a pressed line down his legs."

While I sat on the pile of pants, I felt a stinging on my arms like many bees attacking. By the time Mother returned from sewing for Auntie Tang, the first blister had appeared on the back of my hand. By the time she had the pot boiling for dinner, there were more, then some more, and by nighttime I was covered with itching blisters of a mysterious kind.

For weeks I suffered. The oozing blisters left me tortured by the itching and the flies that followed me, obsessed with my misfortune. When mercifully the blisters all turned to mere ruddy blotches, only one large growth above my eyelid and a second smaller one beneath it chose to keep residence after the dreadful illness. The two growths hardened, then softened, and then wept until they dried into a scar above and below my eye, stretching my right eye bigger, out of balance.

I heard the neighbors whisper, "Poor girl, will anyone ever want to marry her with that pulled eye?"

The condition of my stretched eye came to be called "Pulled Eyelid." I was called "Pulled Eyelid Zhen'er."

I never understood it was anything but a matter of fact. I often heard my sisters singing or reciting their made-up rhyme as they jumped rope:

Che yan pi
Che yan pi,
Mai ban li
Mai ban li,
Mai dao da jie shang
Gei da jie chi

Pulled Eyelid,
Pulled Eyelid,
Selling chestnuts,
Selling chestnuts,
Peddling in the city streets
For elder sister to eat!

All of my siblings sang it, and I did, too.

真

As I grew, I was so proud to be graduated to gathering weeds and plants for the cooking fire and our food while Mother was busy paying Father's debts by sewing for the neighbors.

"I am leaving for Auntie Tang's home. I must sew for her today to repay a debt," Mother said. "You know the house, Zhen Zhen?" She doubled my name to double her tenderness. "If you came there later without my asking, I could be surprised, and they might share a little rice with you, do you understand?" She wanted to be honestly surprised to keep her honor.

"Now, don't forget to gather what plants you can for our meal tonight. When you go out to look for roots and leaves, you can even cut the leftover short weeds. The tall weeds may already have been gathered into our neighbors' kitchens. Then, put them under the sun. After they are dry, we can use them to start the fire." She used one hand to show me how to grab the short weeds in the bundle and the other hand to show me how to use the sickle. Then she handed me my basket and tool. My training complete, I said good-bye to our little pig that sat smiling in the weeds, and I set about my honorable mission.

Sometimes the wind blew tears into my eyes, but on this day it blew a gift into my hands. A children's paper, the first printed piece of paper I ever owned, lifted on wings from some other child's life into my own. I ran my fingers over the characters on the single newsprint page. The characters that Mother had taught me were already enough to read the children's story. I kept it inside my shirt until the long shadows delivered me home.

When I carefully pulled it from my shirt, I saw that the moisture had already seeped into the paper from the hot sun, smearing some of the characters. This only made it more exciting for me because I could add my own imagined words to the faded spots. I used Mother's tedious lessons to read it over and over when I reached home. Smoothing it out on the table, I read "Little Tiger," and then I read another story of a white rabbit. Every single day from then on, I read this single page, staring at the lines to make them come clear, holding it to my heart, running my finger over the little tiger's head. He was my secret friend, and my love of reading made Mother smile.

Although I was not yet the required age of seven, Mother decided to send me to the school to be tested.

"Zhen'er, would you like to go school? Sister Complete can bring you to take the test," she said.

"Yes, yes, I want to go to school," I answered quickly. I had so wanted to hold my own textbook, to be like Puppy sitting in a class-room reciting poems and learning to write the special characters with my own pencil and my own piece of paper.

Sister Complete and I arrived at the school, and I sat for the test.

"What is your name?" the teacher asked.

"I am Zhen'er," I answered bravely.

"Excuse me, teacher, her full name is Zhao Hong Qin," Sister Complete interrupted.

"Ah, yes, from now on, Zhen'er, you will be a big girl with the school name, Qin. Are you a musical girl, to have the name that means a musical instrument?" he asked.

"No, my brother, Repeat Happiness, is the musical one—he gave me my school name. Oh, I played a spoon on our pot once, but Mother made me stop," I answered.

He laughed. "Count as high as you can, please," the man said.

I counted until he stopped me.

"All right, all right, that is enough. You certainly know your numbers."

"I know them from the many steps to the levee for the washing. I can do more if you wish," I said proudly.

"No, that won't be necessary. Let's see how you are at reading," he continued.

I smiled. I could read the characters easily, and I could recognize all of the pictures and match them with the words. I sat rocking from side to side, unable to control my excitement. When the teacher returned with my paper, his look made me feel afraid.

"You did very well, except this one answer is wrong. Can you tell me what these are?"

I looked at the two rounded, dimpled figures side by side.

"Shoes...two dirty shoes," I answered.

A small chill traveled down my back and fizzled onto my arms.

"No, that is incorrect. Have you never seen peanuts before?"

"Yes, but I have also seen shoes. These are the bottom of dirty shoes," I said.

I was afraid, but then the teacher smiled and handed me over to Sister Complete for our walk home. At home, she told Mother of my error.

"She got everything right except she called a picture of two peanuts a pair of dirty shoes."

Mother nodded and looked at me. "Who cares about peanuts? Shoes are more important for us, right, Zhen Zhen? You did very well. You have been accepted to school. That is the important thing."

真

I was standing and reading my Little Tiger paper in the field one day as Mother passed by with her sewing basket over her arm. I proudly held up my vegetable basket and waved, too, although it was a rare day to find a vegetable or to fill my basket with anything but wild weeds and plants. As I left for the fields, I saw a little girl walking on the levee with a new doll dancing its lovely arms and legs as she passed me, chin held high, turning her head around over her coy shoulder to watch my jealousy. I kept the memory of the dancing in my mind as I went about my daily chore.

I felt very important to be responsible for gathering wild plants in the fields for our daily meals and kindling for our fire, but my eye caught a scrap of fabric blown up against the levee, blown by the wind to be my fortune. I squatted down and studied it—one white remnant. I smiled at my find and in my mind, a rabbit smiled back. I plucked the scrap from the briar and ran to the cotton field. My fingers became shredded with little pricks from the picking of the little bits of fluff left over from the cotton harvest. The white softness nestled deep inside each stem was a treasure. I ran the mile to Mother with my discoveries. I quietly entered from the back door into the kitchen of Auntie Wu, where she sat sewing. This rabbit would certainly dance as wonderfully as any doll, I thought.

"Here, eat rice quickly. I am busy with work," she said as I sat on her lap and took some bits of rice and broth from her bowl. "Are you still hungry?" she asked me.

"Finished, DaDa," I said. I did not want to shame her with the truth of my emptiness.

She became very busy with her sewing. I always felt the special connection we had when I sat by her feet as she sewed. At home, I would see her eyes flicker back and forth from her humbling task to the precious box that held her family's legacy. I watched with fascination but saw no joy on her face as she transformed her old jacket into my sister's new coat.

"Little thing, if your fortune is according to my dreams, your life will be what is in that wooden box and not what is in my aching hands," she said.

"May I use one needle and just one bit of thread, please?" I asked. "I have a special friend to fashion." She did not answer. Just then, I spied a long strip of orange fabric in a little pile of scraps left over from her sewing. "DaDa, may I have this scrap?"

"What? I am busy now, Zhen'er! You don't want to learn this skill, I promise you. No daughter who comes from my body will follow this unfortunate path. No sewing for my daughters. You should read."

"Please? He wants me to. Just this once, then I promise, no more sewing." I quickly took the scraps of fabric and the needle and thread without waiting for an answer and ran home on happy legs.

I sat on my straw bed and cut the white cloth to fit the image in my mind, then stitched it awkwardly. Just before my dearest friend was ready, I stuffed the glorious cotton inside, and he came alive, dancing like no doll could ever do. Then I quickly sewed an orange carrot for his lunch. My rabbit would always have a meal.

I remembered my important chore, so I left to gather plants with my new best friend sitting proudly in my heavy, handled basket. It depended on the seasons. In summer and fall, I picked in the cotton fields. In winter and spring, I looked in the soy and wheat fields for whatever I could find. The bamboo basket was so large that I am sure my head and knees were all that showed as I walked into the fields. When so much usage made the handle or rims fall apart, I used some flax fiber to tie the frayed parts together. If the bottom of the basket wore out, I scavenged for scraps of hard paperboard or a thin wood board to cover the holes to make sure my valuable plants would not leak out. It was my basket.

One afternoon, I was singing to my rabbit and feeding him his carrot.

Grandmother said, "You have no plants for the family dinner, and yet you play? The time is getting late."

I ignored her, caught up in the newness of my friend, so proud of my creation. I had so many people to introduce him to, and I had to find a proper name. She came from the house a second time, noticing I had not yet set out. Grandmother, crippled by her painful feet, awkwardly lowered herself and knelt on the ground to beg me, her panic over having nothing to cook for the evening meal weighing on her heart.

"Please, Zhen'er, you put aside this child's play and bring food for your old grandmother and your family. There is an empty bowl waiting. Please, I am begging."

I turned to see the peasant neighbors pointing in mockery to see Grandmother on her knees, brushing their fingers along their cheeks to signify my shamefulness.

"Don't worry, my new little friend. It is not your fault. There is still time. See how our shadows are only so long? Besides, you have your carrot, see?" I explained to my rabbit.

When I went inside to tell Grandmother I was leaving for the field and not to worry, I saw her tortured feet unwrapped. My eyes followed the tail end of the long, wavy strip of cloth that led to her twisted stumps. Her tiny feet were the size of her fist. She was moaning quietly to herself, "Uh, uh," while carefully wiping the blackened crust of blood from beneath her unrecognizable toes, toes that had curled in fear beneath her foot like the root ball of a dense tree. She heard my shock.

"You should be happy this is no longer a girl's fate, Zhen, Zhen," she said, dipping a cloth in warm water and applying cat-tail stamen into the deep creases to soothe the pain.

"Mother said it was beautiful in the past," I said, looking at her feet in horror.

"Not beautiful to a child of four who suffered the daily pain to seek such beauty."

"Why…didn't you stop them?" I asked.

"My mother wanted to ensure my husband's love and admiration by making my feet petite and small. It was tradition for a lady of high status. There were nights I begged her to release the binds, for I could not bear the deep pain; but in the end I, too, wanted to be like a princess. My feet were first bound at four years old, two years before I went to live at your grandfather's grand home."

"Does it hurt?" I asked.

"I have not spent one day without the aching and the pain from this thing of beauty, but you do not need to worry about this, Zhen'er. Go and find our dinner now for Grandmother."

I looked down at my grateful feet and left quickly, running with my rabbit and my basket to the fields, determined not to disappoint my suffering Grandmother.

In the wheat field, there were other children who had been gathering plants, too. But their baskets were full from their labor. They started to play a gambling game. Drawing a line in the dirt, they stood behind it and threw the sickle forward as far as they could. The farthest throw was the winner, and the losers had to give up some of their plants to the winner. As a young Enemy, I was never included, of course.

After a few rounds, some of the children had lost a lot. I picked diligently, shifting my eyes from my bent position to watch their game. The boy who lost the most ran toward me and grabbed a fistful of my plants. He threw my rabbit to the ground, and I swept it up into my arms, dropping my basket. I chased after him with Grandmother's pain in mind, searching for the words to scream at him as his legs took him over the levee.

"Bad...bad egg!" I called, not having a more powerful word, since Mother would never allow naughty words to be uttered in our home.

When I returned to my unattended basket, it was empty, the other children having made up their losses through my small-handed efforts. The sun stayed for another cold hour as I slashed at the few remaining plants in the shadows of my shame, but there was not nearly enough to feed the family. There was not nearly enough to soothe Grandmother's aching worries. I sat down on the cold ground and bit my lip to prevent my tears. Then I turned to see the twin sister of the thief replenishing my basket with an armful of the stolen plants. I thanked her and walked home feeling like a speck of a girl out in the vast field.

After I carried the basket home, I selected the best and most tender tops for the family's meal. I grabbed the remaining stubs, banged the dirt from the roots, and put them aside for our family pig, thinking of his always-present smile despite his bony ribs. After the selection was done, I put all the pig's plants in a big wooden basin and chopped them into a mashed mix. I tried to keep the blood from my left hand, which was tattered from grabbing the rough weeds, from coloring the poor pig's food. I put some dried cattail stamen on the cut. Thinking of Grandmother's feet with a sickness in my stomach, I carefully wrapped my hand up with a long, torn rag.

真

Soon we had to sell the pig, our only option to get food for the family in the fallow wintertime. We had luck; we would not have to do the deed ourselves because it was year-end, close to the Spring Festival, when the butchers came to give their services from village to village. They were in our village and would kill the bony pig for us if we could prepare in time. Although the government took half of everything that was slaughtered as our rightful contribution to the people, Mother said it was worth avoiding the unthinkable task.

Two things stood between the meal and us—a match and a boiling pot of water. Mother opened the little match box and found nothing.

"Zhen Zhen, quickly, take the piece of fortunate heavy paper you found yesterday on the road, and roll it tight into a tube like this." She rolled the paper into a long cone shape.

"Now, run to neighbor Uncle Liu and borrow some fire. Careful, don't lose it on the way home. Twice borrowed may bring us the loss of the future goodwill of our neighbor. Can you do it, Zhen'er?" Mother asked.

"Yes, I will be careful," I said.

I had seen Father borrow fire before. It was the least of Father's borrowing. He said fire was a good thing to borrow because no one was worse off for the borrowing, and unlike the salt and oil, the neighbors had no expectation of its return. So I didn't mind the assignment.

I rolled the paper again just to ensure a tight fit and ran to the neighbor, feeling comfortable with the small favor I was about to request. Taking their fire would leave them with no less than they had, I reasoned. Keeping my eye on the paper in my hand and pushing away the thought of my smiling pig's face, I pulled at my mind to keep it on the fire task at hand, not daring to let my thoughts follow the fateful thread from flame to pot to pig to scream.

The neighbor's fire was blazing. I carefully teased a flame onto my paper from under the pot, stopping a moment to inhale the luscious aroma from the bubbling meal that I could not define.

"Thank you, Uncle Liu." I said politely.

I walked home holding the paper torch upright in one hand and protecting it with the other—fast enough to return quickly but slow enough not to lose the gift. I held my body motionless while my legs moved deliberately in long, slow strides beneath me. When the wind blew the flame back toward me, I slowed my progress. When it flared again, I moved again.

"Good work, Zhen'er, careful of the wind, slowly," Mother said, guiding me.

She took the treasured torch and held it to the pile of weeds and twigs while I had the important job of directing my breath to the flame.

"Alright, Zhen Zhen, blow as though you were about to whistle but with an unending steady stream. Slowly, steady, good, now. Take another breath. More, yes, yes, you have it now."

I gave it just the right amount of puff, and Mother jiggled the little weeds around until they turned yellow then red, and then the pile flared with fire. I felt a tightening in my throat. With my little torch I had been as much the betrayer to the little pig as the husky peasants who would do the deed. I tried to draw the air back in, but the crackling killer had taken hold.

It was the most dreadful time for Mother and me. She had to cook a big, full pot of boiling water for the butchers to dump on the pig to help to scrape its hair off. The sound of their unexpected scalding made my stomach feel twisted, and I feared I would cough up a portion of my heart. It was always the most traumatic time for Mother and me. I had fed the pig for months, not thinking of its fate.

The butchers didn't like us because Mother never did a good job of boiling the water to scalding. The well-built peasants were powerful and had no concern for the feelings of one small pig. They caught my pig, tied it up and put it on two benches. One butcher held the end of the pig, one held the head of the pig, the third one held a long butcher knife. Mother grabbed my little hand, and we ran as fast as we could so we didn't have to hear the pig cry. We covered our ears but could still hear it. We ran past the neighbor's house, but we could still hear it. We could hear the moment the peasant violently thrust the knife into the crying pig's neck, so we kept running up and onto the levee, but the winter wind still carried the pig's destiny to our hearts.

When his cry weakened and stopped, we returned to hide in mother's bedroom from the slaughter and the sight of the blood-filled basin. When Mother was nowhere to be found, all the butchers were angry. They needed her to cook the meat for them to eat.

They said loudly, "Since we already took a life, we might as well enjoy a feast."

Mother did not answer. She always regretted that she had to eat meat. On holidays or Spring Festival, she would fast from eating meat. Hearing the last moments of the animal's fate was enough to spoil any enjoyment.

"Mother, can't they see the pig has eyes and a smiling mouth just like us?" I whispered in her room as we huddled together. I cried for the pig's fate for hours—or perhaps it was for our own fate for which I cried. It was an unbearable sight, an unbearable sound.

Father was pleased. With the pig slaughtered, we would have food for the New Year Feast called Guo Nian, "Survive Year." For us, survival was the only goal. The Spring Festival, as it was called, although it happened in the bitter cold winter season before any hint of spring was felt, was the most important celebration. Anticipating good fortune, family members would travel whatever distance necessary to eat a feast together. New decorations, new clothes, and red envelopes with lucky money for the children were all necessary to welcome in an auspicious New Year. As a result, the rich looked forward to the arrival of the New Year, and the poor feared it. Poor children, unlike their parents who dreaded the New Year, welcomed the celebration for the possibility of a better meal and a day free from any threat of punishment for naughtiness, for it was the period of good-luck creation.

真

I never remember having new clothes. Mother managed to alter her old cotton coat to a smaller one, and that was new to me. She did make a pair of new shoes for me one New Year. That was the most precious thing I owned in my whole little life. If ever I found a stain on the shoe, I worked hard to clean it off with my saliva and my tears. Clean shoes—I loved them!

Having no means to earn money or points to provide for the family, Father borrowed money from others. It turned out borrowing money was often done, but paying back was seldom seen. Especially at the New Year, people flowed to our house asking for repayment. Sometimes they were patient walking away empty handed. Most of the time they were rude and angry, demanding money right there, right then, threatening to tear the house apart or storming away, promising to be back again soon. Somehow, Father always happened to be absent during these visits. So, whenever strangers walked in the direction of our house, our bodies shook in terror, and our hearts sank.

On a cold day close to The New Year Festival, a young girl came to our house dressed in a nice, warm, short, Mandarin-style quilted cotton coat with a lovely pink floral design. She walked toward me as I was standing in front of my home. She asked for my father. I was happy to see a girl had come to visit; it was so rare. I ran into the house and brought him outside.

When she saw Father, she asked, "Do you remember who cut your hair?"

"Yes, it was Sifu Chen," he said, using the title "Sifu," a respectful term for Master.

"Good, he is my father. He sends me here to collect the money you owe. We need money for the New Year."

The smile on my face froze. I looked at Father. The scars on his face grew into the familiar yet still frightening bright red centipedes from the pulsing blood of his anger.

"Yes, I am sorry not to have the money right now. Maybe after the New Year I will find money to pay him back. Please let your father know that, OK?" he said calmly.

"My father said you are a liar, Lao Tsai!" Lao means "old," and Tsai was Father's last name.

Only men of equal age and status would use that term among themselves. She was being very disrespectful. I could not tolerate it. "Listen, my father is not a liar. It is not right for you to call him Lao Tsai, either," I yelled at the girl.

By then, a few of the passing people stopped to watch, and Father was very embarrassed. He changed his smiling face from sweet and solicitous to the girl and turned to me with tortured anger, "Shut your mouth up, will you? Who gives you the right to talk back to her, eh?" he said to me with venom on his tongue.

"I can't let her insult us," I answered, hurt by his attack.

"She is a nice girl. She is not insulting us," he said.

"Yes, she is," I argued.

"How dare you talk back? You'll see how I fix you! You are embarrassing me here in front of others? I will twist your head off," he said. He forcefully grabbed me and dragged me to the door while I protested, screaming.

Mother heard all the commotion and saw what Father was doing to me. She went inside and brought out the sickle that I used to cut and gather the wild weeds.

"Now, here is the knife, you can just kill her, ok? Then you can kill me. We can all die by your hands. Take it and do it. You are a big man. You are strong." She waved the weapon in the air, challenging him hysterically.

The onlookers stepped in and took the sickle away from Mother. The girl in the enviable coat realized that she had stirred up serious trouble and fled the scene. Humiliated, Father touched the rippled, long scars on his face, then turned and stomped away.

真

Soon, it was New Year's Eve, but there were no red envelopes for us. Just Mother and I were home squatting on the dirt floor in the mud-walled kitchen stall, which was attached to the side of the house. When I went outside to the fenced-in storage area to get the last of the cotton stems, twigs, and dried weeds for the cooking fire, I saw a dark figure moving toward the house. I hurried inside but could say nothing, the fear having stolen my voice. The pot sat on the big iron grate over a hole where we stuffed anything burnable to cook food and boil water. Mother stood behind the mud-brick cooking stand, and I sat in front of it, feeding weeds into the fire with our long iron poker in hand. The smoke had turned the kitchen walls black. Even the spider webs hanging from the ceiling could not escape the inky soot.

We looked up to see the shadowy figure standing at the entrance of the kitchen. It was a man we didn't know. But we did know what he had come for and why he had chosen that evening; he thought that my father would finally be caught at home on New Year's Eve. Fortunately, or unfortunately, he wasn't home.

"I am here looking for Lao Tsai! He borrowed money from me and said he was going to give it back to me in two months. Now two years have passed."

"It is New Year's Eve. Your family must want you to be with them. I will tell my husband you have come here for the money, and I will ask him to prepare it for you after the New Year," Mother said with respect.

"No, I am going to stay here until he comes home," the man insisted.

"He has been out finding some food for the celebration, and we really don't have anything to pay you at this moment."

"Well, I am willing to wait as long as it takes," he shouted at Mother.

He sat himself down on a pile of mud bricks and watched us cook. Mother appeared calm, chopping the tender parts of the weeds I gathered from the fields and soaking them in the boiling water. Then she took them out quickly, squeezed the bitter juice off, and mixed it with a small amount of rice. With shaking hands, I fed fewer cotton stems to the fire to let the pot simmer for a little longer. When the food was ready, Father was still not home. The man had waited a long time, so Mother offered him the not-so-festive meal. He took it, smelled it, and threw it against the wall. We jumped from the sting of it—the hours to pick and pound the weeds, the hours to boil and cook the porridge, the wasted cotton stems for the fire, the back-to-the-sun labor to earn our only bit of rice remaining for the New Year. All of this work made his gesture a shocking one, a cruel one. I scrambled to retrieve the bowl and any of the precious remaining drops. He stared at Mother with fury, shook his head, and stood up to leave.

Mother sat next to me as I mindlessly held the poker, drawing lines in the ashes. We were both quiet. The fire had burned out, and the kitchen became cold again. I just couldn't hold back my sobs. Mother and I started to cry hard, letting all the bitter tears out like the bitter juice squeezed and lost from the wild weeds.

"Tear down the east wall to mend the west wall," Mother quoted the old saying. I knew my family did things differently. We tore down the east wall and then tore down the west wall, too. There was no mending, no making amends. We borrowed from here and then we borrowed from there, expanding our circle of debt.

CHAPTER 6
CITY DREAMS

I always thought that I was more fortunate than my unwanted sister, Enough Complete Happiness. She must have had to hold her fists so tight clinging to her little life in the womb while Mother was engaging in all those unsuccessful and desperate tricks to prevent another wide-opened mouth from entering the nest. In a way I felt special, more wanted, more welcomed, because I had heard no such horrible stories about my entry into this life.

One day, I just had to ask Mother why it was that she did not try to rid herself of *me* because she had been so determined not to have another child after Enough was born. "Were you thinking the pregnancy felt different and the baby must be more special, perhaps?" I suggested.

Mother brushed the thought away like an annoying fly. "No, I wasn't thinking that way."

"Well, thank you, DaDa, you make me feel so precious. I should have known better by just looking at my name, Really Enough Complete Happiness, or else you might have called me something else like Precious Pearl," I said.

"I didn't even know I was pregnant," she added.

"If you knew you were pregnant, would you have gotten rid of me?" I felt sad asking the question, but once the lid was off the pot, I had to eat the rice.

"I might have. My tired belly had no break, and we had the uncertainty of our being able to stay in our home. In fact, if ever I had ill wishes for someone, I would wish them to be pregnant," Mother said.

Now in the face of those harsh words of truth, I didn't feel that special anymore. As my name made clear, it was simply the continuation of her pleading words for mercy, a message of her patience wearing thin—thin like the children she daily tried to feed—really enough.

"It doesn't mean I would have been successful in the deed, so you don't have to worry. As you know, you are even more stubborn and feisty than your sister, and she survived unmentionable things."

As Mother noticed my deflated enthusiasm, she comforted me in her own limited way. "Let's go to the city together."

Mother had always wished we had chosen life in the city. She complained a thousand times about how Father had made the wrong choice to move to the countryside with the hope of relying on his friends, who never did anything to help us. She wished he had chosen to move to the city while the policy still allowed it so all of us could have had a job instead of being field workers. By then, it was too late. The rules by that time forbade any choice in residence; we were told where to live.

"There is nothing wrong with being peasants," she explained. "We all have our role to play. It is just that our family has no skill in farming, so we should never have come here so far from the city. It is said that the cruelty against the Enemy of the State is less severe in the city. Had we been in the city, we may never have been treated as Enemies at all."

Mother made a plan to give me a taste of her yearnings, perhaps to plant the seed in my heart. On the day we were to go, there were preparations. I was scrubbed and cleaned, and Mother cleverly altered my humble clothes to give them a sense of newness.

She had her own routine. As a pampered child in her past, she always appreciated beauty and held her dignity. She took the treasured, used matchstick and smiled into the rippling mirror—like looking into clear moving water, she drew each eyebrow with the charred end with precision. Fixing her short hair a bit, she paused, and I saw that look again, the look I never quite understood that always made me stay very silent in my place, waiting.

She turned to hold my face. "You look like a movie star!" she said, eyeing her handiwork up and down, and added, "A perfect fit for a star."

I looked into the mirror for a moment to see the star. The dreadful blisters that had covered my body from my former illness had all long ago healed with the herbs Mother had applied. I smiled. They were gone, but I did not see the star my mother saw; I saw the scar. I unconsciously touched my pulled eyelid with my finger, and the strange little rhyme resurrected once again in my ears:

Che yan pi,
Che yan pi
Mai ban li,
Mai ban li.

Pulled eyelid,
Pulled eyelid,
Selling chestnuts,
Selling chestnuts.

Mother stubbornly held on to the dream of the better life in the city as intensely as she held my hand when we walked toward the ferry to Sand City. We walked for hours. All the while, she entertained me with stories and reenactments of the details of her life before there was me.

"I will tell you everything, Zhen'er, even though your young ears may not hear the lessons. I will not let my last little thing follow the wrong path to the fields. Do you understand?" I did not.

67

The ferry brought us to the North River land at Sand City. As we inferior South River people approached our destination, we arched our necks to see one hundred stone steps that would take us up to the top of the bank of the levee that protected the city. One hundred steps up, more than one hundred steps down, and we arrived weak-legged but smiling at the edge of a sea of dull, green jackets buttoned to the neck—and bicycles, so many bicycles. We weaved across the street through the string of bikes. One wobbly bike carried a large dining table across its narrow back wheel; on another perched a father with his three smiling children.

Safe on the other side, we stood in front of a factory, watching workers with their privileged badges go in and out of the gate. We imagined they were in paradise. Mother wished to have that paradise for us, too.

"See, look, Zhen'er, if you live in the city, you may come and go from work with a full stomach. You would earn real money to buy food and water, even a thermos of hot water to bring home to heat your bath."

"DaDa, I want to be in the city, like Double Happiness," I pleaded.

"Oh, yes, you will do that someday, I am sure. You see, you see, Zhen'er, why I wanted the city?" she said.

We walked through the street in flow with streams of people dressed in sameness—drab green, blue, and grey, all having a place to go to. A calendar shop, with the most beautiful colorful pictures I had ever seen of mountains, flowers, flowing robes, and temples, captured my eyes. I had never seen a color picture. If I could have left my eyes behind to gaze at them for a hundred years, I would have—and it would not have been enough. How I wished these pictures could join Chairman Mao on our wall so I could brighten our dull room with so many colors.

"Shall we go to a restaurant, Zhen'er?" Mother asked.

"Ha! Yes, we can go to a restaurant together and watch other people eat." I knew we had no such money, but she joked about it with me on our long walk. We enjoyed our laugh. We carried only the charred crust of the rice from the bottom of the iron pot, which became the most delicious part when hunger changed your mind about it. We told each other what we would order at the restaurant, but I thought it was just a fantasy to have much beyond rice and a few vegetables and a rare treat of meat. I did not feel envy; it was just a fact. I knew it simply was not possible for an unworthy person like me.

"An ugly toad cannot dine on a swan," Father would say to help us to accept our fate.

"When you have money someday, you will sit in a restaurant and order whatever food you wish. You see, Zhen'er? So much food in the city," Mother said. We gazed up at the hanging quartet of shiny glazed ducks, but only she was able to imagine their delicious taste.

"You see, two levels of eating? You will dine at the top level someday, the better food, the better dishes, the better service."

I counted: first floor, second floor. There at the top floor in a large window, a little girl with a beautiful flower in her hair stared down at me, pointing. Her parents tugged at her hand to sit and enjoy her feast. In my distraction, I dropped my little packet of charred rice. I laughed out loud, wide—mouthed at my clumsiness.

"Really Enough Complete Happiness, you will soon be too old to act this way. Who will marry you if you continue these antics, laughing with your mouth wide open and your tongue wagging?"

"Mother," I said, "you were the one who taught me to laugh out loud. Remember, especially, when we were afraid?"

"Someday soon you will be a grown lady," she said, looking up at the window to see the elegant family dining in the window and staring down at us. "Let me show you. A proper lady expresses her humor in a pretty way, see? Like this," Mother tittered sweetly with her lips closed fully over her teeth, her straightened fingers touching her top lip gently, her head tilted demurely to one side. Three little tweets emitted: "Hmm hmm hmm." Mother continued, "and no bending over like you are a peasant planting rice with your rear end to the sky. You dip with your back straight, like this." She lowered herself elegantly to pick up my humble meal.

"But now we *are* peasants, DaDa. Can't we just bend over as a small benefit of our losses?" I asked.

We looked at each other for a moment as we both held our laughs tight-lipped. She put her face in her hands and shook her head no, side to side, trying to restrain her laughter. Then, throwing her head back, laughing open-mouthed, she stopped abruptly.

"Only in private from now on, you understand, my Zhen, Zhen?"

I could not answer with the loud laugh still growling in my throat. We happily sat on a bench and opened our little packets of charred rice balls with no concern for the peering eyes above us.

Mother was quiet on the way home. I walked comfortably in her silence and in my own. I had seen things, things that colored my dreams. I needed to find a place inside me to keep them. We arrived home weary, but the weather was too hot to sleep, so we took the chairs to the top of levee to enjoy the cooler air. We moved our palm fans in rhythm to chase away mosquitoes. Again, I was alone with her. She had said very little to me since our long walk home. We looked at the stars and the moon and each other. In the golden moonlight, I saw her face go dreamy as I had never seen before, so I left my eyes there quietly to enjoy it.

She broke the buzzing silence, waving her torn palm fan to cool me. In a low voice, she said, "Someday, you can even wear long, dangling earrings. Did you ever see real dangling gold earrings?"

"No, only the pretend ones we made out of the sweet-potato stems," I said. She put her fan on her lap and measured, spreading her thumbs and first fingers as far as she could beside each of her ears. "They can be as long as this...thin and long and gold. When you have them on, and you move your head, they dangle and dance around your happy face."

"Did you once have them, DaDa?" I asked.

"Oh, yes," she said. She closed her eyes, turned her head slowly from side to side, lifted her shoulders, tilted her cheeks up to the stars with a smile, and I could almost see them swaying.

"I can see them, DaDa," I whispered.

"Yes, you will have them someday, I am sure...maybe you will even let me borrow them?"

"Of course. We both will be wearing long and dangling earrings," I said.

We started to laugh. Even the moon was smiling in her eyes. It caused a feeling in my chest that I discovered was the meaning of a name that we all shared but had not been blessed with, for in that fleeting moment, I discovered...happiness.

Swat! "Acch!" The screaming of mosquitoes in our ears interrupted the magic of the spell. Swat! Mother let out an abrupt sigh, adjusted herself in the flimsy chair, and resumed her normal posture. As quickly as the moment arose, her palm fan brushed it away, and it was gone with no sign that it had ever been at all. The butterfly that had lit upon my finger escaped my gentle grasp and came no more.

真

The reality was that food was always scarce, and the dream of earrings became faded and remote, so I tucked it deep within me, along with my city dreams for another time. Days later, Mother shared the exciting news: Sister Double was coming home for a visit from her teaching job in the city. I was excited to tell her of our trip to Sand City. Sister Double Happiness had not been home since she graduated from college. She did not bring home an illegitimate baby after all, as predicted by our critical villagers who thought educating a girl was a waste of time. Instead, she delivered a single piece of paper, more precious than any paper that had come into our lives before—her college diploma. Mother held the paper to her heart. She had long ago put this moment in her dreams and sent it to the sky with each day that she watched three of her precious children shrink off into the distance to another day of wretched labor. For the first time in my young years, I saw her cry with joy. This hope, this single grain of snow-white rice she had secretly kept as an offering in the hands of her forbidden goddess statue, Kuan Yin, buried in the dark, earthen corner of her bedroom floor, had somehow sprouted. A tiny green promise of a future had emerged in which I imagined that perhaps our barren field would finally fill itself with enough to satisfy us all.

She and Father looked down lovingly at the paper, seeing way off to a place beyond my eyes. Inside its golden characters and blood-red stamp lived my mother's ill health, grew my sister's bent spine, breathed my brother's angry soul, ached my grandmother's raw club feet, and lived my hope, as the youngest one who had not yet felt her flesh in the sharp teeth of the commune fields.

As the first female of the county to earn a bachelor's degree, my sister was elevated to the Cadre classification. An honored civil servant, she became a teacher at the county's number one high school. Although her success meant she officially belonged to the Cadre category, guaranteeing her fair share of food and commodities for life, she would never wash the stench of her family's Enemy background from her hands.

In her continued good fortune, however, she met a young man who was also a college graduate. Most importantly, he was willing to marry her, despite her bad classification.

"See, I knew this name was right for your sister," Mother said with pride. "Two blessings at one time: college and an educated husband make Double Happiness a wise choice for her name, after all."

We took a long trip, about 30 kilometers, to Sister's school for their wedding. Mother and I rode a donkey, no doubt a loan from an admiring neighbor for our newly gained but fleeting status. She rode with the look she must have had when those eight strong men and a golden sedan lifted her on high on her wedding day. Brother Ox walked along, guiding the luxurious animal down the road. Unlike Mother, the up and down poking of the donkey's boney hips into my tender end made me envy him, but the look on Mother's face and her slightly elevated chin kept me mesmerized and grateful for the ride. Then she spoke. "Zhen'er, Sister Double Happiness will be married at the school where she teaches. This is very important, you see?"

"Why is it important, Mother, because there will be food?" I guessed.

"No, because it means she will not have to be enslaved to her mother-in-law. She will have all the powers of a man, her own household at the school where she teaches," Mother explained.

"I don't understand." I said.

"Someday you will," she said, smiling.

We entered the room where several teachers had gathered. I ran my eyes over the fabric of their city clothes. I could not imagine having two or even three clothes—one for the teaching days and others for special days off and holidays. On the table was a jar of candies making me ache to have the ceremony over. If stories of my mother's grand wedding were in my sister's mind, I couldn't tell. It seemed Mother could have been wrapped in silk in the simple schoolroom for the way she smiled. Sister appeared to be so tall, wearing a new jacket with long, thin cotton buttons. She had a little crocheted red flower on her jacket, and I loved it. I had never had a possession that had no purpose but to just be there for the looking. How wonderful that flower was.

"May I have the flower, please?" I begged. All of the people looked at me and laughed, excusing my audacity due to my age.

Mother said to me gently, "No, you can't have the flower. It is for your sister. She is getting married."

"Then I want to get married, too!" I said.

"It is too shameful to say such a thing as a little girl," Mother said sternly. I saw that her eyes were hiding her amusement.

After the ceremony, I had the most delightful candy. I was sorry that Sister Complete had to remain at home to search for our evening meal and gather kindling for the cooking fire, so I slipped one candy into my pocket for her. We posed for a very rare and special photograph of Sister Double Happiness; her husband, Arrival; Brother Ox; and me in front, holding Mother's hand. I wished Sister Enough could have been there, but she already had the dream of living with Sister Double Happiness in the city, where she was going to school.

真

With the long-ago wedding memories in mind, I was excited when Mother told me that Sister Double Happiness planned to come home for a visit from her teaching job in the city along with her young son. I hoped to tell her of my dreams of the city, too. It would give me something to talk about with her. She stayed only one day. The morning before she left, she was treated with pure white rice and an egg. She was like an Empress. While I watched her eat, Father called me to do chores. I could not bear to leave her sight; I had not yet had the chance to speak with her about my city trip with Mother.

"Can't you wait a minute? At least let me watch her a little longer?" I yelled.

Sister Double Happiness raised her head from her food and said disapprovingly, "Don't be so unteachable!"

"Unteachable?" The insulting word thrust into my heart, shattering my admiration. *I am not one of those young, worthless, unteachable people,* I thought as the pain refused to subside in my twisting stomach. I was so proud to have a sister who lived in the city. I examined her lovely clothes, her quilted jacket with embroidered flowers, and her beautiful, clean shoes. How I wished she would like me. I would be willing to do anything for her. I wouldn't ask to eat her pure white rice or her egg; I knew she deserved only the best. I would simply hope to watch her lift her chopsticks to her lips and see her smile at me. Instead, the same admiration that made it impossible to leave her sight caused her to see me as unteachable.

I felt ashamed and worthless. Tears flooded my eyes, and they became red and swollen like ripened peaches. There was no way to wipe away the sadness. No one paid attention to me since Sister Double Happiness was at home.

I ran outside to find a friend to play with, the sting of my sister's unkind label on my mind. On the levee, older children were flying kites; dozens of swooping, dancing, indecisive kites decorated the sky over the fields. When one kite broke free of its string and drifted down to my feet, I picked it up to examine it. I memorized its bones and shape before a boy ripped it rudely from my unwilling hands. I ran home and searched for just the right parts and pieces for my plan. As the kite blew in, so did my idea to borrow just one test paper from the stack of corrected classroom papers Sister Double had brought the family. It was my great fortune, paper being so very precious a thing for us.

I fastened some chopsticks to make two pieces for the spine and took the fine threads of a plant to lash the longer stick to the shorter one. I cut a tiny slice through the paper and fastened the bones to the wings, as I had seen. Then, for the tail, I was too desperate to wait, so I tore some tiny strips of fabric from an unused piece of clothing in the laundry, just one small strip enough for the knotted tail for my undersized creation. Mother was so clever that she could mend the damaged shirt or make it into two for Sister Enough and me. It was threadbare anyway and due for a renewal, so worn out that it was ready for the collar to become the cloth for the unmentionable red my sisters spoke of in secrecy with Mother. I justified my small crime to myself.

Then I needed the string, my connection to my paper friend when I set her free. I searched the levee and found it, a discouraged roll of string that had been given up when boredom took the boys' attentions to another game. I attached the string just so, keeping the image in my mind. I would show Sister Double as she left that I was not a hopeless unteachable. I would celebrate her with my kite.

I saw her walking from the house, and she looked at me. I ran with everything my legs could give me along the levee. I jumped down the slope into the field, tumbling, losing my footing. Looking over my shoulder, before my face was thrust into the dirt, a miracle happened: I saw it take off above me. For one moment, I was like the other children, flying my kite on a late afternoon. I jumped up, running, laughing, running, imagining the admiration on Sister's face. My kite began to resist, twisting desperately with such unhappiness that I thought to let her go, but in my selfishness I could not. Swirl, swirl, lower and lower, violently tugging at my hand, begging for her freedom, she crashed into the side of the levee, shattering into splinters, tearing her crisp paper wings. When I stood over her bones and gave her my farewell love, I knew I should have set her free.

CHAPTER 7
COMPLETE HAPPINESS

Sister Complete Happiness did very well in elementary school, getting the highest scores on the middle-school entrance exam. Like me, she shared the love of learning, the natural scholar bloodline of Mother, but her timing was not fortunate. Just before the start of middle school, when Mother had finished sewing her renewed clothes for school, Sister Complete Happiness received an unexpected notification. The policies of Liberation became even more hostile. Children of the Enemies of the State classification were no longer permitted to be educated beyond elementary school. She was banned from middle school for her Black Element status. When she watched her friends and classmates skip down the path to start middle school, she cried inconsolably over losing the learning she loved. She cried, Mother cried, so I cried.

"There is no other way," Father's voice drifted from their bedroom that night. Sister Enough and I huddled together, wondering what choice was causing the tension between our parents.

"She was the top student in her school. She is only fourteen. Education is the only way, and now she cannot attend. We have to hide her," we heard Mother say from her bedroom.

Their words, their tone made me quiver with some inexplicable intuition that I could not explain in my young mind. It felt so much like spoiled food churning in my stomach, like the fleck of a bird in the distance that grew larger and larger until its form was clear, a vulture circling a wounded child, signaling her fate.

Mother pleaded with him to help her to find a way.

"Complete Happiness is big enough and strong enough to earn points with Ox. We have no choice," Father said.

"Is she old enough to face torturous back-bent labor with no chance of any gain?" Mother asked a question to which she had no right answer, as was her way.

"We have no choice. She must go or she and the entire family will pay. We have suffered too long to give in. Something will change, in time, for now she will be safe with Ox," Father said consolingly.

Mother was not consoled, having heard the stories of taunting and cruelty from Brother Ox, who already had his back to the sky.

"Without the points the children would earn, there would be no allocations of food. We may lose them to the fate of your father," Father pleaded.

Mother had told us of her memories, picking the linseed husks from her wasted father's beard—the bits of animal feed that were his only sustenance in his final days.

"My brother could have shared a mouthful of their rice and saved him," she said.

"We need to have that extra mouthful of rice now to save our own children," Father said, settling the argument.

In the morning, Father took Sister Complete Happiness by her small hand. I watched her long braid slip, knot by knot, through Mother's pleading grasp. He walked with her, all the while posturing optimism as though they were to take a stroll together along the Yangtze, but the truth hung on Father's shoulders like an oxen yoke as he walked her into the distance. Her twisted head strained to lock eyes with Mother, Sister Enough, and me, until the last moment. Enough Complete Happiness and Really Enough Complete Happiness locked in a yearning plea with our sister, our eyes to her eyes, until their two figures disappeared over the levee. A long and silent one hundred minutes passed before he placed her slender, soft hand into the rough and punishing hand of the peasant woman in charge. She gave no pause at this painful moment for the father and the young girl, but instead she shattered their tender goodbyes, shoved my sister toward the field to meet the overseer, and babbled on about her duties, the rules, and the consequences. Back to sky, face to earth, Sister Complete Happiness joined Brother Little Ox in the brigade of our commune for decades—long walks, long days, sick or well, little pay, the promising youths lived the peasant life.

真

She was shorter than the young cotton stems. As they would grow, so would her burden. The overseer assigned her patches of land as he would any strong adult, with no consideration for her age.

"You, take up your hoe and clear this area. You see, from here to there? Do it right. There are no points for poor work," the overseer said.

Sister Complete picked up the hoe and began awkwardly scraping away the weeds in the field, not knowing whether to chop, dig, drag, or scrape to eliminate the entire weed, to do a job of excellence. She worked for hours, her back aching and her thin neck weary from holding her heavy head. Sweat dripped from her forehead to her blistered, inexperienced hands, making her lose her grip mid-stroke. At the end of the clearing, the patch still wore a few tufts of brown and yellow, but only here and there. She was relieved.

"Are you so stupid, you cannot even clear a patch of worthless weeds? Even if you have never had the meat, you have seen the pigs walk, haven't you? Return tomorrow and redo it. No working points for you today," he stood over her, screaming. Then he picked up her hoe, ran his fingernail over the dull blade, looked at my fragile sister, and laughed. "Useless," he said.

When cotton was in full bloom, the picking began. Tying the burlap square into a pouch hanging from her waist, Sister Complete Happiness was told to pluck the tufts of cotton and tuck them away into the sack until it was pregnant with white fluff. Moving forward in the row, her unskilled hands endured the evil scratches from the outer shell of the cotton bolls, shredding every bit of skin around the nails on her thin fingers. When a bleeding prick stained the white cotton, she hid the tainted ones in her shirt. As the swelling of her fingers and the soreness of her hands worsened, she became less adept at picking, leaving small bits of white behind nestled in the stubborn bolls. Her sack was filling slowly.

"Better be putting a few rocks in that sack to make the weight go up," a fellow peasant said, sharing her trick with Sister. Mother's sense of honor was deeper in my sister than the cuts in her hands, so she continued slowly until she had finished her assigned rows.

"This is how the rich girl picks cotton. Look at the wasted cotton on those bolls. Tomorrow you can redo these rows, here, there, and over there. You have proved quite useless with those scholar hands of yours." A red-spotted cotton tuft dropped from under her shirt to the feet of the overseer.

"I see you have already taken your allocation," he said with a sneer as he walked away.

Unlike the other peasants, they had no family or housing nearby. Sister Complete and Brother Ox were left to fend for themselves with no one to care for them, no one to feed them, no bed on which to rest their tired bodies. While others returned to nearby homes for lunch and a rest, Complete and Ox ate what little food they were able to carry from home in the hot sun or under what shade they might find.

Sister Complete's unusually large chest was such an embarrassment, inviting frowns and harassment daily. In summer, she had no jacket to hide herself. When she could no longer tolerate the constant taunts of the other workers, especially the men, she took to walking back and forth to her assigned patches bent over in the deeper muddy ditches to hide her shameful anomaly from the peasants' eyes.

They were mere children in a world of hardened peasants with no family legacy of farming. At the end of each day, they walked for nearly two hours to return home on spent legs, only to eat our sparse family meal, sleep, and return to do the same, day after day. At the end of the season with the subtraction of points for poor work, Complete Happiness gained nothing but her calloused hands and stooped young back for a year of 12-hour days. She lost much, for there was a time when Complete Happiness loved to dance and sing, but she buried those joys in the open fields. When there were no points, there was no point.

真

Because Sister Complete Happiness was younger than Little Ox, it was customary that she would delay marriage until her brother was married. Tradition was threatened when the impassioned son of the brigade leader, who wanted her for his wife, pursued her. Finally, word came that his family was coming to propose the arranged marriage.

"Do you know this young man?" Mother asked Sister Complete.

"Yes, but I have never spoken to him. He is a helper at the brigade school, but he is so unappealing and much too tall for me. I don't like this boy. Mother, please, can't we tell them no?" Sister Complete pleaded.

"I was so hoping for some happiness for you," Mother said.

"I will be happy if I can stay with you and Father and Grandmother for the rest of my life. I promise I will take care of you all in the future. Please?" she begged.

Mother looked at petite Sister Complete thoughtfully, then, left the room to talk with Father.

"I refuse to treat my daughters differently than our sons," she said to him. "I promised myself I would send every one of them to school, just as I was sent. I will not let that be taken away from them like it was taken from me. Now look at the situation we are in—our young daughter follows her mother's path." Mother was distressed.

"You could not have known the law would reject us and forbid them to go to school. If she is married to a brigade leader's family, she will be guaranteed to have a better life," Father said.

"Yue Xia Lao Ren, the old man in the moon, makes these decisions, not a brigade leader. How do I know that the marriage god of the moon intends our daughter to be this man's wife?" She was asking the unanswerable.

"If it happens, it is meant to be," Father said.

"I would like to have a peek at his record book right now. I do not have a good feeling about this arrangement. She finds him unfortunate-faced and unappealing," Mother said. She was silent for a few moments. "I do not want to marry her off to another family that sees her as an inferior, as an Enemy. That is not a better life. I am sure our moon god would not make this choice," she said.

"It is tradition for her to be an in-house daughter-in-law, and they are of high status," he argued.

"High status? They are poor peasants who were turned on their heads into the ruling class by the Liberation. We may carry the lower classification, but they carry the lower class. You cannot turn a common sparrow into a regal phoenix by turning it on its head," Mother argued.

"I am saying your strange ways already draw criticism," Father said.

"What criticism?" Mother asked, confronting him.

"When you insist the children of Double Happiness call you the honored title, 'Grandmother,' people are confused. You know that title is reserved only for the son's parents," Father said. "And what about having her children call our daughters by the honorable title of 'Uncle'? It is too odd for everyone, against all tradition!"

"I do not concern myself with the criticisms of others. I concern myself with the happiness and honor of my daughters."

"We should keep with tradition and allow them to use the standard titles of 'External Grandmother' or 'External Grandfather,' as is customary," he continued.

"That is a lesser term, as though the daughter's parents are insignificant. I ensured that Double Happiness was married at her school, not at the home of her husband. She was never an in-house daughter in-law. Her lineage is not through her husband's family, so we do not merit the insulting tradition of being called 'External Grandparents,'" Mother said, explaining her logic.

"Careful, you are riding the tiger's back, and the next destination is his mouth! I don't understand. You could not have suffered so much as the eldest and most pampered one who wore the finest clothes. You have certainly never suffered at the hands of my mother as her daughter-in-law, and certainly not by your mother, who loved you. What makes you defy a tradition that has worked for centuries?" he probed.

"You know little of me," Mother said quietly.

"Then you must tell me what is beneath this anger and stubbornness of yours when it comes to your daughters."

"Fine, maybe it is time we broke the silence that has been our marriage. I will give you the despicable truth. I went from eating from a porcelain bowl of scented lotus seeds after school with a beautiful book in hand to carrying a chamber pot filled with the vilest of things that splashed over my small hands as her insane words chased me from the room. I lived as a servant but much worse, for the mistress I served was my own mother. This was the love of DaMa, the woman who turned from tender words in one moment to torturous, hateful screams in the next, when my true mother disclosed the sham that was my life."

She turned to him and said slowly, "I have known the helplessness of living with a woman who was not my mother. It began with loving indulgence and ended with unbearable loss. DaMa's loving eyes melted into the evil eyes of a monster simply because I was not her own."

Father had nothing to say. Mother walked into the house and sat down next to Sister Complete.

"Your grandmother was betrothed at merely six years old to an older man, and she was widowed and alone by the age of twenty," she began. "I was the victim of an arrangement at sixteen to a man I had never seen, but I had hoped for you to at least be married to someone to your liking. You are only eighteen. There is still time, so I will try to discourage this one," Mother said.

"Oh, thank you, yes, please. I cannot spend my life of nights with such a man," Sister Complete Happiness said.

真

When the prospective father-in-law came to see Father to make the arrangements for the marriage of Complete Happiness, Mother had a goal.

"No daughter who sprung from my body will cross the threshold of her future husband's superior household to live under a repressive roof," she said to Father.

"A fake smile is better than a genuine frown when it comes to your dealings with this man," he warned.

Father had not made the journey from unrivaled rich man to subservient poor man gracefully, while Mother held her poise, intelligence, and dignity throughout the painful path from Puppy to pauper. Therefore, when the time came for serious negotiations on my sister's marriage, Father, knowing Mother's audacious and rebellious position on bestowing her daughters with equal rights to males, conveniently made himself absent. This came as no surprise and caused no disappointment to Mother.

According to tradition, wives were too insignificant in the eyes of their husbands to participate in such important negotiations; therefore, the future father-in-law came alone. In an unheard-of twist on tradition at the time, the powerful man met head-to-head with Mother, an unexpectedly worthy opponent, to make the deal. With the skills of a keen businesswoman in her past and a passion in her heart, Mother, true to her name, exercised her own upright justice on the unsuspecting, powerful man.

She served him tea and then politely asked a question: "Does your son wish to marry my daughter?"

He answered, "Yes, he is quite insistent and says he will have no one else. Although he would be marrying beneath his classification, he is determined, and we are willing," said the prospective groom's father magnanimously.

"How generous," Mother said, hiding her sarcastic tone in a warm smile.

The man peered over his shoulder and around the room, looking for the head of the household. He was a bit surprised at her boldness in representing her family in such a matter.

"My apologies. My husband has been delayed and asks you to forgive his absence. He asks that you be gracious enough to allow me to speak on his behalf."

The man nodded reluctantly.

She continued, "You have heard stories of the poor treatment and abuse that some young women endure in the households of in-laws of a higher ruling classification, have you not?" she asked casually as she uncustomarily poured her own tea first.

"Well, uh, yes, I suppose such situations are not so uncommon, he said, "but I—"

Mother interrupted. "Do you have a daughter?" The trap was beginning to be set.

"Yes, we do."

"Would you agree to risk your daughter to such a situation, to a family of even more power than yours who might abuse her, demean her, or perhaps beat her?"

"Of course not," he answered passionately. "We will make sure we choose a family who will treat her right."

She let the silence hang to allow the idea to germinate in his mind. "Neither would we want to see such a gentle, kind, and intelligent daughter of ours abused or treated unkindly," she continued.

The prospective groom's father stood up, indignantly. "But we have no intention of abusing your daughter!"

"Of course not. Please sit and know that I do not speak of our specific situation, just an observation of society in general, which you admitted that you, yourself, have often seen," Mother said.

"May I ask, is it your plan to marry your daughter well? To an even higher status than your own?" Mother continued gently, pouring his tea. She wrapped her words in the softest silk.

"That would be a goal, of course," he nodded, calming a bit.

"Perhaps with your honorable status, you could use your power and forward thinking to make sure some bourgeois family does not break her spirit or her heart. Make sure she has the best protection in her future."

"How would I do that?" he asked.

Mother tugged on the line to set the lure. "By providing your daughter with a home, a household of her own," she said.

"Nonsense! It is tradition that a daughter will become a daughter-in-law to her husband's family. What are you suggesting? It is unheard of," he said.

"If I am not careful, my daughters may fall into the claws of another family," she said.

"You call us claws? You have little room to discuss such things with your lower classification. You should be grateful my son is willing to marry your daughter. Imagine!" the man said, chastising her.

"I am not in favor of this arrangement. I do not think this marriage is a match," Mother said simply, putting down the pot of tea, signaling the end of the discussion.

"Unthinkable!" Unused to being questioned or defied, the man stood up and stormed out of the house.

For two years, Sister Complete Happiness fought to brush aside the young man's desires, but he persisted, stalking her while also preventing the interests of other suitors. The threat of the consequences of her refusal was real, for she was vulnerable and dependent upon the mercy of the brigade leader. It was only the persistence of the young man's infatuation with Sister Complete that kept her safe from the retribution of his father.

Two years later, his heartsick son convinced the prideful brigade leader to return once more, intending to speak with Father, whom he assumed could certainly make Mother, a mere foolish woman, change her mind and be reasonable.

Once again, Father was missing when the negotiations resumed. Mother knew she had no power to stop the marriage, but she planned to do her best to protect her daughter. She took control.

"I assume you have come to your senses?" he asked her.

"May I ask you a question, first?" she asked.

He nodded impatiently.

"You are a man, as you said before, who loves his daughter and would want to see her happy and safe in a family of even higher status?"

"Yes, I would want our daughter so protected," he answered. "Aaahh!" he said and smiled, shaking off the spell that Mother had cast. Avoiding the trap of their previous conversation, he said, "But here we came to speak of my own son, not my daughter."

"Aaahh!" Mother answered gently. "But here we came to speak of my own daughter, not our son." Then she closed her argument. "It would be a shame to lose both your daughter to abuse and break your son's heart so young."

"I will not have both my daughter and my son unhappy!" he said, his pride at stake. "Would you not treat your son as well as your daughter?" she asked, setting the hook.

"Even better! He is our heir!" he protested.

"Then you agree. It is even more important that your first son be positioned in a place of honor in a family and that you give him a house of his own to start his married life out right. Your son will be most respected at the brigade to have a home with a household of his own, thus expanding and strengthening your own."

"Forgive me," she continued, "only if it is within your means, of course, if the price is worth the gain, that is…and if it is affordable for you."

"Of course it is within my means. I am a man of means."

"You are a clever man as well," Mother said. Then she closed her argument. Seeing the beam of light escaping from the previously closed door of the man's inferior mind, she moved in to capture the small ray of hope like a firefly in a jar. "Then we accept your proposal. You are a wise man, indeed." She took the reins of the conversation to drive the oxen home. "We accept and are honored by your clever plan to give the couple their own home," Mother said to the befuddled but nodding man.

She watched him shake his head, trying to calm the bees that buzzed inside his confused skull, suspect as to how this came about, wondering how this was a win. He found himself agreeing with her. "Yes, my son will have the best, a household of his own," he said as he set his fist down on the table.

She added quickly as the deal was set, lest it be misunderstood, "Then we are honored to welcome your son as our in-house son-in-law, such an honor for us. He will hold a position of power in our family, as well as have the power of his own household. I can only imagine his bright and powerful future."

"I will give my son a home, but I am not in favor of his belonging to your family as your in-house son-in-law. I will not have it!"

"Yes, fortunately, in our case it is inconsequential that he belongs to our family, a mere formality since he will be the master of his own home at the brigade hours from our home at the levee. He will not be tainted by our classification at all," Mother said, needing to make sure it was clear that his son was still considered married to our family as an in-house son-in-law, which linked her daughter's line to her own.

Then the extra bait she needed to finally hook the fish appeared. Mother saw her future son-in-law pacing along the high levee in the distance. She nodded her head toward the window to direct the father's sight to his own tortured son.

"Such a nice young man," she said. "He will be pleased with his father's generosity in securing his future. You must be anxious to tell him of your plans for his own house and your successful negotiations."

"Yes, he will be pleased, and I will gladly be finished with these considerations."

With his son's "Complete Happiness" at stake, the outfoxed man gave in to the final detail of the agreement. Mother let her breath of relief out slowly like a little ribbon waving in the air to keep the celebration inside her smiling self. Sister Complete Happiness thus could stand tall with her in-laws rendered powerless to control her or diminish her in any way.

That was how Mother was a revolutionary of her own kind. With the deal accepted and as a matter of pride, the man was obligated to provide a house for the couple in the brigade. This meant Sister Complete would never have to walk the long distance to work again, and they would be married in that house, creating a household of her own. She was to be a rare woman with all the powers and benefits of a son, carrying on the line of Mother's Book Fragrance Family.

Along with this arrangement, Mother cleverly ensured that the powerful father-in-law and mother-in-law would never have the right to live with her daughter. Mother would have the rare option to live with her own daughter in her old age, breaking the ancient tradition of living with the daughter-in-law. She would never have to say the words "married daughter, poured water," to her own daughter.

In spite of the victory, there was still the disappointment to endure; there was still the unavoidable arranged marriage for her daughter to an unappealing man not of her choosing.

When Sister Complete returned from the fields that day, Mother, dark in the face, sadly shared the compromise she had negotiated.

"I am so sorry. The weak cannot beat the strong. It was a choice between two evils—your life with a husband who wants you, whom you did not choose, or a torturous life in the fields held in the crushing grip of his resentful father," Mother said.

"Mother, I don't want to leave you. Please?" Sister cried.

"I did protect you from being their in-house daughter-in-law, and I will always be able to be with you," Mother said, trying to comfort her with unconvincing words.

"If you want me to go, I will," Sister Complete said through streams of defeated tears.

There was no celebration when Mother had to watch Sister Complete walk off to her new life in the brigade fields. We stood as we had when she was fourteen, when Father took her to the fields. Sister Complete held onto Mother and cried. She was twenty years old. Father peeled her hands away from Mother and slowly walked her away, up and over the levee, to deliver her to her new husband. The contagious feeling passed through my heart, and I cried with little understanding of her fate.

真

When they had their first baby, the father-in-law fought hard to have the baby carry his last name, the only battle left to win. Realizing over time the deal was not in his favor, he was determined to take back what little power there was to be had. He cornered Father in the brigade.

"I am sure you are happy for our recent fortune?" he said.

"Of course, the couple is fortunate for certain, a beautiful baby boy," Father replied.

"I am sure you will understand when the child takes our family name, considering our status? It is the tradition and would be in the best interest—"

Father interrupted with a humble tone. "In that regard, I have no part. I am sure they will have a plan for the naming, since they have a household of their own."

"I demand they use my family name!" the father-in-law bellowed.

"I will let our family household son-in-law know of your suggested name to consider in their decision. Of course, had my daughter been married into your family," Father said, "that would be your dragon to slay." He couldn't help but throw the last straw on the fire.

The brigade leader turned on his heels and walked away with the dust spinning around his angry feet.

Sister Complete Happiness called their son Yang, "Sun," with my sister's proud family name, Zhao, which was quite unprecedented. Others said it was like the sun rose in the west. She would have complete power if she could not have complete happiness.

CHAPTER 8
THE ENEMIES MOVE IN

I was drawing water into an old bucket through a crack in the ice that had sealed off our only nearby source of water. I should not have taken the dreaded muddy pond for granted in summer when its brown eyes stared back lazily, when I resented its slimy smirk. I should not have turned my nose up at its less-than-sweet scent, for every winter it had its revenge, becoming so smug as it held a mirror to my angry, frozen face. Chiseling away at the gray ice with the rusty poker I had stolen from Mother's kitchen shed, I saw my own reflection split into slivers as the ice broke through and reluctantly the stubborn pond gave up its life to me. In time, I opened a bucket-sized hole to access the unsavory water, dropped the bucket through the hole, and lifted the heavy vessel, but it wouldn't budge.

I sat back and felt the temptation to surrender to the spell of daydreams that often tapped my young soul, just one minute to rest, to wrap myself in the deepening snow, to hide my eyes from the thought of the family impatiently waiting for the water to cook another meal of no sustaining worth. Then I saw the bucket elevate completely by itself.

"Aiyaa!" I yelled as the splashing bucket of water was lifted up by a long, strong pole and miraculously rose toward the skies, swirling around behind me two meters above my head. As it left my vision, the thick bamboo pole slid under my stiff, sleepy arms and lifted me from my frozen squat as well.

I held on tightly, and it swung me high into the air. Turning my head, I watched the bucket as it bounced in rhythm with me balanced at the opposite end of the thick pole that was stretched over the shoulders of a tall, bearded stranger. I bounced in silence as he sang a familiar song that Mother sang to soothe us children. It was a song of hope.

He carried me to our house, stopped at the front door, and kept me hanging there for a moment. Then he drew an imaginary rectangle on the mud wall with his long, graceful finger. He cocked his head and looked at me confused as if to ask, "Where is your placard?" In his high voice, he quoted with great formality like a frightening Party Representative announcing something very threatening. He read the imaginary sign, accenting the memorized words with a tap on the wall for each rule:

"Number One: Not allowed to speak freely
Number Two: Not allowed to act freely
Number Three: Not allowed to move about freely
Number Four: Not allowed to commit arson
Number Five: Not allowed to commit crime
Number Six: Not allowed to steal
Number Seven: Not allowed to form a gang
Number Eight: Always obey the Communist orders
Number Nine: Willing to be reformed
Number Ten: Ready to receive punishment."

Then he asked, "No sign on your house, little devil?"

With frightened eyes, I moved my blue lips to answer, using the term of respect, "No, Uncle, it was, uh, we had no paper for a sign," I answered to cover up our family's disregard for the government's rule. *Mother would never have a sign by her front door*, I thought.

"Very defiant," he answered sternly.

My stomach tightened. My eyes ran along the pole to its nearby end, where sharp metal points had been affixed. His intense eyes softened and gave up their game of teasing, unveiling a warm message in his smile that was immediately contagious to his eyes. I let out the breath of fear I had been saving in my shivering chest and enjoyed his conspiratorial smile while my heart's cymbals quieted.

"Ha, ha, ha!" he bellowed with his head arched back. "I think I will like this household."

Even at my young age, I knew to shiver at the words. The Obedience Placard was a required notification I had seen on the wall next to the entrance door of every house in which Enemies of the State resided. Because we inhabited the old, abandoned house, we were not officially listed as the owners. The hated sign that served as a reminder to the public of the shameful past of the Exploiters of the poor was never hung on our door. This was our great fortune because our status wasn't openly identified like others'. I thought we could walk in and out of the house holding our heads higher, although in the end there was really no fooling the brigade officials or the neighbors; they knew just who we were.

My bold savior lowered the pole with bended knee and delivered both the full bucket and me safely to the ground.

"What is your name?"

"Zhen," I answered. There was no need for the adult to share common courtesies with a mere child.

He smiled and said, "You can call me Uncle Bu."

At that moment, even in my unrefined mind, I knew our lives had changed as he opened the door to our humble house.

In the winter, when we most desperately struggled to keep our blood flowing liquid to our laboring blue hands or to fill our stomachs with even a pot of those despicable weeds, I so ached to lure closer the distant flocks of birds to symbolize that our plot still had hope. I searched the unkind sky daily and prayed for any bird to land, and finally, land they did. But I had never meant to lure this kind of bird to nest within our own home. Unlike the flocks of birds that instinctively passed by our pathetic patch of foodless land, it was another species that invaded our home that winter, without any option to move on to more fertile ground. The tall stranger, Uncle Bu, was the first of these unexpected odd birds to nestle into our home.

They say birds of a feather flock together. Well, the Enemies of the State were flocking together, but it wasn't their nature that was driving the strange migration; it was the rule of the upside-down world created by the government, Mother told me. It was Liberation. Those fallen leaders, classified as Evil Exploiters, the former upper class like my own family, were stripped of everything and assigned to do menial labor in the thousands of hectares that stretched across the country. The peasants and laborers, however, were liberated and made rulers of the ones who had ruled, made masters to the ones who were once served.

The importance of these leaders of society was diminished by their meaningless assignments—projects artificially created to break the bending backs of these uprooted people with unbroken nails and unblemished hands. Those who had never filled a blister with the homemade ointment of the poor peasant were put to work digging ditches from sunup to sundown for no purpose, or to build roads to nowhere as punishment for their sins of affluence, education, or faith. With not a choice, nor a chance to return to their homes for the winter, they bent like young bamboo to adjust to their indentured lives, digging a path to their own deaths or an unknown future. This was their "liberation."

真

It happened during the time of Spring Festival that year, a most frigid time of year for a celebration. While the liberated peasants were busy hustling to prepare to celebrate the New Year with red and gold and showing off their newly inherited belongings, twelve victims of the times arrived in our village. On that winter, when I was in the second year of school, our home was designated to house a group of so-called "Evil Ogres," all of whom were branded with the classification of Enemy of the State. They came from different commune brigades from near and far, a dozen of them, all male.

One by one, they arrived at their new dwelling place to be reformed. From industrialists to small businessmen to wealthy men, they were all transformed into paupers by the government's laws. They each brought with them a bundle of straw for their bed, a bundle of cotton branches for their cooking fires, a bag of rice, a sack of home-grown vegetables, a shovel, baskets, carrying poles, and a few precious personal things such as smoking pipes, tobacco leaves, or a tea mug.

The first to arrive of these Ogres, as they were officially called, was my savior, Uncle Bu, dubbed with the title "Rightist" for his outspoken nature and his fearless criticism of the Communists that, by all rights, should have meant a bullet to his head. Even a naïve child of the Enemy classifications knew that.

Amazingly, with a little cleverness, our main room managed to serve them all. Their bundles of straw were unrolled in a tight criss-cross line across the dirt floor like the side of a woven grass basket. Above the straw were laid thinning, tattered, cotton mats, covered again by aging faded quilts, some torn, some patched, with only traces of their former elegant patterns clawing to hang on like the phoenix on Mother's own family heirloom. Still, I could see the beautiful, barely visible designs that faintly marked their well-to-do pasts.

As the men were setting up their cooking area, the last man arrived. He introduced himself as Lao Kong; he had the same honorable family name as Confucius. He wore a black winter jacket with mismatched colored patches and holes here and there that revealed a lining of old, dark cotton. Around his waist, he had fastened a belt made of straw twisted into a strand. The belt helped to keep in what little warmth there was, hugging the thin layers of cloth to his body. He caused instant laughter from the tattered crew when he showed up at the door with his shabby belongings.

"Next door, please," said one of the Ogres, an expression commonly used to tell a beggar to skip this household and beg at the next.

"Yes, I have been to the next few houses already, and I was told 'next door' at every single one," said Lao Kong. Everyone laughed. "I don't see any Obedience Placard on the front wall," Lao Kong continued while carefully examining the surroundings of our overcrowded dwelling. "I was told to live only with the same evil class elements as my pathetic self."

"Oh, we hope you can survive without the obedience rules," one man shouted with a humor even I could understand.

"For a change," added another.

"Ha ha ha!" Our house was filled with their raucous laughs and coughs.

Mother said it was hard to believe these Enemies would have the mind to laugh at themselves or to find a bit of humor in their gloomy futures with a thousand reasons to feel miserable, depressed, and betrayed. Listening to their tales, I learned there were far worse ways to reform the "bad elements" during the time of Spring Festival besides being sent away from their families to dig aqueducts or work the fields like those who moved into our house. And so they made the best of their bad fortune, settled in, and brought the yin and yang of both sobering truth and laughter to my life.

"So many roomers, so many rumors," Mother said as I tucked myself into my parents' bed on the first night with our new visitors.

I heard the men talking, so I sneaked out of the bedroom to listen and huddled in the cold, dark corner of the main room, where they sat on their bedrolls. The men introduced themselves to each other, one by one.

"Spy Lake," one man said. The other men looked confused. "My real name is Hu, but in Catholic Missionary School, they called me by the English equivalent of Hu, 'Lake.' I miss the freedom to be called by my English name, especially since the government added my required tag of 'Spy.' Since we are all Enemies in this house, I thought you might indulge me in a small revenge," Uncle Hu said.

"Yes, we can stage a small underground revolution of our own," said another man.

"That is, if you don't mind consorting with a spy," Hu said, smiling at Uncle Bu.

"Ha! You already live dangerously by consorting with a Rightist," Uncle Bu said.

"So you can both get us all killed," one serious-looking man said, shaking his head to say "no."

"This is really quite unheard of, a very strange request," a man in the corner said.

"To be called a foreign devil name in these times is insane, asking for trouble," another man said.

"What trouble? Who among our ruling peasants speaks English anyway? Only we will know what 'Lake' means. I think we can indulge the man within the solid walls of this house," Uncle Bu said, looking around at the crumbling walls and laughing. "The government takes everything from us. Let's help him regain his name from his happier times as a gift to our stranger."

"The danger in it does have a certain power for me, but only in this house away from other ears. Yes, I agree, Spy Lake," said the man named Lao Kong.

"It is agreed. We will keep it among our bilingual selves," Uncle Bu said. The men all chimed in to his laughter, chattering in strange, babbling words I could not understand.

"See how we have learned the foreigner's English already," the man sitting on a faded red quilt said.

"Well mimicked! Thank you kindly. It gives me a little sense of my old, free self," Spy Lake said.

Then I heard their shocking words.

"What pot or piece of metal did you contribute to the backyard furnace today?" Rightest Bu asked.

"What do you mean?" asked another man.

"Our great leader, Chairman Mao, commands that we 'peasants' double the steel production in our country for the Great Leap Forward. On my walk here, I saw hundreds of people in frenzied lines contributing their battered belongings to the hot jaws of their foolish ovens to meet his goal. They even gave up their only cooking pots!"

"Yes, I saw a man suddenly stop his pedaling to join a line of metal-lugging people—anxious to passionately toss his only transportation, his beloved bicycle, into the inferno," another man said.

"Can you imagine the sturdiness of the steel beams they will produce, made of pots and spoons? I would not want to cross that bridge," Spy Lake said, laughing.

"So, what do you think of the genius of the government's other latest plan?" one man asked.

"The Four Pests Campaign? Eliminate all rats, all sparrows, all mosquitoes, and all flies from the entire country. Ha! Another *failed* campaign," Doctor Wong said.

"There is always a new campaign," Uncle Bu said to the short man. "First they spray all the people with DDT, as well as the mosquitoes, to see who dies first. Then, just have all the people in the entire country kill every sparrow so they won't eat the seeds in the fields. Even children with slingshots are knocking over the little fellows. Teach them to kill while they are young, I say," Rightist Bu said.

"Your commentary is stinging, Brother Bu," said Uncle Huang.

"How could it be stinging when there are no more mosquitoes?" one of the quiet Ogres said.

"Exactly," answered Uncle Bu. "I compliment your insights." Bu nodded to the man to encourage his new outspoken friend.

I stretched my neck to listen closer.

"There are always consequences in nature," another man said. "Touch one thing, you touch a thousand others."

"You are the expert. How has this campaign failed like the others?" another asked.

"Like so, now there are no birds to land on the fields to eat the worms that destroy the cotton, no birds to devour the insects that eat the crops," he explained.

"Aha! So that is why the people were made to scour the fields to hand-pick the worms from the cotton plants; we now do the work of little birds," the man who chewed a straw said.

"At least the birds could eat what they picked," Uncle Bu said, laughing, "but we may get to eating worms yet, if this campaign causes even greater famine."

"So how will they eliminate the flies?" a man asked.

"Easy—no food, no flies."

The men laughed through their noses.

"And the rats?" asked another.

"That's easy, too. There are no crops left in the fields for the rats to hide in, since the birds were not there to eat the insects, so the insects ate the crops and now we starve, so we eat the rats," said the man they called the expert.

The men shook their heads and laughed as one by one they flattened out on their beds.

"This is called 'The Great Leap Forward,' my friends. Fine if you are a frog," Rightist Bu said, yawning, as his voice faded. "I am sure they will get to them soon as well, in the next campaign against all things hopping."

I crawled quietly into my own bed, thinking of the little birds that no longer landed on our garden patch. With many fearful things to think about, but with no fear left of our new guests, I fell asleep to the sounds of their rhythmic snores.

真

On a late afternoon, after I came home from school. I couldn't find Mother.

"Have you seen my mother?" I asked the cook of the Enemy Ogres who was starting to prepare their meal.

"Your mother had to go to a little meeting. She will be back," he said.

"Meeting? My mother went to a meeting? Do you mean she was taken to one of those meetings where people will shout at her?" I asked.

I had often heard Brother Ox and Sister Complete talking about the cruel accusation meetings called 'struggle sessions.' I had watched them reenact such meetings for Mother and Father at night. I knew these meetings were a way for the ruling peasants to put down the Enemies of the State, as well as a way for them to earn easy working points for their attendance.

"Stinking intellectuals," they would scream at teachers. "Stinking Enemies of the State!" they yelled at the former people of good fortune, like us. *Mother has already suffered enough,* I thought. I couldn't tolerate the image of her being on the stage, being humiliated by those who didn't even know her. I panicked thinking she might die since she was in poor health. She had fainted before, and I knew she never was good at walking on the muddy or slippery road, having so little history with such places.

How can she return home? I asked myself.

What little warmth we had that day was quickly escaping off into the gray sky. The dropping temperatures met the melting snow that had become muddy in the sunlight, hardening it to an icy surface, slippery like cow's skin. Our assigned brigade of the commune was far away from where we lived, which was the reason the previous owner of the house had left. It was too far to walk to work for them. For us, the two-hour walk each way was not a choice.

I climbed onto the top of the slippery levee, seeing only the massive snow-covered fields, white fields stretching endlessly. I wished to ride the back of that undulating snow-white dragon to arrive at Mother's side, but the north wind was drawing the hope from my face. So I lost myself in remembered evenings, a summer night heavy in my chest, the whining insects. The icy wind became the brush of Mother's broken palm fan on my moist red face as I held on to the promise of fancy dangling earrings. I touched my earlobe but felt nothing. I was by myself, alone in all the whiteness.

I couldn't tell from which direction she would return. I started to cry, and my frozen fingers, red like carrots, were too stiff to wipe away my tears. My small voice was lost in the night. "If DaDa dies, I want to die, too!" I pleaded out loud. "I always want to be with DaDa!" I called out to the expansive nothingness. The sound of my wishful plea went far out over the fields. Just then, the wind blew to my ears the call of the most beautiful rising phoenix I had ever heard: "Zhen'er, Zhen'er!" It was Mother. She was alive. She was home and looking for me.

Walking down the levee would take too long and be too painful. I dropped my body and rolled down to the bottom of the ravine, gathering a thick pack of snow and stiffly I rushed home to DaDa.

"You are back at last. Did they hurt you? Did they make you stand on the stage?" I was out of breath.

"Why didn't you stay in? Look at your hands." Mother took my hands to her mouth and blew on them. "How are your feet?"

"My feet? Fine. I don't even feel them," I said, smiling with her face in my eyes again.

"So young for such jokes—they are not fine! Let me look," she said.

She tried to take my shoes off, but they were stuck to my feet. Taking me into the kitchen, she put me at the mouth of the cooking stall so the warmth from the fire could melt my happy, frozen feet.

Uncle Huang, the Ogre whose turn it was to cook, took great pity on me, and he let me sit there for a long time until the feeling in my feet returned to me. He also scooped a big dollop of hot, white rice right from the pot into a bowl and handed it to me. This was not the rice water in my bowl but the sticky, beautiful white stuff itself. Mother was so grateful. She thanked him a thousand times, knowing the rice was needed to keep the workers' bodies strong through the next day's long punishment. Uncle Huang gave me the chopsticks and urged me to eat.

"Eat quickly! It will not look good if my Ogre friends come back from their labor and see you eating their rice," he said.

I wanted to share it with Mother. When Uncle Huang was out of sight, I whispered to her to open her mouth so I could feed some to her. She shook her head, urging me to eat. Then I urged her to eat. We were pushing back and forth when I accidentally dropped the bowl. The rice fell to the ground, sticking to the small crumbled leaves, dust, and ashes on our earthen floor.

"Look what you did! That is just too great," Mother said, shooting me a blaming look while swiftly scraping off the dirty parts.

"OK, eat. Better not fight with me again," she said as she chanted, "Gu gan bu jing, chi le bu sheng bing—Unclean, unclean, not sick after eaten." It was a saying that served as a prayer to comfort us when we had to eat something we knew was not clean enough. It seemed to always work, too, because many times we ate spoiled food or rotten vegetables, but we didn't get sick. Whenever we did get sick, we blamed it on something else. It was too unbearable to admit the truth, lest we fear some questionable food that we might have to eat another day.

The next day, Mother got up earlier than usual, telling me to stay inside after school if she should come home late. She had to go to an accusation meeting again. I dropped my school bag on the floor.

"DaDa, listen please, you are not going there today. I am staying home to protect you."

"Don't be silly. You are a child. This is an adult matter. You just go to school."

"I am not going to school today."

"Small arm can't wring the big leg. We adults must follow orders," Mother said.

"I am not an adult, so I don't have to follow their orders," I answered.

"Wang Zheng Yi, Wang Upright Justice," Mother's name was called out from outside the door, "Are you ready to go now?"

I pushed her back into the bedroom and closed the door behind me. All the Enemies were out to labor, and the main room was nothing but a lumpy mess with all of their various belongings scattered amid the straw beds. Stepping over the chaotic campground, I showed up at the door with my arms stretched out, blocking the way.

It was the peasant, Party Representative Lai. His son, named Bao—"Treasure"—was in the same school as me, although he was a few years older than I was.

"Is your mother home?" Lai asked.

"Yes."

"Just tell her to arrive earlier at the accusation meeting today."

"She can't go."

"Why not?"

"She is sick," I answered.

"She was fine yesterday," he said.

"But she is not fine today. I am going to the accusing for her."

Lai's eyes blinked. "What are you saying? You are going to the accusation meeting for your mother?"

"Yes."

"Don't be childish. There is no such thing in the world." Lai tried to dismiss me, with his hand signaling me to back up.

"You back up," I said with force.

"Ho, you are fierce, aren't you? Who taught you that, eh?"

"Mulan. Mulan taught me."

"Who is Mulan? I will have to report her to the Party," he barked.

"Oh, do! She will only laugh at you. Go and ask your son, Treasure. He will tell you Mulan was the one who went to war for her father. We read it in our story book, she was only a child, too—so I am going to the accusing for Mother."

"You just don't know how high is the sky and how thick is the Earth, do you? The world does not work that way. I don't have time to waste with you here. I am here to follow orders. Let me see your mother. She must go."

From the corner next to the door, I spotted the heavy, strong carrying pole from which I had once swung in tandem with the water bucket. Rightist Bu had sharpened each end and installed sharp iron spearheads to make easier work of thrusting into the bundles of crops—and perhaps for a time like this. I lifted the pole, which was twice my height. Mulan was in my imagination, and I found my strength to lift it high.

"Stop right there!" I ordered, like Mulan in the battlefield shouting against her enemy. Hitting one tip of the pole to the floor, I dug into the dirt.

"If you move one more inch, the spear goes right through into your head," I said, pulling it out of the dirt. The world of my young suffering had turned me into my heroine.

"How dare you! Are you crazy? Did you eat leopard's gall?" he yelled, trying to grab my pole, but I screamed and pulled it back.

"Aiyaaa, you kill me! Go ahead, kill me!" A scream came from my little throat that was the voice of someone else. "I'll become a ghost. I'll haunt your son, Treasure, haunt him, haunt him until he is dead!"

Mother broke out of the bedroom, and a space opened up in the room and filled with a powerful silence. Lai loosened his grip, glaring at Mother, glaring at me.

"If my son misses one hair," he held up his index finger in front of my face to emphasize the number one, "don't expect to keep your little insane muddled head," he threatened. He turned to Mother. "If it was not that you helped Basket to have our son, I would drag you to the accusation meeting right now. Don't let your children plant thorns on your path," he said and stormed away toward the levee.

Mother stood there motionless. I started to tremble. The reality sank in, and I knew I had caused huge trouble. I dropped the pole back into the corner of the wall, losing all of my Mulan powers. Anxiously, I took a glance at Mother and then lowered my head, examining the little hole in the dirt floor I had just poked with the pole, trying to mend it with my pointed toe while suffering the long silence.

"I guess I never knew that I was a heroine's mother, eh, you little thing?"

Lifting my head, I saw Mother looking at me, her big eyes shining with light. We both looked out at the levee, where Lai's body, then head, disappeared behind the mound. We looked at each other, again. I feared her anger. I studied the direction of the corner of her mouth, and I joined her in a long string of laughter that was one part shock and two parts relief.

"He forgot how he got his son, thanks to your underwear, DaDa!"

"Young girls shouldn't talk about adult things like that."

Even in our stomach-aching laughter over my outrageous and dangerous behavior toward Representative Lai, Mother reminded me to be proper.

"He should hurry home to check each hair on his own muddled-headed foolish son's head, right, DaDa?" I said.

"But you did scare his gall into breaking by threatening to haunt his son," she said with pride.

"Yes, not just haunting, DaDa, I said haunting him dead!" We both were exhausted by the time the fear had laughed itself out of our minds. I was left feeling fearless yet fearful of my own feelings.

真

Mother began to realize that housing so many people was not easy. She and I always hid in her bedroom, hardly ever encountering anyone when they came back from labor. It was there that she told me more of our history and the stories of her life, and we told funny stories over and over with great drama. Waiting in the dark at night was familiar. I waited for Mother to light the kerosene lantern, but not too early so as not to waste the precious fuel begged from a sympathetic neighbor. I scrubbed the black soot from each of the tiny glass windows of our only lantern every night to invite the most light into our house.

"Don't turn it up too high—the fuel, the fuel," she warned. This little moth yearned for the light, and I was drawn to its power, for in the lantern's fizzling amber circle I could read my precious textbook, and I could do homework well into the winter nights when the sun was so stingy with its light.

One night, Mother had a clever idea. Instead of doing my homework in the bedroom at night, she suggested we save fuel by borrowing light from the same lamp that was on the table for the camp of the Ogres. I quietly slithered out into the golden arc of light when I heard the Ogres blanketed by their most boisterous laughter. I watched my own shadow wavering on the wall from the kerosene lantern as I listened to every word the men said while still completing my school assignments. I did my homework quietly with my head down. They soon forgot that I was there. In time, I began receiving many good comments from the Enemies, who said I was smart and hard-studying.

"It is a shame," I overheard one of the Ogres say. "Regrettably, she would have been very successful if only she hadn't been burdened with this kind of classification." I did not grasp this truth. They behaved well in front of me, too. If someone said something with the slightest impropriety, there would be a warning: "Be careful, there is a girl here."

"Yes, and she has Mulan on her side. Be careful," Rightist Bu said.

Had rumors of my courage involving my threat to Party Representative Lai leaked to our guests? I had never heard Mother's boasts.

One night, Lao Kong burst out with a loud, abrupt sneeze and at the same time, uncontrollably, the enjoyment of his meal escaped into the room from beneath his garments with a clear announcement. It was quiet, and everyone pretended not to hear anything. Uncle Lake, an old scholar who still maintained his pedantic grace, responded, "Look at you, look at you, there is a girl here. Be polite!"

His intensity in making his point produced a similar end result that sounded like the squawk of a duck and the pop of a gun from under his layers of clothes. Now all rules of social grace evaporated into the gales of laughter, threatening to bring the crumbling tile roof down onto our laps. Every time Spy Lake shamed the men into ceasing their roars of laughter, one of them sputtered and another round ensued. Finally, everyone looked at Bu, the cook of the day. From his own look, it was clear he knew he was in trouble.

"Hey, wait a minute. Comrade Bu, what did you feed us today? Are you trying to undermine the Communist's Reform Program, gassing us right to death?" asked Scholar Dong.

"Not left, but *right* to death," added Rightist Bu, "just in case the full meaning of my comrade's words were not absorbed."

The men enjoyed their barbs, but I held my hand tightly over my mouth to prevent my laugh from causing offense, lest I be banished from the room.

Uncle Bu was a tall man who spoke with a high-pitched voice. He was educated and liked to voice his opinions, which got him into trouble. He was accused of using his sharp tongue to attack the Communist Party, which was worse than a gun because it would influence people's political views, he had said. This was why he was a Black Element with the label "Rightist." I was particularly fascinated by the words of Rightist Bu, the man who had lifted my bucket and me out of the water with his heavy pole and gently set me down.

Rightist Bu and Spy Lake often talked a lot, even squabbling hard about things if they didn't agree with each other. One night, they started to talk about China's history, and the topic soon turned to the first woman emperor, Wu Ze-Tian. I was so interested that I put down my pencil to listen. Rightist Bu saw me all ears and joked, "If you keep studying hard, you can become a female emperor, too."

"Wait a minute, Rightist. You'd better not corrupt her with any emperor ideas. Empress Wu Ze-Tian was the first and the last. There will be no Communist Empress," Spy Lake said, disagreeing with Bu.

"I was just joking. Girls should have imaginations, right? She could marry an emperor, like Wu Ze-Tian did, and became an empress. And she could produce a prince and princess. She could be a grand empress." Spy Lake gave Bu a look of warning.

"OK, OK," snapped Bu. "Let's forget about the whole imperial thing and emperors and princesses from the past. Thankfully, those days are over. We are living in a new liberated China now, and we are enjoying the honey-sweet life. Look at us, relieved of the burden of all of those horrid possessions and wealth. Now we can be close to the Earth working under the poor ignorant peasants as our kindly overseers. Isn't that modern? Isn't that the good life?" Bu's sarcasm was not lost on anyone, including me, as I sat in the shadows listening hard.

I was a little embarrassed and pretended to write my homework again, but my mind went wild. If that woman emperor wore her big towering headdress on the throne today, would she order the other students to stop bullying me? Could I be chosen as Student of the Three Merits? Could I be nominated as Young Pioneer to receive a red scarf on the stage? Could we have pure white rice for dinner? I suddenly saw hope that a woman emperor might help me; at least I was sure that she would like to.

"Was Empress Wu Ze-Tian a good emperor? Did she kill many people like the men emperors?" I asked. I pulled back out of the lamp's light, knowing it was not right for a young person to interrupt when adults were talking, but I was just too curious.

"All of the ruling classes killed. You think the Communists don't kill? At any moment, any one of us could be—" Rightist Bu looked at my frightened eyes and suddenly stopped.

Spy Lake immediately took over to answer me. "I think the woman Emperor Wu Ze-Tian was a great leader. She was born to a humble family, and she became so beautiful that her beauty could shame the fish to sink and the birds to drop…and she was a scholar too, like your mother and her family. She dared to stand against the feudal society—uh, that is, the men controlling society—and proclaimed herself the Emperor of China."

"What is proclaimed?" I didn't understand everything he said.

"Oh, she called herself 'emperor.' She took control and announced it herself," explained Scholar Dong, "and she lived in the same area you are living in, and she drank the water from the same Yangtze River you are drinking from, too. So perhaps she is part of you now. Her spirit is most surely running through you."

"I cannot believe it!" I jumped up, looking down at my small self.

"Yes, it is true," Rightist Bu confirmed, "Empress Wu Ze-Tian was living in Jing Zhou town when she was your age, over a thousand years ago. It is just thirty kilometers away from here. Many local people here don't know about the facts, but you know now."

I admired the woman Hero Mulan from our stories at school, and now I had a new woman emperor to admire. They were to be my imaginary friends and protectors.

CHAPTER 9
THE UNEXPECTED PAPERS

Father often walked a long distance to pay uninvited visits to Sister Double Happiness, asking to borrow a few Yuan here and there to help buy rice, salt, oil, or matches so the family could carry on. Sister was not always happy to hear him use the word "borrow" because she knew he would never return it.

One time, Father brought home small bundles of papers from the student tests that Sister Double Happiness had collected. These had so many uses for our paperless family. Each sheet was treated like white silk as he set them on the table with reverence.

"So many possible uses." he said.

We talked all night about how these papers could change our lives. There were many ideas. "Perhaps to line our worn-out shoes for better warmth in winter," Sister said.

"Maybe we should save them to make cones to borrow fire from our neighbor," Father suggested.

But in the end, it was Mother's prerogative. In her dignified way, the papers became our indispensable necessity that helped to recapture one bit of the elegance of her former life—toilet paper. With so many people in the house, the single, unisex, backyard toilet shed became busy during the time when the Enemies were home. Compared to other people, our toilet shed was in good shape because Mother was always picky about the cleanliness of the toilet area. She refused to visit people again if she found that their toilet was too dirty.

Unlike many other people's toilet places with only a half round of sorghum stalks to make a partial wall, our toilet shed was a real shed with a grass roof. It even had a short door made out of cotton stems. The container was a big vat with two wooden boards to squat on. It was not just a big hole like everyone else's. Just like everyone else's shed, though, it was a hotbed paradise for the green-jacket flies to hang out. After they were well fed, they laid endless eggs, and the hatched eggs turned into swarms of waggling white maggots with long tails, swimming busily below, piling on top of themselves, circling and rotating in the ever-filling vat.

In the daytime, the gray-winged flies and big, bug-eyed green jackets took over the territory, while night-shift duty was taken over by the blood-sucking, bountiful mosquitoes, playing their incessant high-pitched songs as if on tight-stringed instruments.

Before the beloved teaching papers arrived in the shed, we had a nice bamboo basket with an unbroken handle hanging on the front of the sorghum wall, much nicer than our neighbors' broken baskets. It held different "papers" we reserved, such as tattered rags beyond use, torn straw papers too fragile to be used to wrap anything anymore, and the cigarette boxes, luckily and rarely found on the side of the road. Other people would use the leaves of bamboo, corn, or pumpkin, but our family never used those, for reasons unknown to me. Either Mother was too picky, afraid of the bugs, insects, and worms attached to the leaves or we were not able to grow anything with big enough leaves for the toiletry.

Once something made its way into the toilet shed, you wouldn't want to take it out to use for any other purpose. The stinky odor glued itself to everything that entered there, including our poor selves. It didn't matter how much better our toilet shed was, it was not a place one wanted to stay a second longer than necessary. You just had to hold your breath, rush in, and dash out, escaping as fast as possible before being unmercifully attacked by either the green jackets of the day or the mosquitoes of the night. One or the other stood guard, taking their shift at annoying us daily.

After Sister Double Happiness got her teaching job in the city, our toilet shed was upgraded to an even higher class. The toilet paper was not your ordinary paper, but highly educated paper. The previous essentials—the tattered rags, the coarse straw papers, or cigarette boxes—were humbled by the luxury of these papers. Plus, the supply was dependable, taking merely a four-hour walk to Sister's house for Father, and they were free. Mother and I were so thrilled with this supply of special papers until the Enemies moved in.

Going to the toilet was quite a challenge with seventeen people to one pot. Mother and I had to stand guard for each other. By the time you realized someone was walking in, it was too late for even a loud cough to signal a warning. Both the squatter and the intruder would suffer an astonished startle when encountering each other in this compromised position. It didn't matter how many times you experienced it; each encounter with the strangers caused a unique shock.

One morning, a dilemma happened to Rightist Bu. There was a line waiting for the shed's availability. After a while, the Enemies started to be anxious about being late.

"Who's in there? Are you giving birth to a baby?" Spy Lake yelled.

"Can anyone bring me any paper?" the shout returned in Rightist Bu's high-pitched voice.

The Ogres in line looked at each other, shaking their heads. No one wanted to do this job. Finally Uncle Huang, the one who gave me the rice to eat who seemed the most generous, took out his tobacco wrappers and put them on a long stick to transport to Uncle Bu through the cotton-stem half door.

I rushed into the house. "I saw the paper," I said out of breath. I couldn't wait to report the surprising discovery to Mother.

"What paper?" she asked.

"Guess where Uncle Huang's tobacco wrappers are from? They are from the basket of the toilet shed," I said. "Who would think those papers could ever migrate out of the shed? They were only meant to wipe that certain place, and that someone would even put it in his mouth?"

Mother's eyes were wide open, and then she began to laugh, "If he keeps smoking those toilet papers, he will stink, we will stink, all the Enemies will stink. As the Party Representatives say, we will be the real 'stinking Enemies of the State,'" she added.

"So we all will be stinking together," I continued, and we laughed.

Those precious papers had many uses. As the supplies of the papers were running low, we decided that we should allocate a certain amount to each person so they each could use it according to their preferences: for their sanitary needs or for another use such as rolling tobacco cigarettes. Mother let me bring out all the test papers, and I handed them out. First, the Ogres just took whatever I gave to them. But soon, after they read the contents, our educated houseguests came back for exchanges.

"Hey Little Sister, I never was good at math. May I change to the history papers?" asked the short Ogre.

"Well, I don't expect to get a college degree out of them," said Scholar Dong, "but I am happy to look at the history tests."

The allocating job was getting complicated because the papers were high school level, and I was just in second grade elementary. Spy Lake was easy; he said he welcomed any subjects because he had a wide range of knowledge. So I just gave the exchanged math papers to him. When it came to Rightist Bu, he said he didn't care which subjects, but he wanted only the highest-scored papers.

"Why do you care about the scores?" Spy Lake was curious.

"Because I care about my 'genius rear end,'" he replied.

"If those westerner Ocean Devils you went to school with only knew how you learned so much so fast." They all laughed. I was impressed to learn that Spy Lake even knew Foreign Devils from across the ocean.

The campground in the middle of our main room became our university. Everyone was busy reading their papers and making comments. It was to my great disappointment when a favorite paper finally met its filthy fate.

"Anyone know where the Di Zhong Hai is?" someone raised a question while reading a geography test. "The student's answer is wrong here. I mean, before I use this, I would like to know."

Everybody turned to Spy Lake. He was the one who seemed to know everything. But Rightist Bu was quicker to respond. "What does Di mean?" he asked. Everyone knew what Di was, of course—"earth"—many answered at the same time.

"What does Zhong mean?"

"Middle." Even the first-graders would know that.

"So what does Hai mean?" Uncle Bu continued.

"Sea." That was easy.

"So, now, put Di-Zhong-Hai together. What do you get?"

We get, "Earth middle sea." Someone came up with the answer fast.

"Now you know where the Di Zhong Hai is. It is the sea that is in the middle of the Earth. Simple," Bu said.

It made sense to many of the Enemies, and they were nodding. It made sense to me, too.

"Besides, Zhong Guo means 'the Middle Kingdom,' so the Middle Earth Sea should be right in the middle of the Earth in the center of China. Again, simple," Uncle Bu said.

But Spy Lake fiercely disagreed.

"Wait a minute, you can't be more wrong!" Everyone turned to listen to him.

"Rightist, are you sure the Middle Earth Sea is in the middle of the Earth in China?"

Rightist Bu toned down his volume. "I was just playing with the words for fun." Still he challenged Spy Lake, saying, "Ok, now you tell me. I will wash my ears to humbly listen to you."

"It is somewhere in Europe. I believe it is called the Mediterranean Sea. It is definitely not in China," the scholar insisted.

"No need to argue. We are only passing the time here. Let's move on," Uncle Huang said.

"Good, good. There is a question about China here in my history paper. What were the Four Great Inventions of ancient China?" Spy Lake asked.

"Sparrows, rats, mosquitoes, and flies," the Ogre who was the expert on such things joked.

"He said inventions, not afflictions," Rightist Bu said, laughing.

The answer was easy for everyone. Shaking the paper in his hands, Spy Lake said, "Paper, compass, gun powder, and—"

"It would seem we Chinese invented everything of importance," Scholar Dong interrupted.

"If we invented everything of importance, why do we import everything of importance from the Foreign Devils, the so called evil capitalists from across the ocean?" Rightist Bu asked. "If only we could get our hands on some of those important imports," he continued, laughing.

"Like some soap for you, my friend, to wash the rebelliousness from your tongue," Spy Lake teased.

The men began the competition that I loved so much—one funny and the next funnier until they all were roaring with laughter at their own cleverness.

"Or a match to light your toilet-paper cigarettes," Rightist Bu said, nodding his head toward Uncle Huang. I hid my small titter in my hands so as not to insult the man who fed me rice and shared the warmth of his fire with my frozen toes.

The day was long, and the oil in the kerosene lamp was sputtering. Before they remembered to mention the last invention, one by one, they dropped to their beds of straw and started to snore. The lively conference went silent, leaving me with the question dangling temptingly over my hungry mind, for always the weight of their twelve-hour workdays lay heavier on their minds than the flimsy quilts that barely warmed their bodies by night.

They slept, but their words always stayed up longer than they did. They left me with so many questions. Who were these Ocean Devils who made the special soap we had no money to buy, who made the precious matches that were always missing by our stove, requiring me to borrow fire from our neighbor? If they made such wonderful things, why were they so rudely called the Foreign Devils? Why were they so evil?

It was then, before the light flickered out, that I stared at one paper and then the other, understanding only some of what I saw, trying to hold onto the words and characters that spread across the sheets before they met their awful destiny. I wondered if I used them for the purposes Mother intended, could I perhaps effortlessly become an educated girl, as Spy Lake suggested? And like Sister Double Happiness, would everyone in our family household, even these uninvited Ogres, sit nearby to watch with admiration as my elegant chopsticks touched my lips, as I smiled down upon a bright yellow egg upon my snow-white rice?

I could not wait for the next evening to arrive so I could sit by the glowing circle of the Ogres' lantern, head down, pretending to write my schoolwork, my eyes stretched wide, the corners of my mouth reaching to my ears, my ears open and deep like a well waiting for a precious good-luck golden coin to drop, waiting for the answer.

Scholar Dong began the evening's court. "As for last night's question regarding the inventions of the Chinese that was discussed before we slept—"I straightened and paid close attention—"it would seem I was correct. We invented everything of importance," he said. The men nodded.

"It is an accepted and known fact," Spy Lake added.

"Except perhaps for a cure to control the insanity of our leaders. Scholar Dong, if I might interrupt, I believe the final and fourth Great Invention was never named as it was lost amidst our snores," Rightist Bu said, "and that provides a hint in itself."

He looked in my direction. "What is there that has the same explosive sounds of twelve exhausted Ogres snoring?"

I thought for a minute, and then I giggled.

"Another hint? The sound whines up and up and then, poof, it explodes. Go on, I see you have turned up the lantern in your mind and you have solved the riddle," Bu said.

"Fireworks?" I asked tentatively.

"So you have had the pleasure of hearing our nightly entertainment from your room, I see." The group laughed, imitating each other's various styles of snoring that sounded like explosions of fireworks at the Spring Festival.

"Yes, just so, it was fireworks." Scholar Dong cleared his throat, inviting the men to focus.

"I am impressed by your well-honed skill from your professor days to bring our little wayward group to attention," Spy Lake teased.

"Yes, I have been thinking about the profound impact our simple invention of paper has had on life, commerce, scholarship, and now here, the unimaginable, our sanitation," Scholar Dong said with great seriousness.

The Ogres, caught off guard, looked up and laughed in a sudden burst.

"Since when have you, Scholar Dong, been one to create the merriment in our group?" Uncle Huang asked

"Yes, colorful umbrellas over our heads and now our education from below from our ever-precious educated toilet paper. Surely, no wealthy foreigner has had such a luxury," one of the Ogres added.

"And how clever for us to absorb our learning with such ease," Doctor Wong unexpectedly continued the theme.

Scholar Dong reeled in the crowd by standing and assuming command of the group. He extended his withered arms straight out and slowly lowered them, palms down, as every student had seen their teachers do so many times to quiet a room. The volume of the laughter in the room went from a boil to a simmer, then sat still in the pot.

"Still, it brings me great pride," he continued.

"Who was the great man who invented paper, Scholar Dong?" The question was out of my bold mouth before my politeness could stop it. I half rose to leave the room as an apology, but once more they welcomed my question.

"Please, girl, you may stay. Rules are changing in our lives, and formalities sometimes seem absurd under present conditions. If we can teach you something here, this place shall be our classroom."

"The success of the invention of paper brought great pride to the Chinese people. It was one of our ancestors, named Tsai Lun, who expanded the knowledge of making paper from used silk and cotton fabric, who invented a complete paper-making system over two thousand years ago," Scholar Dong continued.

I could not imagine two thousand years, having less than eight myself, and I could not understand why something invented so long ago was still so rare and precious in my life.

"If only we could invent something that would bring us such joy, move the Earth to right itself, bring us back in time before the world spun upside down," Uncle Huang said.

Scholar Dong continued, looking in my direction. "It changed the inefficient ways of writing on stones, bricks, tree leaves, bark, bronze, animal skins, or bones. Tsai Lun used such materials as tree bark; hemp fiber; and old, useless fishing nets and pounded the fiber into thick, wet mush. He spread the fiber liquid substance on a cloth mat framed with bamboo to dry under the sun. Thus, the lightweight, convenient fiber and textile material was born, which was called "paper." In the year one hundred five AD, Tsai Lun presented his invented paper to the Emperor, and His Majesty was greatly pleased."

"What happened to Tsai Lun? Was he held up on a sedan and carried through the country to receive his praise?" I asked. "Did they hold parades and dance and swirl silk as he passed by?"

"No," Scholar Dong continued, "as extraordinary an inventor as Tsai Lun was, he couldn't escape the tragic ending to his life. The politics of the Imperial inner power struggles were not suited to his simple and creative soul. He was crushed by the powerful greed that grasped at his skill and his invention. After the Emperor summoned him to appear in court, he took a bath to cleanse himself of the contamination of the corrupted court, put on his finest clothing, and killed himself."

"Huuuh?" I drew a small pocket of air into my lungs before my chest deflated with sadness. There was no "Careful, there is a girl here!" Instead, Scholar Dong turned to me and continued. "Throughout the history of this home we call China, great injustice has been done to so many innocent people, from common farmers to imperial officials, from national heroes to helpless concubines. One person's persecution led to the entire clan's slaughter with cruelest torture to complete the kill, or if the victim was of great fortune, he was rewarded with his own suicide as a gift of leniency. Now the Enemies of the State epitomize the victims of that dark part of our China's tragic history."

"Scholar Dong, that is too much and too deep for a young ear," Uncle Huang pleaded, but it was too late. I had taken this thought into my mind and held it there as I curled up at Mother's feet and stared into the darkness of her bedroom. Scholar Dong's uninterrupted words on that night were my true initiation into this circle of truth that would shape me, frighten me, impassion me, and empower me far beyond my courageous heroine Mulan had, far beyond the Empress Wu Ze-Tian. The sound of his voice on that night broke my innocence like a hammer on a paper drum. My ears could never hear things in quite the same way again. The stark reality they shared was stretching my mind beyond the levee, beyond the brigade—far, far beyond.

真

It seemed the Ogres accepted their fate and made the best of each day. They would leave early in the morning and come back in the evening. The cook carried their lunch to the worksite. I looked forward to enjoying the evening homework time under that kerosene lamp on the table, watching my shadow blending with theirs, laughing with them at the jokes, and listening to their chats, like the wonderful performances in the city squares that Mother had described but that I had never known.

One evening during dinnertime, some Enemies were sitting at the table, some were sitting on the threshold, some were simply squatting. Rightist Bu sitting on the wooden bench next to Uncle Lao Kong holding his rice bowl.

"What is your crime, Lao Kong, besides your last name?" Bu asked.

"I bought too much land because I needed it to grow healing herbs."

"So are you a doctor?"

"I was, but not anymore. All the land was confiscated. I can only secretly practice Qigong myself," Lao Kong said.

"I have always been curious about Qigong. I heard the energy from it can both heal and kill, and the master can freeze someone when he wants to by just pointing his finger at the person. Are all those things true?" Rightist Bu was excited.

"Some grand masters can do those things," said Lao Kong.

"Where are the grand masters? I was always interested in becoming a disciple, but I didn't have a chance. I suppose I am too old now. I read martial arts novels, and they were described as very powerful but secretive."

"Firstly, you will never be too old to learn Qigong for healing purposes; secondly, grand masters predicted that big disasters were to fall upon our massive land, so they ran to hide, deep in the mountains. They will not come out until the world is ready for peace, which they will also be able to predict," Uncle Lao Kong explained.

"Fascinating!" exclaimed Rightist Bu, but soon he became sympathetic. "Also, I feel sad, for not only do you have the stigma of an exploiting Landlord and the labels of Witch Doctor and Devil Martial Artist, but you are also burdened with the remnant of the feudal past that you still wear as your last name, Kong."

"Well, uh," he looked around at the other men who were distracted with talk of the government, "just between you and me"— Lao Kong lowered his voice a little—"I don't mind my last name. It has given me honor to know that I am one of the descendants of Confucius. I can't change my last name, nor do I want to."

"I don't blame you. I feel the same way. They can take all the rights from us, but they can't take away our family names."

"But you must change your last name in the western countries if you get married to your husband," Spy Lake joined the conversation without being invited.

"Guess there is no worry that I would get married to any husband," said Lao Kong.

"No husband would want to marry you, either. Not me, ha ha," laughed Rightist Bu.

"Not me." Spy Lake laughed, too.

"Don't put your eye on me, kind doctor!"

"Not me, not me." The other men repeated the last part of the conversation and laughed without even knowing what they were laughing about. They welcomed any distraction to draw the aches from their bones.

Soon, Rightist Bu came up with another question for Lao Kong: "Were Lao Tzu and Confucius really good friends?"

Lao Kong looked at Spy Lake, wondering if he should answer the question.

"Hey, don't look at me, Mr. Kong. You are the Inner Kong, the real Kong offspring."

"What is Inner Kong?" I found myself asking out loud.

"This means he had a family-generation middle name that belongs only to the true offspring of Confucius, unlike the 'outer Kong,' which means the Kong name was given to them as servants or related family personnel, but not as the true bloodline."

Lao Kong looked humble and spoke slowly. "I can tell you an anecdote, and you can judge for yourself."

It was a story that I would carry forever. I listened carefully.

Confucius was always eager to learn from Lao Tzu, the most holy and knowledgeable one. One time, he brought with him his close disciples, Yan Hui and Zi Lu, to a city called Luo Yang. After days of waiting, finally they met Lao Tzu. Early in the morning, Lao Tzu took Confucius and his disciples into his main room. After being seated, Confucius eagerly expressed his intention. "I have heard Your Master's famous name, and I've been longing to pay my respectful visit. May I humbly ask, Master, how is your progress in understanding the essence of life and the depths of man's cultivation?"

Confucius and his disciples were anxious to hear him. However, Lao Tzu opened his mouth and, laughing hard, he asked, "What do you think of my teeth?"

The baffled Confucius took a look, finding many missing, some blackened, and only a few remaining. He and his disciples shook their heads, looking at each other, puzzled.

Then Lao Tzu stuck out his tongue and asked, "Now, how about my tongue?" Confucius and his disciples carefully examined it. Immediately, Confucius's eyes lightened, answering Tao Tzu with a smile. "Master indeed deserves the reputation of having the greatest knowledge and wisdom."

"I presume now you are clear about the level of my understandings of the depths of man's cultivation?" asked Lao Tzu.

Nodding with great comprehension, Confucius answered, "Yes, I am suddenly and humbly enlightened with Master's wisdom."

Later, on the way back home, his face shone like peach flowers, and Confucius was happy, as though he had received a great treasure. The disciple Zi Lu was skeptical and baffled, so he told Yan Hui, "It seemed to me that Lao Tzu was rude by showing only his mouth instead of teaching us something."

Upon hearing the comment, Confucius started laughing softly while smoothing his beard.

Disciple Yan Hui answered, "It was a very worthwhile trip. Lao Tzu has taught us the greatest wisdom that we could not have learned anywhere else. He opened his mouth to show us his teeth to teach us that although teeth are hard, they become weakened and lost after a long time grinding at our food; he showed us his tongue to teach us that although the tongue is soft, it can endure the hard, so it remains intact forever."

Zi Lu finally understood, and Yan Hui continued. "It is like flowing water. Although it is soft, it can break through powerful mountain rocks and eventually leave them behind, diminished.

It is like wind—although invisible, it can uplift a big tree when angry."

Confucius was greatly pleased after he heard the disciple's comprehension and praised him highly. "Yan Hui can see the significance of the small and understand the sophistication of the simple, the power of the soft over the false strength of the hard."

After the story, the Ogres who were listening turned their eyes, looking at each other, pretending they were Lao Tzu, grinning to show their yellow-darkened, gapped teeth, then sticking out their tongues to show the strength of their survival. I was quite amused. Although they looked like scary, strange creatures, I wasn't afraid of them. They were like family to me then, offering confusing lessons and clear wisdom.

真

That night, I dared to ask a question: "Uncle Lao Kong, I used the 'hard' when I held the bamboo pole up to the mean representative. He wouldn't listen to my soft tongue when I asked him to leave Mother alone. Was it wrong to use my 'hard' to make him go away?" The men all grinned again and sat quietly.

"There is a time to use the hard to meet your goal and a time to use the soft. I myself am committed to the soft, for I have found it effective for getting what I want—peace of mind, the power of remaining my true self in the face of evil, and the miracle of surviving to this day. Knowing the difference only comes with wisdom, Little Zhen," Uncle Lao Kong said.

"I used the hard because I am soft, Uncle. My soft cannot be heard."

"And so your wisdom blooms," said Scholar Dong.

I did not understand the smiles on my Ogres' faces. Rightist Bu squatted down beside me and said, "You had courage and used just enough hard to protect your soft. It is about saving your hard only for the fewest of times. When you feel the resistance is too much, breathe and let go. This is often the softest way of being hard."

"I am confused, Uncle," I said.

"As are we, Little Zhen. If we all had this wisdom, we wouldn't be here. We would be levitating above it all." They laughed again.

"Just remember, if you use the hard too often, it will crumble. The soft will always remain your most powerful force," said Uncle Lao Kong.

"How do I know when to use the power of soft or use up some of the weakness of the hard?" I asked.

"Take your message from your heart and soul, not your mind," said Spy Lake, "just as you did when you protected your mother."

"I will save my hard for the hardest of times, then," I promised.

Lao Kong shared many lessons with the group. Different from the others, he was always calm. He never rushed. He spoke slowly, ate slowly, and drank slowly. Sometimes I saw him standing outside alone with no movement in his body for a long time. Uncle Huang said he was in meditation. He was practicing Qigong.

Each cold morning, all of the Enemies tightened their waists with their straw belts and made sure to be at the work site before the overseer arrived. No one dared to be late or miss any time from their labor because the punishment could mean transferring them to another camp, only to begin their punishment time all over again. They could not afford to have their labor reform extended because their families were counting on them to return home to earn working points, which meant desperately needed food and fuel.

On one bitter morning, a misfortune fell upon the kindly Uncle Huang. He was sick in the morning with a fever and headache. Rightist Bu brought Lao Kong back to Uncle Huang's bedroll, where he lay shaking. Lao Kong made him stick out his tongue just like Lao Tzu did in the story, and then he touched his forehead. He got some warm water and covered the mug with his palm, and with his eyes closed, he gave Uncle Huang the water to drink. Meanwhile, Lao Kong used his fingers to press certain spots of Uncle Huang's hands, chest, and legs.

"You are good now, Old Huang. Get ready to work. But while at work, you can just sit there and rest; no need to labor today," said Uncle Lao Kong.

Rightist Lu said, "Have you lost your mind, to rest at the aqueduct? The overseer would kill him."

"I will take care of that," said Lao Kong.

Amazingly, a short time later, Uncle Huang was able to drag his feet to work. The Ogres recounted the story by the lantern that night. The overseer was a man in his thirties belonging to the Poor Peasant ruling classification, of course. He hated the fact that he had to supervise the bad elements. He had the habit of showing up in the morning, counting the heads, yelling at anyone as he pleased, and then leaving, only to sneak back to check on everyone at the end of the day.

When Uncle Huang finally arrived, the overseer was furious.

"What excuse do you have for being late?" he asked.

Lao Kong held up his warm tea mug and slowly walked up to him. "Don't waste your energy with Lao Huang here, Comrade," he said.

"Who are you calling 'Comrade? Do you have no shame, fool? I am not your comrade. Ha! Comrade with the likes of you?' yelled the overseer. "As for your lazy friend here—"

"Sorry, Comrade," Lao Kong repeated the word, making the overseer furious to draw the focus away from Uncle Huang once again. "Why not go home and drink your hot tea, and we will make sure to work hard. I already have my own hot tea with me right here." Lao Kong held up the mug and calmly looked deep into the eyes of the angry overseer.

"Working hard with your hot tea mug in your hands like this— absolutely not allowed!" The overseer snatched the tea mug out of Lao Kong's hands, drank the tea and dumped the rest to the ground, breaking the precious mug. He wiped his mouth and took off.

As soon as he was out of sight, Lao Kong said to everyone, "Let's eat our lunch early and finish the day and go home and put our feet to rest." Everyone looked at Lao Kong, thinking he must be insane.

Rightist Bu took Lao Kong to the side and whispered, "How is it you are so sure he won't come back today?"

"My herbs tell me he will be busy visiting someplace else today without the option of leaving," said Lao Kong.

"Your herbs tell you what? Ah, I see, the tea was a very special tea with very special powers to keep our comrade in one certain place for many hours," Bu said, smiling.

"Yes, very special."

"I know nothing of the 'special' tea," said Rightist Bu, agreeing to keep his secret.

"I know nothing about the tea, either," Lao Kong said, sharing a grin with Rightist Bu.

To the Enemies, half a day off was like a long vacation, a rare gift. They came back to the house, washed their underwear and socks, and set them in the sun to dry, wrapped their tobacco leaves with the test papers, and simply sat around, lazily holding their tea mugs with their hands to get some warmth while telling the story of the day.

Uncle Huang went to lie down to rest while Lao Kong rubbed his palms very fast, then planted his palms on the top of Uncle Huang's head and abdomen. Rightist Bu watched with amazement as the good color returned to Uncle Huang's face. We all watched Lao Kong's healing hands in awe.

Uncle Huang was feeling much better. He said he felt the strong, hot Qi energy circulating in his body after Lao Kong's healing hands were on him. Lao Kong went outside and dug some roots and peeled tree bark with which to make herbs for the purpose of inducing a sweat.

Mother was surprised by their early return. Normally, she avoided the main room and stayed in the kitchen when the Ogres were at home. Lao Kong came to the kitchen to ask the cook to borrow the pot to boil the medicine. She was at the back of the kitchen cutting some weeds when she heard his deep, slow voice. She stopped her work. When Lao Kong left the kitchen, Mother followed him out into the main room. The beautiful, petite, and refined host, still maintaining the grace that was her legacy, entered the room. The faces of the Enemies looked refreshed by her presence because she seldom appeared amid them when they were home. They humbly and respectfully greeted her with "Nin Hao, greetings." Mother just kept staring at Lao Kong. Everyone turned to Lao Kong. He stood up from tending his patient and looked at her.

"Are you Mei Fu, my brother-in-law, Qing Yuan Kong?" she asked.

"Yes, Sister Upright? This is your home?"

"You changed so much," she said.

Lao Kong rubbed his neck. "Yes, time has no mercy," he said.

"I know, I know. It has been so long. I wouldn't have recognized you if I didn't hear your voice." Mother took him to the quiet corner of the bedroom, tears flowing down her face, the taste of joy and pain. She had a thousand questions about her younger sister, Upright Abundance, and her oldest niece, Xi'er, "Joy."

"I have not seen them since my father's death," she said.

"Yes, Sister, we last saw each other at his funeral."

"We have aged quickly since then," she said.

"We are far from large bowls of rice and brimming, meat-filled soups. I regret our families were moved farther and farther away since then."

"I thought I would never hear of my sister again," Mother said, smiling, "but now you are here!"

"Abundance is doing fine, despite—" he shifted the subject. "After our home was confiscated, we moved to our farm tool shed. Joy—" he said, pausing. Lao Kong, my newly found uncle, squatted down and, holding his face in his hands, he sobbed. I sat in the corner listening. Uncle Kong suddenly stood up and walked to the wall that held the soot-covered portrait of our country's leader. He plucked it down, leaving the only clean, square space on the blackened wall. He placed it face down on the floor. Mother quickly looked over her shoulder toward the front door. "I cannot have those eyes on me, if I am to tell you this," he said.

126

I felt a shiver travel down my arms.

"Joy is dead," Uncle Kong continued. "Please let us sit for this since I cannot honor my daughter with just a few words."

Mother sat across from Uncle Lao Kong. He began slowly. "Our beautiful daughter did not have any good offers of marriage due to our Enemy status."

"I understand," Mother said.

"Then, a young man visiting from Si Chuan Province asked to marry her. We could see a love between them, so we approved. He was from a good classification and eager to take Joy back to his home," Uncle Lao Kong said, leaning forward and looking into Mother's eyes. "Imagine," he said, "her feet had never moved beyond the fields since she was a young girl, and he would take her to her freedom on a ship up the Yangtze River."

"I have prayed for that freedom for my own daughters," Mother said.

"The Party Secretary denied their request. They married secretly and made plans to escape, but they were both captured and beaten. He was sent back to Si Chuan under threat, and she was left pregnant with a blessing from their wedding night."

Mother dropped her head, as did Lao Kong. I could only look into my clasped hands. "She's dead," he said again. "She delivered our granddaughter, White Chrysanthemum, in the fields. The taunts of the villagers were so cruel and constant. I could see the pain in her lifeless eyes." Uncle Lao Kong turned his face to the wall, and then he continued softly. "One morning, the overseer could not find her. We searched for her. Baby White Chrysanthemum was still sound asleep in her brick bed. Next to her we found our daughter, Joy, hanging, motionless."

Mother sat very still. Uncle Lao Kong sighed and finished his tribute slowly. "She escaped to where she could freely wait for her true love's promise when he would someday join her in the beyond," he said.

We were silent for many minutes.

"I am beyond words," Mother said. "We hear of these horrors too often, but somehow you never expect it to happen in your own family."

Mother spent the next few days secretly praying with Lao Kong in the evenings. I tried to paint my cousin's features in my mind, to imagine her face, to understand those impossible things. For days, thoughts of the little baby lying alone in her bed haunted me. I felt an emptiness, and the chills came back to run down my arms each time I saw my uncle's face.

真

After one month, I had finally come to know each Ogre by listening to the group talk about their stigmas and the classifications that the government had assigned to each of them. The brands officially inflicted on them by the government confused me. They made no sense to me. Spy Lake was branded an "Evil Intellectual" because his parents had sent him to the temple school that was built by the Catholic missionaries, the English-speaking Foreign Devils. Uncle Huang was labeled "Spy" and "Traitor" because his uncle followed Chiang Kai-shek, the leader of the Nationalist Kuomintang Party, to Tai Wan in opposition to the Communist Party. Uncle Bu, of course, was called "Rightist" for his liberal thinking and tirades against the State. And Scholar Dong, a religious scholar shunned for his audacity to worship any god but Chairman Mao, was labeled "Ghost Seller." Each one of the many Ogres—the Evil Doctor, the greedy industrialist, the tainted one who traveled across the sea to be contaminated by the Ocean Devils, the artist, the one who dared to pray out loud, the capitalists—all very "evil" men. I loved them all.

"What would my brand be, Uncle Bu?" I asked. The men exchanged glances and smiles.

"My mother told me that I was born with a strong fate. She said I would be either at the front of the boat or the back of the boat, the first or the last."

"What do you think it meant, front of the boat or back of the boat?" Uncle Bu asked.

"As to the front, I do not know, as to the back, I was the last child. I know—" Tears came pressing, so I stopped speaking.

"You may be close to finding your brand if your eyes fill up like that, Little Sister. Finish it now," Spy Lake said.

"My baby brother had to die because of me, since my fortune was to be at the back of the boat, the last child. I am sorry. I didn't want Baby Brother to not have a chance because of me. Maybe my brand is also 'Evil,' like all of you. And besides, I have already been branded," I said.

"How so?" asked Spy Lake. The men were all poised to listen to me for the first time since I was first permitted to float around the edges of their evening talks.

"I am branded 'The Unteachable One' by my eldest sister," I said as I sat down hard on the dirt floor. With my words, the men laughed in concert and in unison chanted, "Oh no, of all brands, that one does not suit you!"

"Not at all."

"Oh, no, not you, Mulan."

I tucked my knees into my chest and held them with two tight arms, shying from the possibility of their words.

"Stand up here, Little Mulan," Rightist Bu said, pointing to a place in the middle of the circle of men.

"We will brand you before you can brand yourself, do you agree? Will you accept your brand from us local tyrants and evil gentry, us Ogres, to wear it forever like a medal on your proud chest?" Spy Lake asked with formality.

"Yes, Uncles, I will accept your brand," I said, nodding.

Smiling, they all stood, and Rightist Bu spoke, walking back and forth in front of me with his hands clasped behind his back. "Well, let's see, according to our discussions of you, Little Zhen, while we were digging in the foolish mud side by side, yes, you could be branded 'Spy' for hovering near our lantern until our snores rocked your roof." I giggled.

"Just one moment," Scholar Dong interrupted. "No, no, there are better brands for this learned young girl. You could be branded

'Defiant' for the time you boldly lifted the bamboo against the Party Representative to protect your mother."

I did not think their eyes spoke the same words as their tongues, so I became worried.

"Or," Uncle Bu suggested, "for continuing to go to school right under your roof when it is forbidden for you to be a student of the Ogre School, you could be classified as 'Anti-revolutionary.'"

"Shh, the neighbors! That joke's too harsh," Spy Lake warned.

"Or perhaps 'Courageous like Mulan'—yes, that is the best," Uncle Huang added. All of the men hummed in agreement.

"We, the Enemies of the People, brand you 'Courageous Scholar Zhao.'" Their smiles and gentleness blossomed out of their teasing words, and I bowed my head, quite pleased with this brand.

"You must promise, after we leave tomorrow for our homes, you will carry your brand with you forever," Spy Lake said with a smile.

"Tomorrow?" I said. I had become lost in their magical spell for weeks, never thinking there would be an end to the nights by the lantern.

"We will be returning to our families now. The festival season is over, and our punishment has been effective, has it not, Bu?" Spy Lake asked.

"Oh, yes, I have moved far left from digging in the mud for weeks. There is no way for them to label me 'Rightist' in this new state of mine. The pain in my back makes me bend in a completely different direction now."

The men laughed. I was too sad, too shocked by the news to smile.

"Do you understand, Little Sister? We have been freed to return to our burdensome lives."

"Will you be far away?" I asked.

Uncle Bu bent over and said, "We are each from faraway brigades in different communes. Twelve families form a work team, twelve work teams form a brigade, many brigades form a commune, and there are many thousands of communes. We go where

130

we are told," he explained. "Sadly, we will most likely never see you again."

My eyes squeezed, and I cried.

"Courageous Scholar Zhao, now you must live up to your name," Spy Lake said.

Mother called me to bed, and I rocked and cried myself to sleep to their musical snores for the last time.

In the morning, they ate breakfast and packed up their personal things. As they were leaving, Uncle Bu said to Mother, "You will forgive us for the forbidden things that we allowed to reach your daughter's young ears, won't you?"

"You have said what I could not have said," she answered. I did not understand.

They gathered and rolled the straw from their bedrolls, bundled it, and generously tucked it in the kitchen stall on the side of the house as a saving gift for the remainder of our winter. They thanked Mother, one at a time, twelve "thank yous" in cold, foggy voices. Then they nodded to me, each one, and said, "Goodbye, Courageous Scholar, goodbye, goodbye, goodbye." Their lips sent out cold, frosted goodbyes until they were all in a jagged line walking up over the levee.

I rushed into the house, found all of the remaining educated papers, and ran as hard as I had run with my little kite. "Wait, wait!" I called. The line of weary bodies stopped on the ramp to the levee. In ninety-nine steps, I delivered my gifts to them, history papers for the short man, Uncle Chang; math for Spy Lake—one by one I handed them each their favorite papers. Uncle Huang's warm eyes were on me as I delivered him a geography test.

"Thank you, Uncle Huang for the defrosting of my feet and the rice," I said.

"I will send you good energy, good Qi for your courageous scholarly path," said Uncle Lao Kong, smiling. "Perhaps someday you will practice Qigong for good health and to learn how to manifest good things in your life."

"Oh, I will Uncle, I promise," I answered.

Finally, for Rightist Bu, I shuffled through the papers and handed him only those with a perfect score.

"Since I am always perfectly correct…right, Little Sister?"

He bent over, picked up his bamboo pole, slid it under my arms and delivered my bouncing self to the top of the levee, where I could watch them growing smaller and smaller, walking away to their faraway homes. We were Evil together, Enemies together. They were Evil Ogres, gentle men.

CHAPTER 10
UNWORTHY CHILD

I t took some time to feel the Ogres had really left our home; I
clung to them for many weeks. The scent of their homemade
cigarettes and the sounds of their laughter still wafted through our
main room. I sat alone by the lowly light of the lantern to write my
characters, waiting through the long, hot nights to start my third
year of school, waiting to be my brand, waiting to use my "soft."

I entered the third grade with excitement. After two years, I
had gotten used to the school name Brother Repeat had given
me, Qin, "Musical Instrument." He had named me for the one
thing that gave him the most joy: the beautiful two-stringed instrument that he soothingly stroked back and forth for hours with his
handmade bow. I was Qin, a schoolgirl, but at home with Mother,
I would always be her Zhen Zhen.

The winter visit of the Ogres had planted a love of learning in
my mind. I imagined Mother's scholarly blood flowing through
me. Until that time, I had not been made to suffer the embarrassment of my classification at school. I was treated the same as the
other students from better peasant classifications. I thought they
had finally understood Mother's truth about our deserving their
acceptance. I was happy and felt so proud to be sitting in the class
of Teacher Xia.

I so looked forward to reading at school. Like Mother's books, my textbooks were sacred to me. That alone gave me a sense of pride. Each year, I yearned all summer to finger them, feel the smooth pages, spread them open like my little tiger paper and care for them like the special friends they were.

Teacher Xia brought the special textbooks to class on the first day. "Students, we have been sent these wonderful books by the government as far away as Beijing. Let us thank our Chairman Mao."

"Long live Chairman Mao," we all chanted.

"We will read them to learn about the world and how fortunate we are to be in China in these abundant years in which everyone's hands have work to do. This first story in your textbook is about the poor children in the capitalist countries, such as Taiwan and their friends, the United States of America. There is much suffering there in a country where an exploiting government does not take care of its people. The first story," he held the textbook up for all to see the page, "is the story of the two Louises." I fluttered my feathers like a baby bird opening its mouth to receive its mother's feed. Sitting straight up to listen properly to take in the words I loved to hear, I gently touched my clean finger to each character in the freshly opened book.

"Let's start with the two Louises," Teacher Xia said, beginning the story of the two Louises. "Lu-eez," we repeated. I listened so carefully to learn about America. Louise number one was a dog, and Louise number two was a girl. They were both living in America. Louise the dog lived with a very rich family, eating luscious food from a full silver bowl whenever she wished. Louise the girl was hungry, living on the streets with no food and no one to care for her. There were no allocations for the child Louise, while the dog Louise sat snugly in her house feeling the soft strokes of her owner's hands. Little Girl Louise felt only the frigid cold of the street and the pain of hunger in her flattened stomach. How sad the life of an American child was, I thought.

It was then that I first understood the conditions that children faced in a capitalist Foreign Devil country, where children were suffering in deep water and hot fire. Even in my fragile life, the children had some food, and I had Mother and Father and my sisters and brothers. Even though our roof opened its mouth to the sky here and there, we had a home. I felt such sadness for the little girl, Louise.

I am sorry, little Louise, I said to myself. *I would share my rice water with you if I could.* This is how I imagined poor America—poor, poor America, where the life of a dog was better than the life of a child. I felt fortunate and cried.

Teacher Xia, a tall, skinny man with a bony face, made me realize once again that nothing could protect me from my family's past. "Everyone who is from a poor peasant family, please raise your hand," he commanded. Some children raised their hands. They were delighted to be acknowledged for their families' contributions to society.

"Yes, keep your hands up. Now those from the middle-class peasant family," Teacher Xia said. Some more raised their hands. "And the rich peasant families?" A few raised their hands, not wanting to reveal their former affluence, coming from a bad, but not the worst, classification. Everyone looked around at each other waving their thin arms. "You may all put your hands down. Lastly, anyone from a Landlord family, raise your hand." My hand was so heavy that I could not move it. I was the only one left to raise my hand, and I had to because I belonged to this category, Landlord, the worst Enemies of the State. He gave no option for the Industrial Business classification. When my shaking hand reluctantly stuck up, the entire class fixed their eyes on me.

From then on, I wasn't just an Enemy of the State; I was the enemy of the class. My classmates were not classmates any more—they were my superiors. They called me names, they laughed at me. They wanted me to suffer because before Liberation, in their eyes, my family had exploited them and had made their families poor and made them suffer. This was the government's reason for punishing all of the rich. They ganged up on me by singing together, "Landlord hog, Landlord hog." I used my lesson of soft.

135

Sometimes the school would hold huge meetings for the poor peasants to come to the stage to talk about how terrible their lives were before the People's Liberation. They declared that the Communists had saved them by giving them a new China, by giving them the ruling power. After the meeting, the hatred was even worse against me. Then there was a "Bitterness Remembrance Meal" made with very little rice mixed with the bitter wild plants, the peasants' former diet that I ate daily. Everyone had to eat a bowl of it to taste the bitter life of the poor peasants of the past to appreciate the new life in which everything was provided by the government through the communes.

I was given a bowl of the "Bitterness Remembrance Meal," too. Just as I was raising the bowl to my hungry mouth, a boy kicked the bowl out of my hand, and the porridge fell to the ground. My teeth were bleeding. The other students were laughing and clapping their hands. The boy acted like a hero, announcing, "She can't reminisce our bitter meal. She should reminisce how she was exploiting us."

"I was not even born when my family was Landlords. You don't know my grandfather, who was kind to all the poor," I stammered.

"Exploiter!" they screamed and laughed.

真

Even though my grades were always very good, I could never become the student of the "Three Merits": Morality, Intelligence, and Strength. I couldn't be accepted as the Young Pioneer who could wear the triangular red scarf. That was an honor that I could only dream of to be recognized, to get to salute, to stand tall, to feel proud, to know my value. At each school meeting, when the new Pioneers' names were proudly announced, my body shook nervously. I listened, holding my breath, wishing my name would be announced, but no.

Each chosen student stood proudly, stiffly, to receive the red scarf around his or her neck as the entire school and teachers sang:

We are the Communist Successors,
Inheriting the glorious tradition
Of our revolutionary forbearers,
To love the motherland, to love the people,
Our beautiful red scarves float on our chests

Not fearing difficulty,
Not fearing our enemies,
Tenaciously learning,
Determinedly fighting

Go bravely forward to victory,
Go bravely forward to victory, victory,
Go bravely forward to victory,
We are the Communist Successors.

In time, I knew my destiny was to never wear a red scarf on my neck, to never have it float on my chest. I did not want to wait until mine was the only neck without a scarf like my lone hand raised in the classroom on the first day of my third year. I could not accept it. I felt deserving. I went home one day, cut my own scarf from Mother's only red blouse, and honored myself, strutting back and forth like a chicken, singing and staring into the dirty pond at my wavering, tarnished reflection. I sang:

We are the Communist Successors,
Inheriting the glorious tradition
Of our revolutionary forbearers.

Mother discovered the space left behind in her blouse by my crime of the red scarf. She walked to the pond, a distasteful route for her to tread. At the sight of me singing and marching, she strutted back and forth as well, but with far more force than a mere chicken, waving her injured blouse like a flag.

"What? You want to be honored? You want to inherit a glorious tradition? Whose successor do you intend to be, cutting the imposter scarf from my blouse?"

There was something tucked inside Mother's words that I sensed but could not understand. There were many things that I knew were not said for fear we children might say something to put the family in danger. This was one of those confusing times.

"It is only an honor if honorably given; it is only to be proud of if earned; it is only worth something if given by someone worthy," she said.

"I want you to be accepted, Zhen'er, truly I do, but not this way."

Her face seemed sad. Her lips held something on them that she seemed anxious to deliver, but she turned around and went back to the house.

I had no idea what the true meaning of the red scarf was, but I did know how it felt to be unworthy. So, in spite of Mother's words, I tucked it inside my shirt, and the pride and shame burned together into my side. Was I a worthy child in an unworthy scarf or an unworthy child in a worthy scarf?

真

I could sense that things were changing. Adults were talking with heads together and voices low with an intensity that eluded me. I heard Mother say, "Mountain High, Emperor Far." She explained to me that the rule of the government was to accept the people of the Business Owner Landlord Classification, but we were so far from the big cities that the brigades of the communes still continued to do whatever they wanted. "More unfair justice," she said.

If only we were not so far from the city, and if I could get them to understand, I thought I could have a real red scarf. So, the next day I went to Teacher Xia's office to explain to him that my detailed classification was not Landlord, but Industrial Business Owner with a lesser Landlord status, which was less serious. I wanted to explain to him that, in fact, as Mother said, people with this kind of brand were candidates to be united into the society, according to the rule of the Central Government. We should be treated as friends instead of as Enemies.

I really hoped that he could reverse my fortune so the children in my class would treat me better. Perhaps he did not know of the government's rule, and he could teach them as well.

I began to explain. He heard my plea. He looked at me, glancing out the window for a moment, and then he closed the door.

"Come here, and I will explain. Sit right here," he said with a kindly tone, tapping his thigh.

I basked in the gentleness as I did when the Ogres lined my family home and treated me with kindness. He softly spoke into my ear, and I felt his breath dance around my face. For the first time, he was nice to me and gave me comfort I had never received. His voice was patient and gentle, wrapping in me in an unfamiliar embrace of acceptance.

"Your classification is even worse than the Landlords, you see? Your family were Landlords, plus Industrial Business Owners—double exploitation," he said.

"But Industrial Business Owner is our main status, and the Landlord part was lesser," I insisted. "Mother says the government agrees we were candidates for forgiveness to be united with the people," I told him.

"I am sorry. There will be no red scarf for the Enemies, but you may come to my office any time, getting whatever you need such as rubber bands, pencils, and precious paper."

Perhaps he understood that I was not the Enemy of the State. *He probably can't let anyone know that he is in sympathy with the Exploiters*, I thought. I sat on his lap repeating my argument. "Truly, I should be treated nicely. I study hard and wish to stand for a red scarf."

He nodded. "Perhaps," he began to speak as his big hand with bony fingers moved softly across my chest, "something can be arranged." He lifted my shirt and slipped his hand beneath it, caressing me. "What is this?" he asked, discovering my hidden imposter red scarf. "You made this insult to the honor of the red scarf?"

"Will you have my parents shot? Will I be taken away to prison? I am sorry I made the imposter red scarf," I cried.

"Maybe you can earn your red scarf here. Would you like that?" he said softly.

I calmed and nodded, relieved that he was no longer angry about my act of red-scarf pride, grateful my parents would be spared again.

"All right then, shall I touch you farther down, right here?" he asked, grinning.

He moved his hand down my stomach and then farther down, closing his eyes and smiling, which startled me. I jumped off his lap and looked at him in astonishment. Nobody told me that I should not let anyone touch me. Touching was simply never discussed and never done. My instincts responded.

Then he laughed. "Oh, when you grow up, we can do it and you will like it, like the others."

I rushed to leave, my heart beating with confusion. This was not something I understood, but I listened to the curling of my body and my quivering heart, like watching the chicken held down to meet the ax.

As I was leaving, he reminded me, "Don't forget. If you come back here, you may have any supplies you want and perhaps a red scarf."

I went home and told Mother about it. She was so serious; her face showed a pain I had never seen. She coached me to be polite to the teacher.

"Then also, tell him that he is a teacher, which is like a father figure, and he should never, ever do it again," she said.

The next day, I was emboldened to go to him to repeat what Mother had said. Instead, I said it in my own way: "I would like to ask for a transfer."

I had always heard my sister and brother saying, "Maybe we could get a transfer from the distant commune to one nearer the house." Although their wishes were never granted, I thought perhaps mine would be. *I could walk the far distance to another school,* I thought.

Teacher Xia asked, "Ha! And why do you want a transfer?"

He closed the door again. "Come, tell me."

I did not follow the tapping of his bony hand. I did not sit upon his dreadful lap. I stood straight and told him, "Because my mother says you are my teacher and you are like a father, and a father would not want to do that to his child."

"Did you tell anyone else?" His eyes flickered back and forth like a bug-eyed lizard.

"Nobody. Just my mother," I said.

With his warm breath still in my ears, my desire for the red scarf flew out of me and into the sky, and I understood that he did not have the kindness of an Ogre. He never touched me again. But I can say, I forever saw Teacher Xia as a less-than-honorable figure, and bony fingers forever made bumps appear upon my arms and caused a tightening in my belly.

真

My other teacher, Li Wen, did not appreciate my humor or me, either. I couldn't resist making the play on words that defamed my highly respected teacher. I was as unstable in that school as a blossom of white rice upon the chopsticks of a baby, but I knew a laugh could reach inside and shake loose little bits of the wall around the children, making them tolerate being so near an Enemy of the State, making them cease the teasing for a while. I could no longer exploit them as a Landlord hog, but I could make them laugh to keep still their taunting mouths.

The students were playing their usual games, gingerly tapping one foot and then the other in and out of a long rubber band being held, wide-stanced, by two other students. The student attempting the skill moved her feet in patterns, jumping and spinning while engaging the rubber band with nimble feet. Others were dropping a stone on chalk-drawn squares, hopping to avoid the block that held the stone, while still others were jumping rope and unwittingly singing songs about revolutionary heroes:

Dong Cun Rui,
Shi ba sui,
Zha diao bao,
Xi sheng liao,
ta de ren wu,
wuan cheng liao

Dong Cun Rui,
Eighteen years old,
exploding the fort,
sacrificing his life,
his task finished.

Still others were sitting and talking, but not to me.

Li Wen, Ni Wen, I turned my teacher's name into another word inside my head by simply changing just one sound, and a smile pushed its way to my resistant lips. His name so begged the joke, being so close in pronunciation to "you smell." I saw my teacher standing in the schoolyard speaking with my worthy peasant classmate. I wished to share my clever discovery with him so he might see me as worthy, too. I picked a nearby weed flower and held it in my sweaty hand up close to the girl's nose, and it just came out of my wicked mouth. It had to come out. I changed just one sound and Li Wen, my teacher's name, became "Ni Wen." "Ni Wen, Ni Wen, you smell, you smell," I chanted, hoping they would see the three-times cleverness of my words—three petals of a flower: Ni Wen, meaning "you smell," the sound-alike word so similar to Teacher, Li Wen's name; "you smell," meaning my insistence that my classmate smell the flower; and "you smell," the insult. One, two, three—it made me happy to see the three meanings of the word. But there was no applause for me. The classmate only heard the single insult, but the teacher obviously understood all three. He squeezed his eyes at me and marched me to the principal's office, once again for the third time that year.

"What do you have to say, insolent girl?" He eyed my pigtail, and my shoulder rolled forward on instinct to prevent the pull.

"I was only being funny. It was, uh, a joke. Does the cleverness of the joke not make you happy?" I folded myself up tightly like the flowers on the vines in the cold night air.

"So, you think you are funny, is that it? A funny girl, how entertaining. You think you are funny? Then tell me a joke and make me laugh, and I will not keep you every day after school to clean the classroom for a thousand days," he threatened.

"Go ahead, tell your jokes, funny thing."

He bent over, drawing a chalk circle, commanding me to enter the mock stage. Then he folded his arms and glared. I took my place on the punishing stage, repeating a story Mother had told me with great drama many times, after which we rolled and rolled on her straw bed, laughing, while holding our empty stomachs. I knew it by heart and could mimic every gesture, every line.

"There was a man who lived by the Great Yangtze River," I began, "with a reputation as a trickster and a liar. He was known to do anything to create his own fun. He could not stop himself, even when his antics were at the expense of his own friends. The Liar walked to the house of a friend, panting and banging on the front door. A woman, hands dripping in cooking oil, answered the door. He said to the wife, 'Sister Lang, your husband has drowned in the rushing river.'" I told the story with great expression as I pressed my hands in prayer to emphasize her pleading.

"'It cannot be so! Oh, my poor husband!' She grabbed the Liar's shirt and dragged him to the floor, weeping and stammering. 'We argued last night, and that that will be the last of this life we will share. Please, nooooo!' she cried.

'Yes, I am so sorry,' the Liar said, peeling her grip from his clean shirt, 'it is spring, Sister, and the river could not hold its joy, splashing over its banks, celebrating the passing of the frigid winter by taking your dear husband into its arms.'

And so, reluctantly, the woman believed him because there had been such occurrences every spring since she was a child. But his words only made her wail louder, for the river's joy had taken her only joy in life."

The teacher clapped his hands abruptly once. "And this is a joke. A man drowns in our Yangtze River?" His face shriveled, and he glared at me.

"Not yet, honorable teacher, I will finish it for you." I remembered that Mother said some things need time for us to see the humor. He waved his hand, and I knew his curiosity was my friend. He leaned forward to listen, once again.

"The Liar yelled through her screams," I continued, "'Give me your front door, and I will go to the river to bring his poor body back to you for his due respects.'

'No, it cannot be so!' She sobbed and wailed as he took the hinges down and walked away, letting the rise and fall of his laughing shoulders disguise themselves as silent crying, rushing to keep ahead of the screaming wife, who was desperately dragging her weakened self to the river.

"When the Liar arrived at the river where his friend Lang was lounging and fishing by the banks, he ran to him with the door in a panic saying, 'My friend, your house is on fire, and I am afraid it has burned to the ground. Your wife is safe, although wailing inconsolably. She is on her way.'

'No, it cannot be so. I left just one hour ago. How could this happen? Where will we live?' he cried, holding on to the Liar's grease-stained shirt.

'Luckily for you, I saved your door. Although, in truth I cannot imagine you will need it now.'"

The memory of Mother and I gripping our stomachs danced into my mind and with my tongue at my teeth, a sneeze-like sound exploded from my mouth. Another explosion came when I looked up and saw the teacher's angry face.

"One thousand days, I promise you, one thousand days you will clean the classroom on your knees!" he threatened. I knew he had to know the rest of my tale, for there is no one who can stand a story with no ending. I knew from watching the Ogres stay up late into the night to close the circle of a story despite their weary souls; I knew from the long days of hiding in the bedroom with Mother when my tired eyelids could not fail me if a tale was about to end.

"The Liar was taken to the court," I continued, "where the judge heard the details of his cruel and heartless crime.

'Do you think this kind of behavior is funny? Look at the faces of these people who were the victims of your joke. Look at this woman's swollen face and this man, haunted by your so-called joke,' the judge admonished." I mimicked the story just as Mother had done at home.

"'My intension was not evil,'" I continued in a feigned man's voice, "'I only meant to be funny,' the Liar said.

'You think lying is so funny,' the Judge said, 'you tell me a lie, and I will see how good a liar you are, and then I will pass my sentence.'

'But first, I need a stage in order to tell a lie with full effect,' the Liar told the Judge. With a wave of the judge's hand, the clerks scurried and quickly built a wooden stage. A short time later, with ceremony, the Liar stood on the stage and ceremoniously took his final bows. Then he proudly smiled, as though finished. 'Go ahead, tell your lie,' the judge yelled.

'Excuse me, Your Honor, I have already finished,' said the Liar.

'Where is the lie?' he asked impatiently.

'That *was* the lie, Judge, for who needs a stage on which to tell a lie?'" I delivered the final punch.

My teacher let escape a begrudging laugh at my cleverness and the way in which I had captivated the group of teachers who stood around me, laughing endlessly. It seemed a bit of their laughter drifted in the direction of my teacher, making his formal wall come down, and he joined in without control. He could not afford to lose face in that crowd. Gathering his demeanor, he gave me my sentence.

"I will reduce your punishment to one day of cleaning the classroom, since I promised if you made me laugh you would be saved. I am a person of my word, but I cannot let your insolence go unpunished." He pointed to the brooms and buckets in the corner and sealed my fate.

I have no memories of the great East Mountain Temple, the place where the gentle monk foretold my fate, but I do remember the pagoda that floated over the riverbanks across the ferry at Sand City. I dreamed of it while sweeping the hardened dirt floor of the classroom with the late and low sun showing me the way to my punishment. All the other classrooms were finished, and the poor deserted brooms, dustpans, and buckets were lined up against the wall, lonely, wanting to be something else, wanting to be something better. I wanted to give them life beyond the purpose they were told to serve. I leaned my broom against the teacher's desk, set the dustpan down on the edge, and sat down on the floor.

Looking up at the black metal dustpan, it took on the shape of the flying wings of the pagoda escaping from the edge of the teacher's desk. Then the late sun beamed through the window and awakened the tip of the broom handle above like a golden orb, and I stood quickly to begin my unassigned work. The brooms surrounded the entire desk, the buckets were the bones, and on each bucket I carefully perched a dustpan with its curled-up edges praying to the sky. The long-dreamed-of pagoda had finally come to me, the one who loved it the most. I admired the creation of my punishment but my teacher did not.

"Class, I wish to know who did this. Who left these dirty brooms and such on teacher's desk?

"Oh, it's a pagoda," pointed out one student in a whisper.

"Yes, look how clever, our classroom has a pagoda," another student spoke.

"Quiet! Whoever put it up shall take it down," the teacher commanded. No one spoke; eyes darted, peasant eyes to peasant eyes.

"Then the coward will watch the other students do the deed and suffer the guilt."

I innocently and helpfully stood first. Taking the top dustpan down, I walked to store it by the wall to hide my smile and my tear, knowing that soon, like our family temple, my pagoda would no longer be. It was a day I cannot forget; it was a day of building lies and sweeping honesty.

CHAPTER 11
THE EAST IS RED

The rumors of the Cultural Revolution spread from the cities through the countryside. The violence gathered momentum like molten lava, incinerating every drop of civility in its path, inflaming the confused and polarized people. It was the end of my third year of school.

I heard the thunder of a plane overhead. I covered my ears but still heard the sounds of chaos in the streets that flooded our classroom. I could see wild fights and hear the screams of those being beaten. "Da! Za! Qiang!" The three slogans of the Revolution were resounding everywhere—Da, "beating"; Za, "destroying"; and Qiang, "looting." I had never seen the students talk back to the teacher, but the crack in the old wooden bowl had finally given way, splitting my world in two.

"Stay seated where you are!" the teacher cried.

Everyone rushed for the door, ignoring the pleas of the stunned and fragile teacher.

"Students! Do you hear? Sit down!"

His face showed that he knew the reins were slipping from between his fingers. He slammed a chair down in front of the door to block their exit, but the force of the students' passion broke the dam, and I was swept along like a twig in the wild spring flood of the Yangtze River. I covered my head to avoid a beating as the entire school flowed into the chaos of the street.

The love I had for school burned in my stomach as I ran home. I hoped it was just a mistake. I would go back next week perhaps, or the next. In my heart, I feared I would never be my mother's daughter; I would be the one to cause the thread of generations of scholars to fray and break. Was it my own fault? Was I really the unteachable one? I was ashamed that it could end with me.

My school was no longer filled with the voices of children reciting, no teachers leading children in their lessons, no math, no reading. The fear screamed loudly in my ears at the thought of my empty, lifeless classroom; the halls echoed only with the sounds of Revolutionary songs:

The East is Red,
The East is Red, the Sun Rises.
China has brought forth a Mao Zedong,
He amasses fortune for the people,
Hurraheiya! He is the people's liberating star.

Chairman Mao loves the people,
He is our guide,
To build a new China,
Hurraheiya! He leads us forward!

The Communist Party is like the sun,
Wherever it shines, there is light.
Wherever there is a Communist Party,
Hurraheiya! There the people are free!

Some children formed gangs in the streets. Some semblance of order amid the chaos came when young students were organized into labor groups or gathered to participate in the Revolutionary Movement. Students everywhere were sent proudly marching in brigades to pick cotton or carry sand. I watched them pass over the levee that encircled our housing zone carrying their red books, wondering if I would have to join their ranks. I could not avoid the trend, and like all students, I was enlisted to participate.

After several such noble treks, marching out to labor, scarf-less among the red-scarfed children, Mother feared that I would be captured in the net of the commune system, after all. She had hoped I could escape to spend more time in the city with Sister Double, but word arrived that even Sister Double Happiness was to be humbled. She received her assignment for her re-education—hard labor in the fields side-by-side with the simple peasants to ensure that she had empathy and respect for their plight. The government wanted to make sure her shaping of the future minds of the country would be in line with proper new thinking. Sister dropped the chalk and picked up the hoe beside other defeated intellectuals. Doctors, who were stripped of their scalpels and handed a sickle, infected their skilled bourgeois hands with the harshness of the rice paddies, while untrained peasants took to the hospitals as their official unworthy replacements. Honored with the title of "Barefoot Doctor," they treated the sick, and the upside-down world continued.

The only sweet part was the return of Sister Enough. With no school to attend, there wasn't any purpose in her staying with Sister Double Happiness. I was grateful to have her home.

The students were free from their restrictions, their repressed lives of order, out of their minds with their new freedom to hate—their new freedom to punish. An honorable activity for students and teachers was participating in accusation meetings—students against teachers, teachers against teachers, teachers against principals—everyone was expected to take part in these public humiliations.

Eventually, the students were called back to attend school daily, but our days were filled with meetings or labor. The slogans of the Revolutionaries were called out in concert at the meetings.

"Down with the bourgeois anti-revolutionary!" a student screamed at the teacher, holding his red book of Chairman Mao's sayings on high.

Another student spat at the dignified teacher, saying, "You promote education to fill up people's minds with feudalistic ideas."

A teacher shoved Principal O Yang onto the stage.

"You repeat after me!" the teacher commanded. "Long Live Chairman Mao! Down with Tyrant O Yang!"

The crowd thrust their fists and their ever-present red books into the air. I could not raise my hand at first, not knowing quite why. The presence of Mother in my mind would not allow my hand to rise until the energy of the crowd around me drew it up against my will. I murmured with the crowd, "Long Live Chairman Mao, Down with Tyrant O Yang!"

"Down with American Imperialists, down with the Imperialist Soviet Union!"

"Repeat, now," the teacher continued.

"I am principal O Yang. I am stupid, and I am old. "I am Principal O Yang. I am stupid, and I am old," the principal said, hanging his head.

"You think you are above us? Sing it now, louder!"

The principal began the song with no choice with the crowd bearing down on him. "I am Principal O Yang. I am stupid and I am old," he said with dignity, as though giving a lecture on some important subject. An inflamed Red Guard hung a sign around the principal's neck, and the crowd cheered. "Stinking Intellectual" they all called at once, reading the shameful sign aloud.

Sing this: "I am a stinking intellectual," another student insisted.

"I am a stinking intellectual," the poor man repeated.

"No, I said to *sing* it, now sing it!"

The man copied the tune of his accuser, obediently.

"Much better. Now, go on!"

"When I ruled the school, I offended the teachers and oppressed the students," he repeated.

"Say it with meaning, louder," they taunted.

"I ruined their minds with foolish old thoughts," he continued.

"I committed this horrendous crime, and I deserve to die."

Fists were thrust high in the air all around me. An elbow returning from the thrust crashed into my shoulder without notice.

"The Imperialist capitalists are paper tigers. We will burn them with one match!" a young Red Guard screamed, and the crowd became more frenzied. More jeers were shouted at a man in the crowd: "Capitalist Follower, Big Betrayer!" As quickly as the taunting voices had focused on the unknown man, the attention returned to the principal, who stood spent on the stage with his exhausted head hung down.

"Now bow! Bow and say, 'I bow and bow, my apologies, down with me, the stinking intellectual.'"

The principal copied their words, damning himself with passion, keeping what little calm he could to avoid tempting the crowd into more Da, Za, and Qiang. I felt sorry for him. I could not raise my fist again, but no one would notice a small Enemy arm with no red band anyway—an outcast with no membership in the Little Red Guards.

真

Eventually, Sister Double continued her re-education and reform with a reassignment to teach at the middle school of her assigned brigade in the countryside, where she had labored. She would leave the hard labor of field work where she had formed her first blisters on her hands, but she would not return to her well-earned former position at the best high school in the county. With Sister Double teaching again, Mother made her plan to move me to live with her. I was so excited that I didn't think about how I would feel leaving Mother. Although I would be far away from my home, she hoped I would have the chance to go to school again.

On the morning I planned to go, Mother gave me a packet of food for the long walk. My sadness was overcome by my excitement. Remembering Mother's directions, I walked the twenty kilometers to meet my new adventure. It was not what I had expected. I traded attending accusation meetings and carrying heavy bags of sand in the hot sun for carrying heavy bags of laundry, hauling buckets of water for cooking and bathing, and dressing and feeding Sister Double's babies. I had grown, but so had the laundry for her growing family.

Each day, I would take a food ticket from Sister's family allocations to buy steamed rice in a pot for the family. I brought it home for everyone to eat. The next day, I returned the empty, dirty pot to the school kitchen to exchange it for another full one. There, in the kitchen, I saw a dignified teacher, my future dream position, squatting before a wooden basin stacked with dozens of returned rice-encrusted pots. I hesitated to add my own sticky pot to the basin. How could I demean this learned man? I caught the quick look of despair in his eyes as he clicked his head in the direction of the stack. Quietly, I stopped and added my crime to the pile. I felt the disrespect crawl inside me and lodge there, an unwelcomed inhabitant in my soul.

I made sure to finish all of my chores early every day so I could attend the classes of the middle school of the brigade like a regular student. Some days, we spent time reading the sayings of Chairman Mao aloud. Some days, the students were divided into groups according to their classifications to attend various re-education or accusation meetings. I was sent to accuse, while others were gathered to hear the news of Chairman Mao in private meetings. My humble ear was unfit for such an honor.

At my assigned meeting, I recognized the next one in line who was to be accused. It was the gentle woman, Hua, "Flower," one of my teachers who had been demoted to a school cook. She stood before my class to be accused. Teacher Flower was known for her creativity. She made beautiful boards for her classroom wall filled with hand-cut paper flowers and elegant floral drawings. True to her name, she loved flowers.

The accuser stood holding a scrap from her destroyed artwork. "Can you see this?" he asked, holding it high. It was a torn part of a beautiful design. "Can you see how she dares to draw the Kuomintang logo from the hat of Chiang Kai-shek, promoting the Commandant's logo, the party of our betrayer? Down with Chen Hua," he screamed, stripping her of her title to address her rudely with disrespect.

She repeated their words as told, raising her fist against herself.

"Look at her hair, she spends her money to curl her hair like the bourgeois pig that she is, trying to be better than everyone else," a student screamed. I knew her curls were not a bourgeois indulgence but a natural yet unusual trait for a Chinese woman. Sister Double Happiness had mentioned it before. I was at the back of the classroom when she passed by to leave the accusation meeting. I followed her out. I had to say something. I could hear the jeering crowd had moved on to their next humiliation. "Teacher Chen?

She turned around to face another expected attack. I could see she thought my use of her stripped title was less than sincere. When I saw her haunted eyes, I lost my words.

"Um, Teacher Chen, mmm, you will always be my teacher," I said awkwardly, lowering my head with respect. She smiled gratefully.

I could hear the call to the Loyalty Dance, but I couldn't go. I walked down the hallway and slipped into an alcove to hide my sadness. Around the corner from me, two Red Guards who had attended the special forbidden news meeting were talking about the foreign Ocean Devils from America. I stayed quiet, listening, unnoticed.

"Yes, it is true!" I heard one say in a low voice to his friend. "My brother is high up in the Party. He gets the secret newsletter from Beijing, and what they said in the meeting is true."

The young man looked over his shoulder but did not see me pressed against the wall around the corner. He continued, "My brother confirms it. America has sent men to explore the moon in a rocket. They have landed and walked on the moon. Walked on the moon. And do you know what they found?"

I peeked around the corner to see the other young man lean in close to hear the news. "Nothing. Nothing but craters of ash. So our foolish people have been praying and looking for guidance from the god of the moon for thousands of years, and there was nothing—no god!"

"So our government is right. There is proof there is no god?" the listener asked. "And the country which believes in a god the most, our capitalist enemies, the paper tigers, have proved that Chairman Mao is right!"

"Ha! Ha! Ha! They might as well exchange that so-called holy book of theirs for the truths found in this Red Treasure Book of Chairman Mao," the informant said, gripping his little book.

"They will be happier having the power of the people instead of handing themselves over to some god who does not exist!" the other said, holding his book high above his head.

The music for the Loyalty Dance began, and I rushed to join the obligation. Hundreds of people of all ages were gathered in the courtyard, some elderly barely able to stand. We swayed to the familiar music and moved our arms and feet in attempted unison. In one voice, the people sang:

Respect for Chairman Mao,
Our Red sun on our hearts.

My mind was riveted on the American man on the moon and how he must have felt to stand with the thick dust of nothingness around his feet. How devastated he must have been to be the one human being to first learn that there was no god. I felt burdened. I did not want to tell Mother. It would sadden her even more than crushing the family temple, even more than burying her goddess to preserve her life.

真

With time and great fortune, Sister Double was given back her rightful high school teacher status in a school across the river from Sand City. Because I would not be allowed to attend that level of school at the time, there was no benefit in following her, so I moved back home again. It was the first I would see Mother since I had overheard that the Americans had landed on the moon. I debated whether or not I should tell her. I couldn't bear to disillusion her. I couldn't let her know there was no god.

On my walk home, I saw long lines of enthusiastic middle and high school students, the so-called "Up the Mountain, Down to

the Countryside Intellectual Youths," proudly and pa
answering the call of Chairman Mao by the thousands to join in
the Revolution. They walked for days to join brigades, working
with the ruling-class peasants in faraway villages, sensitizing their
minds and hearts to the plight of the peasants and preparing for
their futures as the "Communist successors." These were the "new"
intellectuals who would replace the deposed Enemies—the vilified
adult intellectuals whose heads were filled with the useless "old"
knowledge that was forbidden by the government. They marched
along with heads held high, casting off everything from the past
to embrace the "new," to honor their leader, The Sun Who Rises
in the East.

This new plague of change was eating its way toward our home.
Father came rushing home from herding the cows in the middle
of the day, bringing the news with him.

"Red Guards and young students from the cities—they are
flooding the villages, inflaming the peasants to destroy," he said,
out of breath.

"To what end? What is there left to destroy?" Mother asked.

"They are cleansing the country of old teachings, old things, in
order to purify the minds of the people of 'wrong thinking' from
the past. It is called wiping out the 'The Four Olds.'"

"What campaign do they now launch on us wealthy people?"
Mother said through closed teeth. "What are The Four Olds?
Grandmother, me, you, and our young girls who grow old by the
day in the fields?" she snapped.

He answered, "Old Customs, Old Culture, Old Habits, and Old
Ideas. All art, buildings, religious things, symbols, or anything that
represents the past is to be destroyed to make way for the new."

"What are you saying? My books?" she asked. Her face showed
a fear so unlike brave Mother.

"Even worse," Father said, nodding toward the sadly repaired
wooden box imprinted with the memory of the evil boot.

"My family genealogy book? What do they have to fear of old
books? They will not take my books! They burn the lives of my
children and now my books? We can save them. We can bury them

until this insanity is over," Mother said to reassure herself, but her promise was made too soon.

"You cannot bury them. I am told they have a special wand, and it can find any hidden or buried items down to three feet deep. If they find the cache, they ask no questions. It means torture or, if you are more fortunate—a bullet to the head. Besides, we have no time, no workers, no way to dig a hole of such proportions," he said.

"I have never heard of such a wand," Mother said.

"The rumors are growing. It is only a matter of hours, perhaps, before the burning and the killings will reach this village. They are destroying architecture, temples, everything old of value."

Mother interrupted him. "Temples? Our East Mountain Temple?"

"Word is, yes, it is to be flattened and made into a school. The only people to be spared are those with only modest possessions, if it is the Red Guard's whim. And you must speak in simple terms with no reflection of your learned past when they arrive. You cannot argue logic this time," Father warned.

Father borrowed a match from a neighbor and began to build a fire using dry weeds and twigs for kindling. As the daylight passed, we desperately added the least precious things to the small flames to encourage a fire angry enough to consume everything that reflected the forbidden "Four Olds." It grew in a rage, fueled by the line of furnishings we all struggled to drag from the house. Taking the kitchen poker, Father began to wrench the golden dragon emblem from the front of the beautiful clock that had smiled down on us in our main room. Next, under the stare of Mother's eyes, he worked to a sweat, desperately trying to make our beautiful chest seem of lesser value. The carved words on the chest came off first: Happiness, Long Life, and Great Fortune were each gouged away from the front of the chest.

She watched his efforts. "Just as you have torn those characters from this carved chest, they have ripped these things away from us. Happiness, Long Life, Great Fortune—each of these words now eludes us," she said as she tossed each of the wooden characters into the fire.

When the deed was done, the shadows of the medallions of good wishes were even more prominent than when the carved characters adorned the chest. Father ran his hand through his hair and sighed. He picked up some dirt and smeared it on the lighter areas that illuminated the former best wishes. He called me to help, pointing to Mother's stool that stood at guard by her golden silk chair. I pressed my cheek against its coolness for the last time, kissed it and, rolled it toward Father to meet its destiny. He raised the heavy hammer and shattered the blue and white barrel stool with the pretty cutouts, through which I had seen the boots of the men with the red armbands who had taken over our home years earlier. Clunk—it chipped but did not break. Crash, crash, crash. It took three more determined tries to finish the painful task. Finally, the beloved stool lay shattered in many pieces. I looked over my shoulder at Father, who had moved on to other dreadful tasks, and I secretly took twelve small chips for myself. That night I would place them around the main room where my treasured Ogre roomers used to sit, to give honor to their memory.

Finally, as the sun left us, Mother stood watching the enormous fire that took her soul. She ran her hand gently over the hand-stitched cover of each book that held her family legacy, dropping tears at the funeral of the ancient texts. The poetry escaped in smoky phrases and took refuge in her mind. The elegant brush-strokes, the carefully hand-written characters shattered into the ghosts of the learned as they rose in bursts of red crackles and black smoke, releasing one thousand years of wisdom to the darkening sky. She released each book into the air in ritual like beautiful birds, freeing them, delicate pages flapping, fluttering in the night breeze, innocent of their fiery fate below. With dignity, she honored each book in unhurried ceremony. One by one, they were lifted high with hope, then fell helplessly into the flames.

The last to meet its demise was Mother's book of ancestors, her connection to her past, the genealogy of the Book Fragrance Family with its hundreds of years of handwritten characters. I watched her pry open the fragile wooden box, the survivor of the crushing boot. She grasped the thick yellow stack to her chest, hesitated, then thrust the irreplaceable treasure forward into the hungry fire. Then, in a moment of regret, she reached out over the flames stretching, reaching, her face melting in despair, her hands fanning the smoke in waves toward her face, as if to breathe in the disappearing knowledge from the past.

The beauty of the raging fire that rose far above my head to the sky entranced me, but my elation melted quickly in the eyes of Mother as the centuries of her ancestors' knowledge turned to ash. She stood defeated, holding the only book remaining, the required little red book, The Sayings of Chairman Mao.

Father ran from our home with a beautiful quilt, sewn with skill one hundred years before. When he saw Mother holding the Sayings of Chairman Mao above the rising embers, he called out, "No! That will buy you certain death should so much as one ashen page or one fleck of red cover be found in the rubble. Have you lost your senses?"

She looked down at it with disdain. "I have seen this book in the hands of every peasant who cannot read, quoting the words of wisdom aloud with authority while holding the book upside down. Ignorant for these people to be ruling this country."

"We must hurry," he warned. "You understand you are the kind of person most targeted. You are a woman of the Four Olds. If they find anything that speaks of the past, we could be imprisoned, tortured, maybe killed. This comes from good authority!" He grabbed the little Red Treasure Book from Mother's sooty hands and dropped it in his jacket pocket.

Father held the dragon quilt, the silky splash of colorful gold threads and vibrant peonies that had survived to comfort them in their loss of fortune. He swung the quilt open like a cape to give the treasure its last glory. A flourish of the garden of beautiful hand-sewn flowers and the vibrant golden dragon waved in the air, as if the dragon himself would take wing. He flung it high with the force of his anger. As it left his hands drifting high, floating above the hateful fire, Mother's dull look changed, and she reached out to save it from its death.

"That is enough!" she commanded. "Let them shoot me." She wrapped herself in the quilt and walked away to sit upon the saddened hand-carved chest, and with lifted chin she awaited her damning.

The destroyers never came to our out-of-the-way village, and there was no such rumored wand after all.

"I would still rather I gave my books their rightful passage myself than to have it done by red hands of ignorance," Mother said. She walked into the house intensely repeating an ancient poem, sealing it to her memory. We were burning memories, burning souls.

真

After the burning, Mother was unsettlingly quiet for days. Food was getting even more difficult to find. Sometimes we had rice but no firewood to cook; sometimes there was firewood, but there was no rice; and sometimes we had nothing at all.

I carried two bamboo baskets with a bamboo pole on my shoulders out onto the levee and along the aqueduct to look for wild weeds and grass to gather. The hope was growing thin, along with all my siblings. I could see the other neighbors in their fields gathering vegetables in heavy loads. I put three rocks under the nasty grasses in each basket and fantasized about how proud I would feel to walk home under a heavy burden, pole across my weary shoulders with two happy and abundant baskets bouncing on each end.

We shivered when Sister Enough and I heard the dreaded sound—the scraping of the scoop against the bottom of the wooden rice box. We looked at each other. The desperate murmurs of Mother and Father's whispers strained from the room next to our shared bed made us whisper, too. We knew there would be empty bowls and useless chopsticks unless some unexpected fortune came our way.

The next night, we huddled together to stay warm in our straw bed. Our breath hung over us in the chilled room. Gratefully, the cold put us into a deep sleep. Awakened by her empty stomach, Sister Enough woke me up, too. She shook my shoulder hard.

"We need to help. We need to do something. We can go in the dark now to the commune and borrow some vegetables from their fields," she said.

"Borrow? You sound like Father. I am still half asleep. I don't want to go; it means trouble," I said and turned over in the bed. "Go back to sleep."

Then she used those powerful words: "Did you see Mother's face tonight when we sipped the watery broth?"

This was something that made me get up. "OK, I will go, but I really don't want to get in trouble."

Then Sister Enough became fearful. "I have changed my mind. I don't want to go now, either," she said.

"Well, guess what, I am up and dressed, and we are going. You are the one who put the look on our mother's face in my mind." I said.

I grabbed a bag with one hand, my shivering older sister in the other, and out into the cold and dark I dragged her. Slowly our trembling legs took us to the commune field. Sister begged me to go back because this was the first we had ever thought to cross the boundary of our parents' rules. We groped our way up and over the levee, jumping at the smallest pebble under foot, the slightest noise. Suddenly, we heard voices echoing across the canal. We saw shadows of people off in the distance walking with lanterns.

"Let's see if they are getting larger or smaller," I said.

"No, let's go home. If we are caught, they will take us to prison and kill Mother and Father," Sister Enough whispered.

With an empty stomach and my parents' hungry whispers in my mind, I was still determined.

"Since you are a scared coward, OK, you watch for people, I will do the stealing."

Her shaking and chattering teeth threatened our discovery as I was pulling and digging the vegetables from the soil with a rock—carrots, potatoes, and cabbage, a beautiful harvest. Our plot never, ever had anything like that for me to toil.

As I was working hard at it, Sister suddenly whispered, "Hurry, someone is coming this way!"

"OK, OK," I whispered back. I immediately threw myself on the ground, motionless, face in the dirt, waiting for the answer. Would the hot bullet enter the back of my head or perhaps my beating heart?

Then Enough said, "I was just teasing you."

I stood up and threw a cabbage at her head. Finally, the job was done, and we got back home safely with the bag full of vegetables—many different kinds, too. Early the next morning, Father's loud, angry shouting awakened us.

"You bad things! Get out here! Try to ruin my life, uh? Thieves, thieves, who told you to steal?" he yelled.

"Aiyaaaa! Neighbors, neighbors, they can hear!" Mother pleaded.

Father ignored her. "This is not our family tradition! If they catch you, I am the one to pay the price for your stealing. You just want me to die early, don't you? Eh? Answer me."

"Aiyaa! No mentioning of stealing, are you feng le, crazy? The neighbors!" she said to him.

Cursing, he continued, digging deep in the bag that bulged with the feast of vegetables with a look that hardly matched his ire. With each word he barked at us, he pulled a luscious fresh vegetable from the rough sack and banged it on the table for emphasis: "I (carrot) told you (radish), this family (cabbage) does not (potato) STEAL!" He lifted the potato quickly, examining its skin for a bruise. "Still tai hao le—still perfect," he whispered to the potato and held it to his heart.

Mother banged around angrily and put the pot on the stove, and I saw the corners of her mouth turn up. A small puff of air, somewhere between a laugh and relief, escaped her mouth. She reluctantly dropped each perfect vegetable to swim in the yellow simmering water from the much-despised pond that always served as an insult to her dignity. I stopped to listen as she hummed a song, breaking the silence that had hung around her since the burning.

CHAPTER 12
A HIDDEN ORCHID

Brother Ox passed his twenty-seventh birthday, far beyond his prime marrying age. He had grown to be a very handsome young man and intelligent, articulate, and humorous. He possessed many traits that a girl would yearn for, such as playing an alluring musical flute he had fashioned from raw bamboo. If only he had been from the right class.

"You are so choosy! This is why you have no wife," Mother warned him.

"Yes, your mother is worried. It is only normal that we wish to you to be happy," Father began.

"Me, happy? Walking two hours back and forth, barely straight, then bent again, laboring back to the sky, day in, day out? Not me happy, you happy," Ox answered. "I don't care. I can stay single my entire life. I am waiting for the special one. This is one choice I get to make."

"Don't talk such ways. You are the only heir now. You will have your own household. The family furnishings will go to you and your new wife. That should be some motivation for a good match," Mother pleaded.

"It is natural that your Mother would want a daughter-in-law," Father said.

"Yes, now the pressure is on me to bring you a real daughter-in-law since Brother Repeat Happiness chose to be an in-house son-in-law to his wife's family," said Brother Ox.

"That is a subject separate from you," a voice joined in. Brother Ox turned to see Brother Repeat Happiness standing with his old school friend, Lu, in the doorway. "Yes, I once made the mistake of agreeing verbally to join my wife's family as a son-in-law. Because they had eight daughters and no son, I had compassion for them. You know, I never did join their family, but Mother could never forgive me for that, even though we did set up our own household. I paid the price of losing my status in our family for those words. I did not inherit, and so it goes to you."

"If you refer to losing the legacy of the family furniture, you may have it if I can avoid a forced marriage," said Brother Ox.

"Lu and I were summoned here to spend some time speaking with the stubborn brother who lives up to his baby name, "Ox," he said, grinning. "We have come not to focus on my past but on your future. Shall we get back to the matter at hand, bare-stick bachelor brother?"

"So you have been enlisted to rein in this younger brother?" Brother Ox said.

"It will be a sweet sabotage, if it works," Mother whispered to Father.

Repeat continued. "We think we may have a solution that will work. There is a girl named Buo, 'Pine.' It seems she has lost her senses and has taken quite a liking to you. She is OK-looking but has only a Middle Peasant classification, much better than ours," he said, laughing good-naturedly.

"Knowing how choosy you are, Ox, I, as the rebellious one in the group, also present the possibility of another girl, Zhong, 'Middle,'" added Lu.

"Tell us more, Lu," insisted Mother.

"She is from the Poor Peasant classification, the best status."

"Lu, I know of her family. She would never accept. Her mother has already made it clear that her daughter is not going to even think of someone who has a bad classification," Mother said.

The meeting did not result in a promise from Ox to my parents, but the heat of the fuel put pressure on the teapot lid, and thus, they were hopeful.

Like bees to honey, many girls of his age swarmed Brother Ox with no nectar to be had—even pretty girls from the ruling-class group. To these girls, he was a piece of spicy ginger found by a monkey—they were tempted to eat it but too worried about the burning of the pungent treat. But to the other group of girls who matched our family status, he was thorny like a porcupine found by a dog, not knowing where to land the bite.

Brother Ox remained unclaimed, which became a constant worry for the whole family. Mother wished for only one sweet bird to land from the blue sky into her life. She pleaded to her goddess, for her second son was her only chance to have a daughter-in-law to help in her old age and to grow the family status. Finally, her wish was answered. It was not a bird that landed but the bees that brought the honey, and her name was Orchid.

She lived on the other side of the Yangtze River, the west bank, and was from a poor peasant family, the best classification under the law. Her beautiful elder sister happened to have married a friend of Ox's. She saw Brother Ox as a wonderful catch and brought her pretty younger sister to meet him. She was much younger than my brother, but they liked each other at first sight. Our family was overjoyed.

"Good fortune has not totally forgotten us after all," Mother said.

The good fortune soon waned into dismay for the family, especially me. Word came that Orchid had already been engaged with the approval of her oldest brother, who possessed the ultimate authority because her father had died. Orchid asked her brother to break the engagement so that she could marry Brother Ox.

"This will never happen!" her elder brother said, flatly denying her proposal. "No yellow-furred fledgling sister of mine will have a word to say. Do you want to embarrass the entire family questioning my decision in front of your future husband's family? You want to disrespect us by bringing an Exploiter into this family? Ours is an honorable family that has done nothing but work for others our entire lives. You will be here under lock until the wisdom seeps into your foolish head," her bother announced.

Orchid was locked away for days before she managed to run away to us. I was awakened in middle of the night by a cold body sharing our overcrowded bed. Brother Ox needed her to sleep with us girls until they could make a plan. The night was gone, and the dawn came. We added the fear of Orchid's brother to the longstanding fear we already had whenever strangers showed up at our door looking for Father's debts to be paid. We knew he could come in person or he could send someone else to find his sister. As the lowest of the lowly peasants, he had the highest ruling status, the power to accuse us of anything terrible he would like. Our fate was fully in his hands.

A decision was reached. Orchid would not stay in the house. Just a block away, there were government shelters built for flood evacuations for the brigades on the other side of the levee. Because there had been no flood yet in that season, the spaces were vacant. Father used one of the bare spaces to house the oxen he cared for at night. The next day, as he carefully removed the black fertile mash from the space, he checked to make sure the space next door was empty. It had a front door and back door. That seemed a perfect hiding place for Orchid.

The next day, she moved in without delay. Brother Ox went to the fields as usual, but my chores mounted. Instead of washing five people's laundry, I had to do six. Instead of feeding just ourselves, we had one more mouth to scramble for. My basket for searching the plants in the fields took on another duty: secretly transporting food hidden under weeds to Orchid's private place, where I became her personal servant, guard, and courier. I had to look around very carefully when I went there. The front door had a lock to fool other people. I would always enter from the back door with an eye over my shoulder fearing that the brother, who had the power to destroy us all, would see me.

Weeks later, she was finally able to resurface into the world as word came that her former engagement was nullified by her boyfriend's family, and her brother ceased his persecution.

"A long night would generate more nightmares," Mother said, warning that delaying the union would only allow time for more problems to arise. It was time to choose a wedding day quickly. To honor this beautiful flower, their future ruling-class daughter-in-law, my parents gave up every single piece of furniture from their past fortune and had each family heirloom updated to the current fashion, at all cost. The beautiful five-foot-high mirror came out from its hiding place and was installed on Mother's big carved redwood wardrobe for the first time since we had lost our home. The rich, red high dresser that held my little rabbit and Mother's laughing porcelain bald monk was repainted according to current fashion to hold their wedding ornaments, such as our double happiness vases and pretty china jars. It was paid for with promises and debt.

They had a real bed with a brand-new white nylon mosquito net, which was the most luxurious and popular. I saw every single thing that made me believe we had any chance in our lives for improvement, every remaining heirloom of value, being prepared with care for its departure. No matter, Ox and my family now had the status of a ruling-class poor peasant in our family to crow about.

I ran my eyes over the clean, white, modern mosquito net in Ox and Orchid's bedroom. Our mosquito nets were made of linen-like fabric that was gray, heavy, rough, and patched. Before Spring Festival, we had to wash everything to prepare to start the New Year pure, including the mosquito net. Mine became so heavy that I could not lift it; I could only use my feet to step on it to squeeze the black, sooty water out. And they had a real desk. How I liked that desk, but I had no right to wish for it because it was from Orchid's dowry, which also included the standard double set of quilts.

真

At 13 years old, the wedding was the biggest event in my young life. The greatest regret was that Grandmother did not live to see this happiness, for she died shortly before the wedding. She had met and approved of Orchid, which gave us all some sense of peace because she was so close to Brother Ox. Repeat painted a beautiful portrait of Grandmother for her funeral. We displayed it on the wall at the wedding, which gave us some sense of her presence at the event. Still, her absence cast a shadow and left an ache that weighed on the joy of the day.

Besides the routine work of looking for wild plants and gathering cooking fire twigs by digging up the roots of cotton or sorghum plants, I was worn out after many days of washing and cleaning. The big day was highlighted by the arrival of the bride with her entourage. According to custom, we sent a band with wedding folk drums and gongs to accompany the bride all the way from the river to the house.

All went well with the guests and the food until there was a sudden stir from the wedding room, where all the special guests from the bride's family were seated. One less well-dressed man insisted on leaving. All the important people—Brother Ox, Sister Double Happiness, and Lu, the designated matchmaker for the day—were begging his forgiveness. He was the older brother of Orchid, the man who had the power to bring misery to our lives, the most important wedding guest next to the new couple themselves, and I was the one who caused the trouble.

I was assigned to serve all of the guests a cup of tea from a tray upon their arrival. My cups ran out just as I got to her brother. I went to fetch the refill and continued to serve tea to the others, but I forgot to hunt him down amid the crowd to give him the tea and highest respect that he deserved as the most powerful person in her family. Fear shook in my weak legs as I brought the tray to the insulted man. I used my big eyes to push the apology into his heart. He begrudgingly accepted it and stayed. Orchid didn't have to hide anymore, but I wished that I could.

With the festivities over, Brother Ox and Orchid soon moved to their new home by the brigade. Our furniture was carried off to grace the house of our family's heir and his high-class wife. The only thing of any purpose or value that remained was the broken eating table with the crippled leg. Even my little homework table that sat beside my bed with a lantern was repurposed for their happiness.

真

Sister Enough carried the memory of the family furniture with a saddened heart as she awakened before the sun. There were certain female needs, the unmentionable ones, that were not available to a newly blossomed woman without any money in her pocket. Enough Complete Happiness had taken some of the sweet potato plants that were distributed as their allocation for the points she and Ox had earned, and chopped them into pig's feed. She then tied them into a makeshift sack, to sell.

With the rooster's crow to keep her company, and needing to return to her work in the field, she walked quickly with the heavy load to the town nearest to her brigade early in the morning. She was fortunate enough to find a buyer right away. With shyness and no experience with buying, she took her two-Yuan profit she planned to use for the special pad of yellow straw pressed paper for her monthly needs. Somehow, the loss of the family furniture left her wanting to fill some need, no matter how small. There were so many things she needed, she told me. She considered buying a small piece of soap, a pair of socks, a hat to shade her from the sun, ink to write in her diary, or a new toothbrush to replace the lowly bristles on her well-worn brush. In the end, she decided that the special yellow papers would provide the most relief. With these dreams in her mind and the two folded Yuan in her pocket, she walked to the field and picked up the hoe to get to work.

"What makes you come so late?" Brother Ox asked.

"I went to the town and sold the pig feed."

"Oh, where is the money?" Ox asked. "Can I have it?"

Sister Enough said in a low voice, "I need it," hoping she would gain the courage to make the purchase the next day and not wanting to lose this one benefit to her brother, who had been the benefactor of the entire contents of their home.

"You don't have it? You spent it? On what?"

"I just need it," she answered.

Brother Ox was getting impatient. "For what?" he asked again.

Sister Enough could never say the words to her brother or to Father. She could not even hint at what she needed to buy; it just was not done.

"You tell me what you need the money for, more than my family needs it?" he insisted.

"I need it to buy a blouse," she answered. She hadn't meant to lie, but the unmentionable subject forced her tongue. Once done, she hoped the lie would work. "Look at my blouse. It is worn thin and patched beyond patching."

"What do you need a blouse for, to only have its fabric melt in the hot sun, while my wife and I need fuel to cook? Look at her!" He pointed his chin toward the most poorly dressed of peasants whose clothing clung to her back through sheer will alone. She was the subject of much teasing and was thought to be the most pathetic of them all. "You still have many days left in your blouse," he said.

"You want me to suffer jokes like she does?" Sister Enough felt the punishing sting of his words and moved away to work by herself.

Brother Ox steamed for hours, moving the hoe dramatically. Then, exhausted from his day, he approached her, but before he could resume his inquiry, she relinquished the two lonely wrinkled bills into his open hand. She walked home defeated and downhearted.

At home, there was no table for our little lamp for her to read or write on—the only distractions, the only escapes she had from the harshness of her days. Without our simple little table, she could neither take up her pen to write her perfected elegant characters to escape the thought of the next day nor read by the dim crescent light that fell wasted upon our bedroom floor. She looked around our empty room, and we sat in silence. I felt her sadness wrap around me, squeezing my heart.

"I had only wanted one small luxury to soothe our many losses, but the words were too unmentionable. They could not come to my lips," she finally said.

"I am so sorry," I said, for certainly these were words that could not be delivered to a man without her unbearable shame and his unthinkable embarrassment.

The next day, Sister Enough again left for the brigade fields, carrying with her the heaviness of the loss of our furniture, the memory of the carts as they took away our special things, and the guilt and discouragement over the hard-earned two Yuan. I could not let her come home to the painful emptiness of our rooms again. I went outside to think. There was no hope of having any furniture. Then I saw it in all its glory—the discarded chicken cage behind the kitchen stall. Because we had no chickens left, I dragged the heavy, slatted, wooden box into the sun to see its promise more clearly. *Yes, it has structure and can be given a breath of life*, I thought.

I dragged the heavy coop down to the pond. With a flat stone, I began to scrape the hardened, putrid chicken manure from each slat. Within hours, the soaking and the scraping had their effect, and our new bedroom table began to live. I dragged the rejuvenated, dripping piece back to the house and left it in the sun to dry, eyeing it to plan the next step. I needed to find a way to give it happiness, to bring a smile to Sister Enough's face. We could do the final decoration together to keep her mind from our home's emptiness.

Sitting on our bed, I waited for her return, waited to see the delightful smile on her face—to see, if nothing else, that we had a hopeful table in our room to hold our lantern. She entered with a ghostly look, having passed through the barren land that was our home. I waited for her to see the clever table, but she fell down on the bed and wept.

"Never mind your foolish table. They have taken everything. It is a chicken coop, not a table!" she cried.

I saw the truth. There was no hope of reading or writing sweeping characters by the dim light of the lantern from its lowly position on the scrappy little table. My carefully fashioned coop had elevated our light only just a bit from the bedroom floor, leaving our reading eyes and our writing hands in the dark of my failure.

Early the next morning, I found an old, worn brush with no bristles on the end. Hollowing out the end cleanly, I went to seek some bristles. I spoke gently as I approached the pig to borrow some of his bristle hairs. He wasn't very generous at first, not knowing my intent was harmless. *Perhaps he sensed my part in the killing of our former pig*, I thought. I had to chase the skinny pig around the yard to painlessly trim the dozen hairs I needed from his hide. I hugged him in gratitude and sat down to make my brush.

With a piece of string, I folded each bristle in half and pulled it down into the hollow brush. I wrapped the ends of the hairs with several flax fiber strings around the bristles to stuff and hold the bundle in place. Borrowing Mother's sewing scissors, I trimmed the ends to make the perfect brush.

Later, even as we made the homemade paste and covered the holes between the slats with shameful but clean paper I had stolen from the toilet stash, even as the coop became transformed by the arduous staining of the trim with my little homemade brush, it was not the cure she needed.

I still saw the imposter table's beauty, but finally, I cried, too. I cried for the memory of Mother's beautifully carved furniture repainted in the newest style that now graced the home of Brother Ox. One sibling's bliss was two siblings' loss. The emptiness of the drawers and shelves of the old and dignified furniture had at least held some hope for us, but the emptiness of our home could be heard all night in the echoes of our hopeless crying. Changing something, changing nothing.

CHAPTER 13
TURNING TERRACOTTA

Mother stood me at the wall and scratched a line above my head with a piece of charred twig. It had become too hard to hide me from the eyes of the brigades. I was nearing the size that if they caught me, I would join my sisters and brother in their hopeless lives. She walked me four hours to the city on her pampered feet that had rarely touched a muddy street until the world came down.

Sister Double Happiness once again agreed to take me, the unteachable girl, to help her raise her babies, clean her rooms, and rub her clothes clean with a hundred strokes. I was illegal with no papers to work in the city, a stowaway, working long, sleeping little. I was to have daily food again, and for this alone Mother felt some joy. In exchange for my relentless work, Sister agreed to spare a little money for our parents to survive, which comforted me.

As luck would have it, Sister Double gave birth to twins. With the doubling of her children came the doubling of my labor. Although I was not back-to-the-sky, I was sad-eyes-to-the-ceiling. One day, in one of the long years in which I labored to care for my sister's home and children, Mother made a visit to us at Sister's apartment at her school. It was summertime.

"Father has no clothes to change into. The only shirt he has is falling apart beyond mending," she said as we sat holding the babies.

I looked down at my shirt with shame.

"This will not fit Father, but perhaps it could be cleverly redone?" I suggested to Mother, who could make a cloth turn magic tricks when needed. Then I had an idea.

"Sister has a few white T-shirts, and they are even the right size for him."

"I don't dare to ask for one, even though she is my daughter," she said.

"I don't dare to ask for one, either, even though she is my sister," I added with an idea in mind.

My heart was aching to see Mother leave without a T-shirt for Father. Just as she was a short distance down the road, I felt an urge to just kill first, report later. I stole one white T-shirt out of Sister's pile and left the safety of her apartment. I caught up to Mother and gave it to her, insisting. She relented and took the gift to Father. We knew he would be impressed by Sister Double's generosity. Later that night, I summoned the courage to confess to Sister. Her mouth said nothing, but her angry face spoke.

I felt so desperate for my life. I relentlessly cleaned the soiled laundry of the babies, hauled water for bathing them, and cooked for them—with little time and weary eyes for any reading.

When the twins became three years old, Sister was moved to a new assignment up at the capital of Hubei Province, where her husband was working as a scientist in a research institute. Sister's life became lighter because this was a great change in fortune for her family, but my lot weighed heavily on my shoulders and my heart.

Sister counted out her allocations at night, sorting the tickets for fabric, food, and fuel at the eating table. I stretched my neck to see the precious tickets, the right to buy from the government supply, the right to eat from the commodity grain as city residents, the right to buy soybeans, oil, meat, fabric, and rice. She received six portions of each, allocations enough for six people—four children and two parents. I would share what food they had. Sister Double saw my face.

"I am so sorry, no tickets for you," she said.

One evening, I was babysitting for the twins, and I smelled the most luscious chicken cooking in a neighbor's pot in the hallway of the school housing where we lived. I walked by it several times, waving the aroma toward my nose, breathing deeply. The juices flowing in my mouth overcame my senses. I reached into the pot, took the least valuable of the pieces, and ran back to my room. There, like little nestlings with open beaks, I dropped the fatty little bits of meat into the children's mouths, saving only the bone with grateful threads of delight still clinging to it for my hungry self to suck and savor.

My only real personal joy was books. Sister's husband could read English, the strange language of the Ocean Foreign Devils. This was to be a fortune so great, I could never have known. It was here through my young teens I labored long days as the babies became boys. Grateful not to have my back to the sky, I was still aching for more hours to read a book, to hold the hope of being a teacher like my sister, to see that yellow yolk upon my rice bowl, to no longer be unteachable.

Sister Double thought it was foolish to waste my sleeping hours on a book when, of course, I no longer had any hopes of education. I found some small books in her husband's library, long forgotten from a class in college. These were poems from the Ocean Devils, translated into a language I understood, but containing thoughts that I did not. I read the characters slowly. I had a floating sensation, and the words made me hold my breath and tingle.

"My love is a red, red rose, newly blossoming in June; my love is a melody sweetly played in tune." The blood went to my face, but I read on. I let my mind drift to a look Brother Ox had on his face when he played his flute for his beloved Orchid with dreamy, floating eyes. It was a look that made me feel a yearning I had not had before.

"What are you reading, Hong Qin?" Sister Double asked as she came into the room. I jumped, startled.

"These are yellow books," she continued with anger, "shameful books for a girl to read, too worldly for a young girl's mind."

"But the words are so beautiful. They speak of sweet things like roses and love," I pleaded as she gathered them into her arms.

"They speak of things beyond your understanding. These are subjects for adults. This is a forbidden pastime that I cannot approve of for you. You should read Chairman Mao's Red Treasure Book," Sister said.

"I have read that book a million times in school, so it leads me to no added learning," I argued.

"You obviously have not read it sufficiently to understand. You should read it again and again," she said.

After Sister left, I opened the pages once again to read the wisdom of Chairman Mao, but it caused no fluttering, no beating of my heart like the yellow poems of the red, red rose. Sister Double hid the book under her bed, but I found it when I was cleaning. I rescued them like Mother wished to rescue her children from the fields, her books from the fire. They were my only friends, my paper friends, my only way to float away to places in my dreams.

Besides my romance with the poetry books, the only beautiful memory I had of those isolated years was the day my sister and her husband bought me a new red, white, and black checkered jacket. It was the very first thing I had that was new, starting only on *my* back, an honest jacket that had never posed as another thing, made of cloth that had never lived the life of another sibling's shirt, never hung around a waist or down a leg, and whose collar or cuff would never serve the life of the unmentionable red thing.

And soon to my delight, there came a new pair of shoes. To have a second pair of shoes was a sign I was sure that things would change. I tried them on. I could see the benefit of my house arrest; no soil would ever mar my shoes. Despite my imprisoned soul and the daily drudgery of my lot, I had come so much further from the threat of back-to-the-sky, face-to-the-earth than I could have hoped. As I was moving higher, I still felt I was stooping lower, with no options beyond the repetition of my heavy labor.

When winter came in my seventeenth year and it was Spring Festival time, Sister Double Happiness permitted me to leave to be with my parents. I took off like the free wind with no desire to go back. I could not stop my feet from running as soon as I exited her door, hoping not to hear a voice that would call me back from freedom.

真

When the New Year celebrations were over, I refused to return to work for Sister Double Happiness. After a few days at home, Mother worried because there was no other place for me to stay. I had become taller and noticeable. It was my misfortune that the soft mounds upon my chest grew far beyond the delicate lotus cone-shaped breasts that were considered so proper and desirable in the eyes of all. I was ashamed to have the deformed extra growth of full, soft pillows on my chest. So I gathered scraps of fabric, tied them with many knots to surround my ribs, and wrapped the embarrassment tightly until flat. Sitting on the dining bench with knots digging into my back, I cursed my homely self—full chest, dark skin, and scar upon my eye.

I walked over and turned our required portrait over on the wall so that he could not look at me that way. "DaDa, I have something I have to tell you. I have kept it from you, but it will no longer keep," I started, bravely.

"What is it that gives you such pain? What has happened to you while in Sister's hands?" she asked.

"I was in the hallway at Sister's school, and I heard some Ocean Devil news. I overheard some Red Guards talking. I'm afraid it was the truth, and I have not wanted to share it with you."

Mother closed her eyes for just a moment. I was so reluctant to bring such damage to her soul. "DaDa, the Americans have landed a rocket with men in it on the moon." I finally got it out.

"This is the disturbing news? China cannot be first at everything, silly thing," Mother said, laughing.

"No, it is not that. They found nothing, DaDa, nothing but dusty, empty craters," I blurted out.

"What were they expecting that disappoints you so?" she asked.

"DaDa, they found nothing, you see? There is no god! There is no god of the moon who holds the records of every newborn baby or keeps the lists of marriages. There is no point in celebrating Moon Festivals or traveling to the river to worship under the full moon, or to look up at the night sky. There is nothing there but dust." I started to cry at the loss of our special god whom Mother so loved. "They said the Americans have proved there is no god, proved that the Communist Party is right; we have only the people." I was inconsolable. "We have seen what the people can do to the people. Who can we turn to now?" I asked, sobbing.

Mother smiled. "Is that what has you so worried, Zhen'er? Do you think that a clever god would let anyone see her in her celestial home? They are too clever for that, my Zhen Zhen."

"Really? Do you think so?" I asked.

"I know so," she said. "A god is anywhere he wants to be, any form. My goddess would not have been there for the eyes of a mere human. The Communists are wrong on this account. We cannot see the wind, but we know it is there by the dancing of leaves."

I stood with my head bowed down to Mother, relieved and breathing gratefully. "So, can I please stay here? I cannot return to Sister Double. My mind is as still as the pond while there. DaDa, I am not permitted to even read. Only reading the sayings of Chairman Mao again and again, is allowed by Sister." Those were the words in a long string of arguments that finally worked on Mother.

真

Brother Repeat's wife Lin, "Forest," visited us on the way to see her sister in a suburb of the county. When Forest arrived, we were able to hear all about our old village, where she and Brother Repeat had moved to take advantage of what little honor remained there for our family name. He did enjoy favor there, assisting in teaching the children in the commune school, since he had been educated through middle school in the city while living with Sister Double. He was not awarded the Cadre classification, but at least he was not in the fields.

"My sister and her husband belong to a brick factory, a great privileged status—city residents who eat from the commodity grain. Maybe Hong Qin can get a contract to work there?" Sister-in-Law Forest suggested. "They pay money," she said, looking me up and down.

Mother clasped her hands in hope.

Then Forest asked, "Are you willing to Chi Ku, eat bitterness, accept hard labor? The brick factory now requires many laborers as contractors, and I heard that papers are not reviewed for these workers. I may be able to introduce you so you can be recommended for a temporary contract job," she told me.

It was like the sky opened a crack for me; a warm beam of Qi entered me. "Oh, yes, I can eat the bitterness of hard work. I have much practice in that regard. I promise to do anything, even give up my life to work hard," I said. My mind went to the joy on Mother's face as we watched the workers go in and out of their factory jobs in Sand City. I would be paid money. I could send my pay home each month to help Mother and Father. I could also save to buy a book and read at night, at will. I could not see how there was anything bitter about this offer. I was eager to go.

Together, we walked twenty kilometers to arrive at the brick-tile factory. The same day, I was taken to the tile-making department, and I was accepted. My new position lifted my feet off of the clay earth and swirled in my stomach like the silk kites I once saw from Sister Double's window. I lifted one brick tile and held it up to kiss my good fortune, leaving a ruddy color upon my cool lips that I was reluctant to wipe clean.

They didn't check my background, and I was not required to fill in any forms. There were so many people, and no brigade could keep track of every worker's soul. It was a joy that wrapped around Sister Double Happiness's fury and floated it off among the drifting clouds. Her stinging words came in a long letter, and the unteachable girl, who, according to her letter, had become a "yellow-furred fledgling," alluding to my immaturity. Such a foolish girl she thought I was to leave the graciousness of her own position—long days, hard work, no pay, no books—an ungrateful girl who dared to hope.

"I will send you fifty Yuan, and then I want nothing more to do with you again," her letter said.

Once more, I did not fail to disappoint. I didn't mind her anger at me, and fifty Yuan would be so much money that Father could buy T-shirts and a new red blouse for Mother that would have no red scarf triangle hole to patch. But in her busy life of doing this and that, Sister Double never remembered to send the money.

I lived in the factory dorm with ten other workers from all parts of the county in one room with bunk beds. I had my own bed, and it fit so neatly into a pattern like the straw beds of the Ogres on our earthen floor. I was making thirty-five Yuan each month, enough to fill my parents' bowls for many weeks. It was so much money. I could send almost all of it home and still keep a few Yuan for my books.

The first morning, I was startled awake by yelling. Each day from then on, the manager's abrupt call became familiar: "Qi chuang le—get up, get up, time for work."

The shift was yin and yang, 3 p.m. to 3 a.m., then change in a week to work 3 a.m. to 3 p.m. I rose the first morning and followed instructions carefully so as not to give a reason for anyone to take away my dream. I copied my co-worker, loading the wet mud tiles from the belt of the machine to a special framed shelved cart. I counted twenty tiles.

"Don't leave a slot open. Fill them all," she whispered.

I was so grateful for her hint to a new and lowly worker like me. I would have pulled a load of one hundred tiles to earn such pay. Struggling to get the wheel of the cart to move over a small hump in the path, I strained thinking of the thirty-five Yuan in the hands of my family, the rice in their pot, perhaps a second set of clothes. She didn't need to help me, but my angel, Sister Mei, "Pretty," stepped behind and secretly pushed the cart to start the slow roll to the drying houses. I gripped the bar at my chest tightly, holding on with both hands, slowly pulling the twenty precious gems to the high, narrow, tall towers with layers and layers of bamboo poles, the crisscross racks on which the bricks dried. The bottom shelf touched the dirt floor, the top one reached the high roof, and each empty shelf was waiting for me.

When I arrived with tiles at the drying house, another worker was waiting. We worked together, quietly putting the tiles in their wooden racks onto the top drying shelf. There was a wood board that we had to move into place at the level of the next empty section. I climbed up the bamboo scaffolding, six feet high, to stand on the board. The co-worker lifted the racks to me to put on the higher shelves, where they could receive the benefit of the heat for drying. I was seventeen, and I was free to do shift labor for my first pay.

I became so fond of my co-worker, Sister Pretty, who helped nudge me through my first day. She was a few years older than I was, so I called her Sister, as was the tradition. She had a City Resident status, and she had greater security and rights in the factory than I did. In a very few days, we became special friends.

"Little Zhao, you have made my work much more enjoyable with your wit. And how is it you have so much knowledge as a brick worker from the countryside? I have had to work with many others, but there was little to say. And your spirit is so high; it makes my day pass with more ease," she said.

"Mother is the reason. She was a scholar and taught me much as a child. And I have always had a love of words and learning. My sister is a teacher," I said, as though it could be contagious in the family.

"How is it you have a certain city flair, yet you come from the countryside?"

"I have lived in the city," I said proudly.

"Oh, no wonder," Pretty answered.

"Who would want the luxury of the city when you can have luxury of this brick factory?" I joked.

Sister Pretty laughed. "See how you make me laugh," she said.

We pretended to ballet dance on the board when she passed me each tile. She would do the tiptoe postures, and after I bent my body to catch the tile, I would reach up to put it on the top shelf with one leg gracefully lifted high. We found friendship in the hardship.

We had to empty the dried tiles to have the vacant trays ready for the new wet-mud tiles. It was full of dust. After finishing the shift, my face was covered with the orange coating. The sweat joined in to make a perfect paste that encrusted my face. I wore a hat with my thick, long hair tucked under it. Only my two eyes broke through the human terracotta. The workers called me "big-eyed," not "pulled-eyed," but I never thought I had beautiful eyes. Also, I did not have the preferred light porcelain skin. I never felt I was even close to pretty, but I was happy.

I was a worker, although only an uncertain contract worker. I wasn't burning under the sun like my siblings in the brigades. I didn't dare imagine having a chance to be guaranteed to earn my meals, to be legal with city papers—this rural dweller illegally in a factory, this Enemy of the State far from her home brigade. I was rubbing shoulders with those who were eating the commodity grain, and that was close enough.

Sister Pretty became a formal worker of the factory and was promoted to work in the main administrative office. It was as if I were promoted, too. Every now and then, I was able to visit her for a short time, admiring her office and her status, even listening to a radio. With my new friend came my new status.

CHAPTER 14
IMPOSSIBLE ESCAPE

I dreamed of Sister Enough and things I could not even bring myself to say that happened to her in the planting season. In my dream, she was pressing the bright green sprouts of rice into the fetid soil. She had no salt to stop the torture of the two-headed leech, the creature that was sucking out her soul. I awakened to hot hands and wet clothes.

I made a rare and secret visit to Mother and Father. Sister Enough told me of the imminent danger; she had begun to have suitors. A long string of rejected suitors crossed our threshold with Mother right behind them, ready to close the ill-fitting door. The gossip had grown from a random bee-buzzing to an angry hive of insulted families, and she heard it all.

"Was that Zhao girl too good for everyone?"

"She has already had a half dozen fine young men make the offer. Who is she, to be so choosy?"

"It is that Mother of hers, always so smart, thinking her daughters should be above us all."

"Yes, it is said 'Ignorance is a virtue for a woman for a reason. What man wants a wife who is smarter than him? Isn't that a terrible plague to a marriage?"

"And one educated daughter with a Cadre classification doesn't lift another uneducated daughter from the fields and honest labor," they said.

"She will have to say 'yes' soon to someone or there will be a price to pay for her arrogance," another neighbor added.

"Ignorance, a virtue for a woman? Certainly, that's an old saying created by an ignorant man," Mother said when she came home still full of the gossip she had overheard.

I eyed our chicken-coop table while Sister and I both lay on our childhood bed, deep in troubled fantasy. I hatched a plan with Enough before I left.

When I returned to the brick factory, I lay on my narrow bed, and thoughts kept churning. Dreams no longer came by night but in the dusty daylight. With each brick I loaded on the drying rack, the plan was built. I wished to help Mother in her war to keep Sister Enough from marrying her peasant fate. Once more, I was driven by my uncontrollable dissatisfaction. I wished to bring Sister Enough with me from her tortured place bent in half each day. I wished to rise even higher than the tile department. I wished to have a job from which I did not come home each night to chip away the clay from my dry skin, to scrub my clothes of dust a hundred times. I dared to think I might stand before a classroom in a school, like Double Happiness—me, the unteachable one. I dared to think I might someday have a bright yellow egg sitting happily on my bowl of snow-white rice. I dared to think I might be a teacher after all.

Foolish dreams? Maybe not, I said to myself. *Wasn't the factory once a dream? Wasn't I farther from the fields than I ever thought possible? Why not farther, why not higher?* I kept the nest of dreams warm in my depths for days until an idea pecked its way through the hard shell of my reality and there emerged a hopeful yet featherless plan with which to fly.

I curried a favor from a co-worker at the brick factory, knitting him a less-than lovely sweater, my first ever, in exchange for help from his good friend, a leader in the local brigade. I needed an official stamped acceptance letter for Sister Enough to leave her current brigade to join the brigade near the brick factory. I am not sure what else my co-worker was expecting, but I left him warmed only by the haphazard sweater, my determined self long gone to fetch my sister before I could find out his intentions.

Of course, ours was a less-than-honorable scheme because Sister Enough and I had no intention of having her hands touch the soil again. I did not think to scold my crooked self. She would join me as a contract worker at the factory. First, we had to go through Party Secretary Qin, who ominously shared his last name with Emperor Qin of the Qin Dynasty, known for his cruelty in building the Great Wall of China, burning all books of the times and burying scholars alive. This only served to intensify our fears of this man. We could only hope that this leader, who had power over her brigade, would stamp the papers, allowing Sister to transfer. She would register at the local brigade near the factory, as required, but would never go. If we posed the story in just the right way, we would both be together again and free to earn pay. Dust would certainly beat a bent back.

I worked hard on the story as I walked to our home, where I would meet up with Sister Enough to plan her escape. It was a risk. If I was recognized or questioned, without proper papers I could be taken to the fields forever and feel the bite of the commune trap, undoing all of the hiding and risk Mother had taken to save my fate. If our plan failed, as an in-house daughter-in-law and betrayer, Sister Enough may never have a chance again to straighten her back, and the treatment she would endure was beyond my imagination.

It was wonderful to see Mother, and I told her of the plan. There was no laughter in this story for us. Sister Enough returned at sunset from her labor.

"Are you ready? Do you have it committed to your heart?" I asked. Sister Enough imitated the conversation she would have with the Party Secretary. She was ready.

The next day, she took the inauthentic papers to the brigade to get the necessary red stamp of approval, the one red blur on one white paper that would free her. Sister Enough stood outside the makeshift office of the man who held the power of the precious stamp. When he arrived, she nervously began her rehearsed speech: "Yes, there are orders here. I am being called to a much harsher place to work in another distant brigade as punishment for my poor work," she said from memory with authority, while maintaining just the right amount of disappointment in her face.

"What harsher place? By whose orders?"

"In a place where my family is despised for their exploitation of the people," Sister said, hoping it would be the right thing to say.

"Do you still have family there?"

Sister hesitated. Which was the right answer—yes or no? She debated in her mind. She chose a version of the truth.

"I have no family there working in the fields at that brigade, Secretary Qin." She feigned a dark and fearful countenance. He stared at her for an unbearable minute.

"So why would you go there, and why do they want you there? You are a terrible worker." He eyed her suspiciously for a long and tense moment.

Enough felt the plan fraying but in her fear could not find the words to answer.

"Wait here," he said, and then he walked over to intervene in a heated discussion among his staff nearby. When he arrived at the group, they went quiet, listening to his every word.

Sister watched him talking to his comrades, too far away to hear their words. She studied every expression on his face, trying to determine her fate. He shook his head no, laughed, folded his arms in front of him, pointed off to the field, and scowled. The comrades left. Then, the man who held her fate leaned his back against the tree and took out his pack of cigarettes to extend her torturous waiting, never once looking in her direction. His face changed; the pack was empty. He crushed it in his strong hand and flung it to the ground, growling to himself.

She felt weak, anticipating not the rejection but the punishment after the rejection. Shivering with fear in the humid morning, she regretted the foolishness of our plan. With perfect timing, a woman arrived with a fresh, full pack of the same cigarettes—a brand so popular that Sister Enough recognized the label from the distance. The favor seeker opened the pack for him, flirtatiously handed him one, and in one swift movement struck the match and lit the drooping gift that hung from his indulged mouth. The two stood under the shade of the tree for a long time, Qin smoking and the cunning woman engaging him with her subtle messages, gestures that cut clearly through the swirling smoke. The flattery puffed out his chest along with the long draw of smoke. He drew in slowly until the long, red ash threatened his lips. She looked longingly with hopeful eyes at him as he dropped the butt and crushed it under his boot heal. She shamefully flirted more, they spoke at length, she smiled, and he nodded his head. The victor left hurriedly, obviously pleased with whatever decision he had made on her behalf.

Sister Enough felt the foolishness of her charade flushing across her face as he approached her. She had no gift to entice him, nor would she give it if she did.

"Are you still here?" he snarled.

She turned to leave, giving up, hoping to escape without his fury raining down on her.

"Just one minute. Did you come here to waste my time?" he asked.

"I just thought—" Sister Enough said.

"You thought—well, that's a first!" he said.

He signaled for her to follow him into his small office. She followed, leaving the door open behind her, her escape hatch.

"I have decided what I will do with you," he said, oddly smiling.

She held her breath as he raised his fist and banged it down onto the desk. Chunnkk! But he was not banging on the desk to begin a tirade against her as she had thought. The stamp that was deeply buried in his broad hand had made the mark. With that single movement, the powerful man had set her free.

"I will rid myself of you and gladly send your insignificant self to be someone else's problem." He thrust the paper toward her with the precious red stamp. She was twenty-two and almost free.

I said goodbye to Mother and walked with Sister Enough's belongings to the secret appointed meeting place with angst. It was getting late, and my stomach held the fear of our failure. Then I saw the joyful thing. She ran toward me with the paper held high. Her smile told me the results. I pulled her hand and tried to run, but she stood in disbelief looking back, afraid a voice would call, no memory of freedom, too many years of sameness to break the tether. She hesitated again, looking back. We walked away quickly, holding hands so tightly that her untrimmed nails drew blood from my palm and sweat dripped from our hands like the squeeze of twisted laundry in the muddy pond water.

The moment we were out of sight, a safe distance from the chance of discovery, I turned her face toward mine and stared into her widened eyes. She was trembling. At that same moment, we remembered when we were in the field stealing vegetables, once again. We laughed and ran until our laughs tumbled us to the ground. Then we scrambled to our feet and ran with the memory of Mother's slight smile and the pot boiling over with the harvest of our crime.

真

Sister Enough was accepted at the brick factory with the reference of Sister Pretty and my reputation for hard work. She would stay with four others and me in our room in the factory workers' residence—quite a step up from my former room for ten. With my experience, I knew which job to seek for her that would give her lighter labor after the soul-crushing years of working in the fields.

My seniority helped me arrange for Sister Enough to work the moving line belt, where she stood gratefully for twelve-hour shifts scraping excess from the edges of the wet tiles—no lugging, no loading. As fast as my gratitude entered my heart to have Sister Enough free from the fields, as fast as my smile spread on my face at the thought of her living safely with me inside the factory, the black cloud of my resentment for the life of abuse my sisters and I had suffered as young girls grew inside me like a wild vine without control. For me, it wasn't enough to exchange a bent-back fate in the hot sun for one of dust. Anger boiled up inside me, the anger of a thousand undeserved insults, the anger of a diminished life of discrimination, of a deflated spirit on a path with no choice, a path empty of dreams, unacceptable, intolerable, and endless. I swept up the fragments of my shattered dreams into my mind like Mother swept the red splinters of her ancestor's box into her arms. I needed a place for it to all go. I had to purge it. I had to write it.

That night, with our heads together, I spewed my anger out onto the piece of paper.

"Are you sure about this? This isn't just snatching a few vegetables. This is crazy, insane," Sister Enough said, yet she leaned into the light that focused on my letter, finding the danger of my words irresistible.

"What can he do about it? He has no power outside of his area. He has no reach beyond his own brigades, right?" I said, reassuring her. "He would have no idea where to find us, a four-hour walk away in another district altogether, two meaningless insignificants?"

"You are right. We are insignificant to him. He said it himself. It is less fearful to be writing this with you than being at his elbow waiting for the bang of the red stamp," Sister Enough said, rubbing the chills that had traveled down both of her arms.

"His cruel face is still in my mind," she explained when I looked at her, questioningly.

I was impassioned. "Dear Party Secretary Qin," I wrote. The shadows flickered across the words and our faces, and we laughed nervously at the drama we were creating. We openly told him everything we had ever felt in our tortured young lives, "...escaped from your claws...treated like pigs...not even the compassion to give a day off when the festering infection on my sister's feet...torture... you yourself have a daughter our age who was afforded an honorable place in the army by virtue of your position alone...you know it is said 'one member in the military, the whole family in glory'... how you can justify the horrendous, inhumane treatment...shameful man... " I wrote each character carefully and clearly to somehow demonstrate the outrageousness of such intelligent young women being treated so shamefully. Ignorant of the consequences, we boldly signed the letter.

"I would send this letter to Chairman Mao if I thought it would ever reach him. Our best chance of having it read is to send it to the Party Secretary, whose hand lowered the red stamp onto your corrupt papers of freedom," I said.

Sister and I had a rare day off together before her shift started the next day. We walked with heads upright into the town, and with forthright justice we mailed the letter. Our next stop was to indulge ourselves in a very special luxury to celebrate our coming together again and Sister Enough's impossible escape from the fields—we had our photo taken. It would take weeks to be ready, we were told, but we wanted to capture such an important moment, so we parted with the precious Yuan.

I also wanted to show Sister the fruit in the market. In our home region, there were only peaches. But the county capital near the brick factory imported plums and a great variety of exotic fruits from other areas. Having been very frugal, I had yet to try them myself. I wished to share the experience with her to celebrate our special victory, so I decided to be bold and spend a little more of my money.

We walked through the town from the photography shop to the market. There were so many things we had never seen. The plums were so beautiful, the purple orbs piled on the wooden rack. We bought a bag full.

"Perhaps you would like to try a banana. Very good today." The vendor said.

"Oh, yes," I agreed.

We bought the curved green fruit, but we were too embarrassed to ask how it was eaten. We tried to pry it open, but it was inflexible and hard to fathom. Finally, we ripped it open with effort expecting a joyful gift, but the treasured fruit was bitter and hard. We spat it out and threw it in the field, regretting such an awful way to waste our money.

We moved on to the plums. The plums were ripe and luscious beyond any flavor we had ever known. It was a rare and very special indulgence for us both. Along with the luxury came a large portion of guilt. We looked at each other, then at the plums with watering mouths. I called on one of Father's wise sayings to resolve the conflict: "Get drunk with today's wine and let tomorrow worry about tomorrow."

The blandness of our life's palette was the perfect stark backdrop to enhance the sweet and sour delight. We squinted, then smiled and sighed as the layered flavors unfolded with each bite— the sourness of the skin and the sweetness of the flesh. The flowing juice cooled our chins. We stopped under a tree and ate them all, a decision we regretted with each interruption of Sister Enough's first day of work. We saw each other more often that day, echoing groans and laughter in the walls of the toilet room bent in half, not with hard labor but with the pain of a rare experience—overindulgence. In spite of our foolishness, the luscious, worthwhile memory of the plums remained. It was so comforting to have Sister with me again. We ate together and lived together. My workdays seemed so much lighter with her nearby.

真

A few weeks later, on our way into our residence, we heard our names called. It was Father, walking at an angle toward us that spoke loudly of his seething anger.

"Who is after him for his borrowing now?" I whispered to my sister.

"I have no money, do you?" she asked. "He walked hours to see us."

"Yes, yes, I can give him whatever I have, but I have already sent off my pay to them," I answered, digging into my pockets willingly as he drew closer.

"So, you want your Father dead?" His centipedes had never screamed out so intensely on his pinched face.

"What happened?" I asked.

"You wrote that disrespectful letter to Party Secretary Qin?"

I could not take my eyes off the twitching movements of the long, stitched scars as his face contorted with fury.

"What business did he have with you, when we were the ones who wrote it?" I could not get the words out fast enough.

"What business? You are my daughters, that's what business. We are still family. What one does, we all do!"

"But we are adults. Why wouldn't he come to question us, personally? He's a coward who bullies the old and the weak. We wrote the letter. You should have told him to his face, if he needs to kill someone, he should kill us. It had nothing to do with you, Father," I said.

"I had to beg at the feet of the Secretary with his gang of supporters surrounding me. I had to kowtow, bow a hundred times, beg him to forgive my stupidity and ignorance for raising two of the most disrespectful and corrupt daughters he had ever known. Have you two lost your minds?" he asked.

"We were so outraged! You know how we have suffered. Someone finally had to tell them of the pain they caused, but we never thought—"

"Yes, you never thought at all because you want me dead or your mother tortured, is that it? I had to beg, do you hear me? I had to beg them on my knees in the dirt to honor me with one last wish to allow me to punish my despicable daughters myself in his name in exchange for my life. I told him I had nothing left to give except my word that I would punish you both with no mercy for the unsavory souls you were."

"I understand. Do what you must," I said. Sister Enough pushed her elbow into my side.

Father was quiet. "Fine," he said, pacing with his hands behind his back, back and forth, head down, searching for our punishment.

I saw a solution enter his mind, lighting his eyes up with the revelation. He had decided on the punishment. He looked at Sister and then me, letting his plan germinate in his mind. Then he spoke. "Don't plant thorns on my road ever again, you hear me?" he said sternly, looking at each of us. "Fine, I can see from your faces that harsh words from the father you love is punishment enough," he added as he turned and walked toward home with long shadows thrusting out from his straight, angry legs.

Sister and I exchanged looks of disbelief. We were stunned by his choice of so-called punishment. We pinched our childish giggles behind tight lips and again elbowed each other, but as the grins receded, the effect took place; I felt the shame and regret enter my heart. He had chosen the power of soft, and the soft of his punishment had a powerful effect.

I stripped the secret pocket in my jacket of the few Yuan I had left and ran to press them into his resisting hands. He kept walking, not wanting to give the humbling exchange any focus, refusing to hear my pleading words. Then he stopped. With the money in hungry hands, he looked into my eyes in the most unfamiliar, tender way, a way that spoke of caring, even love.

"My life ended with Liberation," he said, "but your life's road is still long. You must learn not to challenge the authorities. Keep yourself safe. Promise me that?" For a moment, he let his warm gaze stay on my face. This rare tenderness from my father touched me in a needing place devoid of fatherly closeness, and my punishment wrapped in his reward was complete.

When I returned to Sister, I searched my heart for my honesty. I would never have wanted that to happen to him, but once I knew he had survived the unexpected and we had survived the punishment, I was still happy we did it.

Sister Enough looked out at Father's small figure in the distance, bit her lip, let it slide through her teeth, and smiled.

真

As a pretty girl, Sister Enough soon drew the attention of a factory manager, and in him she found her husband. My dream of eating from the commodity grain passed to her.

It seemed like a good match. She could share her husband's tickets and eat from his share of government provisions. As always, marrying out of your classification does not absorb the odor of your past, just as the pretty paper we carefully pasted on our little salvaged table to cover up its source would always hold the putrid smell of chickens.

Although Sister Enough delivered a child to her husband's family, it was by misfortune a baby girl. With little rest, she cared for all the needs of both husband and live-in mother-in-law and was still expected to haul dusty bricks twelve hours a day while scrubbing heavy, muddy laundry; cleaning their small home; and preparing all the food. There were no favors. No easier position was assigned to the wife of the manager in charge who still belonged to a countryside brigade and carried such a bad classification. She had, in fact, the hardest job, working the loading dock, hoisting blocks of bricks and tiles with tongs onto the delivery trucks, the work of a strong man.

When Sister Enough was breastfeeding her young child, her husband took a break from his management job briefly to bring the baby to nurse. Impatiently, he took over her job to keep the system running smoothly, but just long enough for the baby to be fed.

"Hurry, just finish. I am getting tired, and my hands are sore," I heard him complain. Then he rushed off, carrying the baby like a sack of laundry to get back to his office.

Sometimes, it pained me to have brought her to that place. We had only changed her life from a bent-back fate to a dusty fate. In spite of that, she was grateful to be out of the fields, to eat regularly, to have her little apartment at the factory where all would be provided—even boiling water in a thermos to carry home to add to a large basin of water in which to bathe. All in all, it was a luxurious departure from the fields.

With Sister Enough married, I, a single girl, remained the main money source to my family. With my housing provided by the factory, and by being very frugal, I was able to send nearly the entire thirty-five Yuan home to Mother and Father. Brick by brick, I had also saved every extra Yuan I could earn for some needy time in the future that I could not predict. It was the first time in my life that I had any means beyond the meal in my bowl. I counted it every night and tucked it into the secret spot in the lining of my jacket. I felt proud, and it made me breathe easier to know I had some security in my insecure world.

I went to the loading area and saw a woman discussing her purchase with the manager. She seemed to be short some amount of money. She turned, just as I was passing.

"Little Zhao, How have you been?"

I saw it was an old friend, a teacher from Sister Double Happiness's school. We had played basketball on a few occasions when I was able to sneak out for a break from the responsibilities of caring for Sister's children and house. I had not seen Fen, "Scent," for quite a while, but I had fond memories of her. The well-built, athletic woman took me aside. I could see the concern on her face and the impatience of the manager.

"I am so very happy to see you, my friend," she said.

"You seem distressed, Sister Scent."

"I am so humbled to ask this, not having seen you in so long, but I do need some help. I am short thirty Yuan for this final stack of bricks to complete our home. Can you help me?"

I instinctively put my hand over the secret savings place on my right side. It was as though she could see through the checkered fabric. I had exactly the amount she needed, a sign for certain. I did not hesitate. Not used to having money, having all the food I needed for the day, and because she was a teacher, I immediately rescued her with the loan of my thirty Yuan. When the deed was done, I couldn't believe I had parted with the money without inhaling, without any hesitation. I felt I had an obligation to help anyone in need, considering my well-off status. I simply decided it should be done.

真

One day matched the next with one exception, September 9, 1976. I was suspended on the scaffolding on that fall day when an announcement shocked the workers all around me. The news was met with an explosion of emotion, weeping, and sadness. While other workers were falling to the ground in despair, I turned away to hide my secret smile—Chairman Mao was dead. But I had no understanding of the profound importance of the event. I took advantage of the moment for a much-needed rest.

Many months later, Scent returned to the factory but made no mention of the money she had borrowed from me. In fact, she never said a word about it again. She had something better to give.

"Oh, my friend, this dust is no fate for a bright one like you," she said, making no mention of the debt she owed. "I came to tell you that there is a cooking position at my school. The principal is my friend, so I have a connection to secure it for you. Would you like to leave this muddy work?" she asked.

In this way, she repaid her debt with an action, not a word; with a kindness, not a Yuan. My excitement was so intense, I wanted to brush off my dusty pants then and there and take my terracotta self immediately to the school. I owed it to everyone to give notice and to say goodbye to Sister Pretty before I left the life of the brick factory.

I was deeply worried with every minute that passed for fear of losing this miraculous chance. If I could feed the teachers, it was closer to my dream. To be allowed in a school once again, even if it meant boiling rice, was my honor. I decided to never ask her about the money she owed. She deserved the reward. Wouldn't I give one month of twelve-hour days of brick work to clean the clay from my face, to be in a school feeding teachers?

Sister Enough carried me and my humble belongings on a bicycle to the school, and we once more said goodbye. I would start a new job, an honorable job at a high school.

CHAPTER 15
COOKING UP TROUBLE

I walked into the kitchen on the first day, and the hard earth floor took my melted knees. I was delirious with joy until the principal showed me what my cooking responsibilities were—three meals a day for thirteen teachers. I thought of Mother's saying: "The smartest wife can't cook a meal without any ingredients." But for me, I could not cook the meal with too many ingredients. I knew water, rice, oil, salt, and weeds with the occasional vegetable and holiday meat, but I had never been the one to cook.

For the morning meal alone, I had to cook noodles or porridges and pickled, preserved dishes. I walked to the big pond behind the school to pull the water, one, two, three, four times, straining to carry buckets full of water two at a time to fill the enormous pot to cook enough rice for all of the teachers. This time there was no Ogre with a bamboo pole to help me with the overwhelming task, which I regretted when I lifted the first full buckets from the pond.

Still, on that first day, no matter how heavy the water buckets, I knew each time I would happily return to the warm womb of the school. I put the pot to boiling before I had finished fetching, to save time. Looking at all of the ingredients, I stopped to think. My laugh erupted at the thought—a girl who never had a proper meal was hired as a cook. What did I know about cooking, having never eaten? What did I know about feeding, always having been famished? What did I know about the rice, having grown up on rice water and weeds? What did I know about variety, having gratefully eaten whatever was put before me?

When I returned to the kitchen, nervous about the task, the teachers had scooped the first buckets of hot water from the pot, thinking my cooking water was for their morning wash-up. I was trying to be efficient, but my plan was spoiled once again. I had to start the water brigade from the first bucket again to fill the cooking pot.

I boiled more water, and more teachers came to scoop the heated water in their thermos to go back to their rooms to wash. After that, the bell rang—time for breakfast. The line of scholars, holding up their empty bowls, looked at me, then the pot. I looked at them, then the pot. This ping-pong game of eyes went on for a few seconds, ending in my angry departure. I had to complain to the principal.

"If the teachers feel their stomachs are more important than their faces, they shouldn't scoop my hot water away! If they want merely clean faces, then they can forget about their breakfast," I said.

When the teachers complained that the dishes were too salty, I would gladly add water to it. If they complained that the dishes were too mild, I would be happy to dump more salt in, too. This was my strategy for spicing. I was very flexible, wanting to please. Salt, I understood.

On day two, I raised my shoulders high to my ears when I heard both the crunch of the hard and blackened rice scraped from the bottom of the pot from the mouths of teachers who unfortunately had arrived last, and the slurps of the early takers who politely nursed their watery bowls of mush. I remembered the delicious taste of Mother's crusty rice balls from the bottom of her pot that we ate greedily on our trip to Sand City. I understood that expectations tame the taste buds, and experience trains the palate.

"You will do better with time," one of the more generous teachers said to encourage me, but I did not. While cooking every day for just two weeks, I created more than one scene like the Ogres around the lantern with the flapping of the teachers' towels to distribute their disgraceful odors that escaped from beneath their clothes. Unlike the good-natured Ogres, it did not end up in rolling laughter; it ended up threatening my job.

The cooking position was a very desirable position, too. There were many watching to see how long before that job might be their sister's or their wife's good fortune. In the excitement of working at a high school, it had not come into my mind that this was neither my fate nor my skill.

Worried that my time was near, I hurriedly thought through all of my options, but I still could not find a place to go. After my proud departure from the dust, returning to the brick factory wasn't an option anymore. Maybe I should have stayed in the factory, but that door was closed. I started to regret my decision to take the cooking job. The wet tiles were much easier to deal with than the cooking of such a big pot of rice. Pulling the tile cart was easier than drawing the big buckets of water from the pond. The lotus flowers had been so beautiful to see, but I had no time to appreciate them because my only goal was to use all my strength to pull bucket after bucket out of the pond.

I counted the blessings of the brick factory: someone else to cook your food, co-workers to help move the bricks, and the ballet—the wonderful movements of Sister Pretty and me balanced high upon the bamboo stage. They called me "big-eyed girl," and they thought I was pretty. Like the taste buds, expectations tame the feelings, too.

真

My roommate and co-worker, Hui, "Wisdom," told me that she knew a Communist leader in her commune who, as we talked it through, I realized was a remote relative of Mother's. His mother was my mother's aunt, the sister of my grandfather who died of starvation in the early years when my family was first "liberated" to the abandoned house.

Mother and I took a whole day's travel by bus and on foot, passing many towns, communes, and villages. We finally arrived at the home of her aunt, who lived with her son, a prominent Communist leader called Kang, "Healthy." Mother and Great Aunt were so happy to see each other. They talked for hours about my grandfather and their passing lives.

It was quite late in the evening when the Communist leader, whom I called "Uncle Kang," arrived home from his official affairs. He was a short man, soft-spoken and quick to smile. I asked him if he knew Wisdom, the girl who worked in the factory with me. I told him how I got his information from her. Again, he was all smiles and very polite, but his smile faded when I asked him if he could help me to get a job. Then I asked if he knew anyone in our county who could help me. He was hesitant but mentioned a name that he knew, Comrade Han, who was the Vice Party Secretary of Yang Chang Commune. That was all I needed, a name. Mother had reconnected with her aunt, and I had drawn a powerful long straw that I could use to change my fortune as a failed cook.

The headquarters of Yang Chang Commune was about a three-hour walk from the school where I was cooking and a two-hour walk from the brick factory, spaced like a triangle. When I finally arrived at the grand gate of the commune, my heart was clanging cymbals, and I was nervous. Would Comrade Han be willing to help me, or would he scorn me? He might wonder why my own relative, Uncle Kang, didn't do me the favor. But my own relative wasn't corrupt enough; he played by the good comrade rules. I laughed to myself. Corruption was a crooked man or straight man, upside down or downside up, depending on what you needed to get. I pondered the fate of my corrupt self. His response could be either the bite of the dog or the fat of the pig. Would I be fattened or bitten?

I went to the reception office. I held my head high and shoulders up. No ordinary people appeared at such a high-powered place, I knew that.

"I am here to see Comrade Han, please." It was a simply and politely stated fact, not a begging request.

To see such an important figure, I knew it was assumed that I must be an important person, so, I was treated very politely, with a chair offered to sit and tea offered to drink. The receptionist stuck her index finger into the dial of the black phone, "tick-tick-tick-tick, chsssss, tick-tick-tick, chssss." I loved the sound. She informed Comrade Han's office of my arrival, and I was invited in to see him.

He was a tall man with the excesses of his good fortune swelling from beneath his jacket. When I shook his deeply dimpled hand, hot like a steamed, doughy, pork-filled bun, I introduced myself as the niece of Comrade Zhu Kang. I said I had just returned from visiting him, and he had sent his greetings. Comrade Han nodded.

"My Uncle Kang was wondering if you could find me a position in your area, as he regrets he is too far away to come to ask in person," I began.

"I saw him not long ago in the County Leaders meeting, but he didn't mention you then."

"Oh, he said he meant to, but didn't have a chance." I made up my story quickly on the spot. "He said something about the schedules being so tight?" I scrambled to find the right words.

"Yes, I had to leave early to attend an emergency, too," he replied.

Then our conversation flowed well.

"So, what are you good at?" he asked me.

"Oh, I am good at many things," I said, trying to buy time. I realized I wasn't good at anything. "Yes, my sister is a high school teacher, and I follow in her footsteps, I am good at school," I said, carefully phrasing the stretched truth.

Comrade Han thought for a moment. "Go to see Principal Mu in the Yang Chang Elementary School. I believe they are in need of a teacher."

I gave him a gracious thank you and rushed from the building, my feigned sophistication dropping like the lion's costume at the parade's end.

I returned to the cooking job at the school and told them I must leave, knowing my words were within a breath of the principal doing just the same. She smiled. I enjoyed the feast

CHAPTER 16
CIRCLE OF CORRUPTION

I could have lived without shoes then, my feet never touching the ground from the joy of teaching. On my first day of school, I had such Qi flowing through me that when I passed by, each student's face lit aglow. I bathed them in the overflow of my elation, smiled upon them, embracing each one of them one by one in my heart as I had rarely been embraced myself. Each fragile one, clear of their classifications in my eyes, relaxed and thrived in the sunlight of my gaze, excelled in the safety of the enemy who had been set free, free to teach.

Floating outside myself much of the first day, the unteachable one; the yellow-furred fledgling with the eyelid scar; the terrible, awful cook; the escapee from the commune's bite; the dust-covered laborer disappeared, and in her place emerged a teacher. I was finally my brand, as the Ogres had assigned; I was Courageous Scholar Zhao. I was finally the daughter of my scholarly mother. I was a teacher, I was a teacher, I was a teacher.

"This one must be fed in a box," I remembered Mother saying to Sister Enough, who wished to have me help her with her relentless labor just for one day in the fields. I had to be preserved, a little kitten in a box, until I could make my cat-like escape through the fields and on to the city of her dreams. I was not in a big city, but I had arrived.

For the first time, I had my own room, complete with a rectangular mosquito net above my bed, but I was not to be alone for long. The room was not in the section where the teachers lived. It was a concrete room attached to the main building. Its purpose wasn't very clear—storage perhaps, or a place for former furry or feathered beings to live. The large gap between the top of the walls and the roof left a space in all four walls for nature to have her way with me.

The first night I crawled under the net, still feeling the chills on my arms from my good fortune. I lay smiling and had just let out a big breath of relief and gratitude when the first black phantom nosedived down, grabbed a claw full of my protective mesh and lifted it into the air. I screamed. A second creature followed, then a third. I struck a match and saw the dozen bats planning their next attack and a second dozen hanging like clusters of drying tobacco leaves from the ceiling of my infested first home.

I lit matches through the night to discourage their game, trying to be rested and prepared for my class. Finally, at dawn they all settled into hanging quietly, as though innocent of their evil ways. *The sun will bring me peace*, I thought. I was wrong. A swooping sparrow slid in on the first beam of sunlight and took over the game. It called to me and landed on the net above, sending gifts down on my head. At first, I smiled, charmed, thinking it was a rare coincidence, and for some people this perfect target on my head would have been seen as good luck. Too much good luck can happen in one life. One bird sent the signal, and a flock descended to perch on the lovely net, a perfect place to deposit the remnants of whatever berries or seeds they had managed to scavenge that day.

These were the day and night visitors who replaced the green bug-eyed flies and the sharp needles of the mosquitoes in Mother's fancy toilet shed. These were the true enemies of the state that stood guard over me every day, bat and bird, night shift, day shift.

I tried to prepare my lessons the next night by my lantern tucked under my mosquito net. I could hear the voices of the

Ogres in my mind, my secret mentors as they reviewed Sister Double's test papers one by one before they were crumpled into that unmentionable place. I could only laugh out loud at the most valuable sources of my education: a dozen ragtag men, a pile of toilet papers, a single piece of newsprint with a tiger's head, and an elegant woman scholar without a single book, teaching me and telling stories in secret.

When I returned in the daylight, I quickly placed any paper I could find on top of my mosquito net, and the top of my bed became papered like the bottom of a birdcage. Again, my world was upside down, but this time at least it was dry. The noise was deafening as the sparrows let me know who was in charge. I made sure to place any important paper face down in a certain spot so I would have the chance to read it once again, straight above me with only my big eyes peering out from under the safety of my covers.

The persistence of the invaders made it impossible to study in my room, so I took my ever-present, precious fourth-grade textbooks and moved operations to the classroom. I prepared by lantern late into the night, staying one step ahead of the fourth-graders to avoid my exposure for the fraud that I was.

My students already unwittingly outranked me in days spent in a fourth-grade class. I studied the curriculum carefully each night so that I could teach my students with an air of confidence. I had almost gone to fourth grade, had they not closed down the school. I had to spend hours to stay ahead. Even though I had later taken two years of middle school in the floundering classrooms of earlier times, I had never had the benefit of the curriculum of fourth, fifth, or sixth grade, and middle school consisted mostly of accusation meetings and reciting Chairman Mao's sayings from the Red Treasure Book.

I could have handled my teaching more easily were it not for the long evening hours spent sleepless in the classroom to avoid nature's battering that was going on in my room. Exhausted, I would crawl quietly into my bed and pull the cover over my head, hoping the fanged residents would maintain their flaccid hanging. I bounced up daily at first light to the disrespectful chattering of my in-house choir. The birds I had so passionately prayed for in the early days of our seedless land had finally, without invitation, filled my world.

Each day, the class-subject schedule was posted in Principal Mu's office: math, reading, science, geography, and history. I had never taught, but I had a logical mind that told me it was not efficient to have all of the teachers go to the office each and every day to see what subjects they would teach and in which session. Preparation would be so much easier if we planned a week in advance or made all of the weeks identical. *And think how much time it would save for the principal to not have to write all of that text on the board each day*, I thought.

I decided to share my observation with the principal as a contribution to his success. When I spoke with him, he was polite, considering the Vice Secretary of the Commune had sent me to his school. Yet the schedule system remained the same. I thought, *Some habits take time to break.*

真

At the first opportunity, I took the risk to walk home incognito to tell Mother the news about my new position, vindicated and grateful to the woman who was my strength for all of the years of my life. With arms stretched wide, flying in my freedom, I passed hundreds upon hundreds of back-bent peasants in the cotton fields. I shivered, and for a moment my gratitude was overcome by guilt—guilt for my sisters and my brother who spent their youths in such a place while I was hidden like a family gem. My joy swept the guilt away instantly, and I held my arms up to the sun in praise.

Mother hustled me into the house to avoid losing her carefully preserved one to the brigades.

"DaDa, you now look upon a teacher, your most favorite daughter." I grinned at our little joke.

"How did that happen? I thought you were cooking for the school, or did they fire you?"

"No, DaDa, I was hired to teach."

"The child with no food becomes a cook? The child who barely finished middle school becomes a teacher?" Mother was astounded. There was a respectful silence, and then we laughed together like we did when I was a child—a belly-holding, escape-the-harshness kind of laughter that took us to the floor, blending ourselves together once again in one vibration. As much as I loved to soak in the light shining on my happy self, I did not dare to stay too long to celebrate, lest the celebrating end in tragedy.

真

When I returned to my school, the news was buzzing. The government was initiating a "cleansing" to eliminate the disqualified teachers and to bestow the Commodity Grain Status on the qualified ones. I had forgotten the reality of my station, the classification of my Landlord past; I was an Enemy who yearned to exist.

It would be a dream come true to receive a formal teaching status for a contract teacher, a temporary teacher, or a teacher with a bad status, like me. I dreamed of the chance to have a regular ration of tickets that opened my life to buy food, fuel, fabric, and security. I imagined what it would be like to never worry about my false self again, to let my shoulders drop with an easy breath. I set out to do everything I could to earn the lifetime of sustenance, the coveted Iron Rice Bowl.

Inspectors were being sent to investigate all of the teachers who did not already have the desirable status. I thought about it every minute, trying to find a way to break into the privileged life of guarantees. "There is always a way," Mother said many times. But my Mulan warrior self could not be so bold in this tender subject. No bamboo pole with spikes could be employed.

"Teacher Zhao, the inspectors will be at our school in seven days," my colleague Xiu, "Show," said.

"Do you know who the inspector is?" I asked her.

"Comrade Xiao Xiong, I have heard."

I was surprised at my good fortune to have found the secret door to crawl out of the Enemy status so soon. Comrade Inspector was a cousin of my sister-in-law, Forest. He had the power to help.

Surely, as a relative, I thought he would help me in this matter. I paid him a visit, uncertain of my fate, asking for his help to vouch for me at the school. He welcomed me, remembering me from the past, shared a friendly conversation, smiled, and implied that he would help. Hope in my heart, my students' faces in my mind, I felt relieved, tasted the full bowls of rice, felt the fabric of new clothing on my skin.

The week passed. I was standing in my classroom while a student wrote with chalk on the board. I remembered the circle of chalk my teacher drew, in which I told my joke to escape the punishment for the insult I made to Teacher Li Wen. *Ni wen*, I thought—*"You smell."* I could not help but keep a smile on my face at the memory of my audacious childishness. Despite my Enemy past, I was so close to having the yellow egg upon the snow-white mountain of rice in my bowl, to lifting the chopsticks to my grateful lips.

The head of the school, Principal Mu, entered the doorway, and my smile turned. He asked me to join him in his office after class. I had survived in a cruel world long enough to have good instincts when danger was near, and I knew how to read the smallest flicker of an eye.

"Teacher Zhao, I am sorry. You, as a teacher, have been eliminated from the faculty," he told me when I arrived in his office. "You may feel free to leave at any time. I assume with your fine mind for schedules, you will not delay your departure."

The air escaped from inside my dancing dragon all at once, its silken sides deflated as the music in my world stopped.

"But...Why? Why would you do this to me?"

I wished I had not criticized his class scheduling, as inefficient as it may have been. I would gladly have lived by the chalkboard's rules had I understood the consequences of my words. My intention was only to lift the burden of his work. I wanted to explain. He smiled.

"Don't ask *me* why. I am only following the orders. Why so shocked? Why be so surprised? The report has come from the inspector himself. He has completed his investigation. You told us you were from an Industrial Business Classification, but the inspector enlightened me about your true status, not Small Business as you claimed with your corrupt mouth, but Landlord," he said.

"I see," I said, turning to leave the office.

I did understand. I understood that my trust had been broken, and now my heart would be, too. I could not blame the inspector. It was his job to do the cleansing. It was the truth. It was my own corrupt mouth that came back to do the biting.

I could not bear to tell Mother and Father. To take back the laughter and the joy was not something I could bear to do, if not for them, then for myself. Returning to my old commune brigade was not a possibility, for I was the Enemy of my country, and they would make me pay for all my deception. I could not go to Sister Enough's house because I would shame her, making her life more difficult. For everyone in my tightly woven life I wept, sending apologies from the unteachable one.

I lost the strength of my weakening legs, the muscles of my face unable to even lift my mouth to smile on my students as I passed them in the schoolyard.

"Goodbye, Teacher Zhao..." Their small voices faded as I dragged myself away.

I ducked into my room to gather my small bag of belongings to the joyful sound of the sparrows chattering about the news, I was sure. They would no longer have to tolerate my interruptions to their happy lives perched upon my papered net. The hanging bats made no attempt to bid farewell. With no one else to tell of my departure, I silently waved goodbye. I picked up the bamboo pole that my colleagues had given me to kill my little invading friends and propped it securely under the net to give them more support.

My co-teacher and colleague, Show, took pity on me as I passed by.

"Xiao Zhao, Little Zhao, I am so sorry to lose you. You have such enthusiasm, and your knowledge was such an asset to the students. Can I help in any way?" She looked over her shoulder as she offered her assistance to the lowest of the low. "Where will you go, if you are not insulted by my asking?"

I hesitated to admit my circumstances, but I had not the caring to even create a story to protect my vulnerability.

"Perhaps I can help you to care for your baby. I have quite a bit of experience from my past. Just to give me a little time to think."

"Go ahead to my house. I will meet you there soon. You are welcome to stay for a while."

Teacher Show had a good classification and was given formal teaching status. In return for her kind roof and food, I cared for her two-year-old son.

"Little Zhao, why not report your situation to Comrade Han?" Sister Show said, encouraging me. "Was he not the one who introduced you to the local brigade to set your residence here? Wasn't it he who put you in this teaching position in the first place? To beat the dog is to humiliate the master," she added. She was sure that Comrade Han would do something to reverse my bad fortune that was certainly the doing of Principal Mu.

"I should speak with his wife, the school's cook. I know her. She could easily have been a teacher as the wife of the Vice Party Secretary. He can do it as easily as a toad snags a fly. She couldn't even read a single character as big as a bucket, so he handed her the cooking job, the next best privilege. I can get her to put forth the word to her husband for you."

When Sister Show spoke to the secretary's ignorant wife, the truth came spilling from her foolish lips.

"My husband knew of the fate of Teacher Zhao, and he approved it."

When Sister Show returned and shared the words with me, she was angered by the unfairness of his actions, not knowing the trickery with which I had secured the job.

"You should see Comrade Han once more and ask him to place you at the cotton factory. My sister says they are always accepting temporary workers. At least it would be a start. He owes you that at least. He could put you there as easy as brushing off the dust from his hands."

I said nothing of my corruption in using my uncle's powerful name with Comrade Han to get the teaching job. I was ashamed because Sister Show had been so supportive. I followed her advice, with no energy to argue and no options to choose.

真

Waiting at the gate, too mortified to go to his office once again, I felt the heat of the sun on my shoulders and feared it would soon be on my back. I would beg him to help me. He finally passed through the gate riding his bicycle, void of any cares. He saw me waiting, knowing he had cleansed me of my position.

"Do you need a ride? I can take you on my bicycle," he said, smiling.

"No, Comrade Han, I am only hoping you could find a job for me at the cotton factory. If only you would refer me."

"Yes, let us go to see. Just get on my bicycle, and we will go to the cotton factory," he said.

I hesitated. The look on his face was not one that I could read.

"Well? Can you get on, or do I have to lift you on myself?" His jellied flesh was shaking as he chuckled.

"Thank you, Comrade Han," I said as I perched myself on the back of his bicycle. He headed for the factory, and the wind blew hope into my face. I was grateful.

"Are you seated comfortably?" he asked. He seemed to be truly concerned. He reached behind as if to check my safe position and grabbed my chest, feeling the unfamiliar fullness. It was then I knew he was aware that I had tricked him into the teaching job by stealing the power of my distant uncle. He knew he had my fate in his hands. There was no more leverage to be had.

"Are these real melons? They are so nice and ripe." He chuckled again as he massaged my breast.

Again, my oversized appendages were a liability to me, just as they had been when trying to run, play basketball, or simply walk where men would eye me. I brushed his evil hand off me and jumped off the moving bicycle.

"Oh, I didn't know you were so feisty," he said, laughing. "We'll see. Come on, you need the job, do you not? Or will you call your uncle for more help, corrupt and clever girl?" he snorted.

I stubbornly walked beside him as he laughed and pedaled slowly. "So, you like to play? I can play, too," he said.

He reached out and grabbed a handful of my shirt again. I wrapped my arms around myself, remembering the red scarf hidden in my shirt, the bony fingers of my teacher as they tapped upon his thigh, beckoning me to his lap. A sickly vibration spread inside my stomach and pushed the words out of my angry mouth.

"Dirty wolf!" I called. "You are a dirty wolf in the skin of a sheep!" I knew with my two harsh words, "dirty wolf," I had lost any chance of working in the cotton factory. I could have satisfied his fascination with my oversized chest and had a job for certain, but I would not fall into that predator's den lest his filthy claws lock into my flesh forever. I was already in enough danger from the teeth of this wolf. I watched his disappointed shoulders sag as he pedaled away, the bicycle seat disappearing under his enormous bottom.

真

With no one to tell and nowhere to go on a heavy summer morning, as was fitting, I took my worn-out quilt and a few belongings and registered with the local brigade to work in the fields. It would guarantee my shelter. I would be assigned to stay with a peasant family as my host, as the Ogres had been assigned to mine. They would share their food at mere cents per meal. I would make the best of my pitiful situation. There was no option to share my secret humiliation with anyone. I had to go underground, where I belonged.

"I come from the school of Yang Chang Commune," I began with a grain of truth. "I would like to experience re-education and contribute to the brigade during this summer period," I said.

I carefully chose my words, hoping it would work, that they would think it was short-term, loyal volunteering on my part, which was a common way for some intellectuals to be reformed at the time. *If I could hold onto even a speck of hope to not be classified as an official lifetime peasant, if I could only be in the trap without the jaws digging into the flesh of my leg forever*, I thought.

I was handed a hoe to begin the day. The cotton stalks, tall and about to break forth with their white gold, needed tending, nurturing. I hoed and hacked at the deep-rooted weeds and loosened the soil around the roots to ensure a healthy plant at harvest. No calluses, no back strength, no skills for the work of a peasant, I hoed until my hands were blistered, swollen, and weeping.

Moving forward down the row, I dug and scraped awkwardly until the dry dirt gave up the stubborn weeds. The only experience I had with cotton was plucking tiny leftover bits of fluff to make my rabbit in my childhood. The overseer realized I was not a worthy worker. I had no technique to do the job, and I was the victim of mockery from the group for my inept skills.

I listened to the rows of people working in orchestrated rhythm, to the clunking sounds of their metal water bottles tied to their sides. With each stroke of the hoe, the bottles flew from their sides and returned with a glug and a clunk. Scratch, glug, clunk, scratch, glug, clunk. I chimed in. My glug, clunk, glug, clunk, scratch—poor sense of the music of the work—resulted in calls from the line, "Wo de ma—Oh, my mother! Look at her go!"

I heard the chants and sighs go down the line with good-natured laughter as the peasants cringed at my offbeat self.

"Teacher Zhao has no rhythm and sings an off tune song, ha, ha ha!" they chanted, enjoying the brief respite.

Not knowing what to do with this tuneless, worthless, unseasoned temporary peasant, the overseer moved me from the cotton field to planting rice. Thinking I was a teacher with no skills for such work who only needed a little reminding of the plight of the many through some summer manual labor, he was lenient. I was moved to the rice field, "so as not to destroy the entire future cotton harvest," one woman teased. I could not imagine that there could be a job more torturous than the cotton hoeing—I was wrong.

The rice paddies required me to work backward in two tones: hot back, cool feet. Standing in sinking mud, ox manure floating by, maggots wriggling in the hot sun, I placed the bright green tufts into the shallow water and pushed them down into the muck, splitting them into smaller tufts, row after row, until the bell rang for our lunch. I had no lunch to bring, not yet having my allocations.

The woman from my host family took mercy on me and brought me to her home, where I savagely ate from her bowl. She gave me homemade ointment for my painful hands. Each night, the teacher in me was slowly drawn from my soul as I pulled each green and yellow sucking leech from my legs and packed a poultice of herbs and leaves to draw the ooze. The long ones, the impossible long ones, despite my stretching them to twice their size, would not let go without a precious pinch of salt. I had none, and I was not my father's daughter when it came to borrowing. I would not borrow anything without the means to repay.

With mouths at both ends, the leeches tracked me down by the sound of the gurgling of my feet as I pulled them from the deep muck in which I planted the endless rice. With each backward step I took, they wrapped themselves around my legs and sucked the hope from my lifeless veins.

There I stayed week upon week, feeling nothing but the torture of my labor and my despair. My shoulders hung with regret for my fallen state, and the shame that all of Mother's efforts to keep this kitten in the box had failed, although she had yet to know.

I was not used to the discomfort of being fed on by the insects and blood-sucking, heart-devouring creatures. I was not used to the burden of the day-long torture of labor in the sun. I felt, as time passed slowly, it would take only one more minute, one more insect, one more leech to remove any sense I had, to make me break, to have my scholar's mind break free, leaving me forever to the safety of some other bleak, lost life.

I saw a large, dark demon on my leg one day and screamed, shaking my leg, shaking all over like a wet dog. I jumped out of the rice muck and danced around in frenzy. "Get off, get off!" I screamed at the vile creature.

I was close to feeling that the threads of my mind would fray, detach, and blow away the person who I was forever. Like a tailless kite, I would spin and crash to the ground, splintering into too many broken pieces with no chance for repair. A peasant came to help, a short shy woman whom I would never forget. She pulled the harmless piece of bark from my leg and calmed me, sharing her water bottle with my vibrating lips.

The next day, I moved far away from the others in embarrassment and to avoid the teasing tongues.

"Be careful, Teacher Zhao, there is tree bark over there where you are working. Very dangerous!" I laughed along with their taunting.

I was grateful to be rejected day after day, working far from the group where perhaps my ineptitude would be hidden from the overseer.

Those who had the skill planted the young, green rice in perfect rows and patterns. The bald patch where I had worked was a signal to the overseer that it was again time to move me on. I was handed my sickle and pointed toward the cotton fields again, but this time I was assigned the thinning of the plants to prepare for the season. Here, alone, far from the others, I followed memories of Mother's instructions about weeds to thrash down the tall plants. I was learning the all-too-painful lesson—plant backward, pick forward.

真

At sunset, after many days of torture, the need for connection from being so alone overcame my exhaustion. I walked to the brick factory to see Sister Enough, whom I knew would certainly understand my plight. I had little hope that I could keep the truth of my situation from her eyes in my condition with aching back, burned skin, and bleeding hands. I knew she would keep my secret, and I would leave quickly to avoid any contamination in her life.

She met me at her door, still covered in red dust. "Have you heard the news?"

"What news, Sister?" I asked. "The news that I am a failure in the fields? The news that my mind has deserted me and had the sense to flee to the city?" Not knowing about my firing, she smiled at my joke.

"No, my funny sister, the government has opened the test to go to college."

"What do you mean, 'opened?'"

"No longer just the soldiers, peasants and ruling-class children can go to college with a simple recommendation and a red stamp. According to the rule, everyone has to pass the test for acceptance into college. Anyone, with no prejudice, all classifications, even us Enemies of the State can sit for the test," Sister explained.

The recommended students, who were riding high, getting the red stamp to go to college without any qualifications with nothing more than their social status as their ticket, would soon be riding low. Could it be true?

"You must be mistaken," I said with the doubt born of a helpless victim.

"It's true. Sister Complete walked from her brigade to deliver the news. I have heard it not once but twice. The whole town is buzzing about it—no corruption, a pure test, fair to everyone, guaranteed. It has been true in the city for some time, but it only reaches us now."

"Why do you look so sad then, Sister Enough?"

Sister Enough said, "I regret you are too late for an education. At least you are a teacher."

She read my face, and I took her hand and walked with her down to the river, where I could spill the shameful truth in private. I told her about my being fired, and the silence hung between us.

"Then I am so deeply sorry, Zhen'er, that you are too old, that you have missed the boat," she said.

"Why missed the boat? You mean there is an age limit?"

"No, silly, but you have only had school to the fourth grade and only some of middle school. How can you learn that much in ten months? It's September already, and the test is to be given in early summer. You have missed fourth, fifth, and sixth grade and then there are four years of high school—you are missing seven whole years of school. How can you learn in less than one year what Sister Double Happiness learned in seven? It is as remote as the moon. I am so sorry," she said.

That was all I needed to hear. "I will just have to learn faster. People have reached the moon before, remote or not," I said.

"Zhen'er, you are no longer young. It is getting late for marriage. The children competing are fifteen years old who have studied straight through at school, good schools. You can marry and eat the commodity grain. How about the co-worker who followed you around? You know, the one who even carried water from the pond for you when you were cooking?" Sister asked.

"He was just an ordinary friend," I said.

"Yes, a friend who is kind and a good catch. You are ordinary, and he is ordinary. A warped pot matches the warped kitchen stall, and he eats the commodity grain," Sister Enough added.

I did not respond.

"I am sorry you missed your time," Sister Enough continued. "We have all missed our time, but at least now you can marry. He can help you to get your rightful city residence papers."

"Will you at least keep my secret, for now?" I asked. I let the conversation die and left for the office of the brick factory to see my friend, Sister Pretty, needing to confirm this rumor. I had to hear it for myself.

真

"Hong Qin, how sweet to see you," Sister Pretty said using my family generational name and my school name, which was our tradition. I have missed our ballet performances," Sister Pretty said, smiling, reminding me of how we balanced on the flexing board to put the tiles on the drying racks.

"Those fantasies of dancing helped me to survive my days with the tiles," she said. "What are you doing with the summer, my teacher friend? I am so proud of you. We have done well, have we not? You and me, eating the commodity grain—me in my office, you in your classroom."

No one except Sister Enough knew of my firing or my bad classification, except my sister-in-law Forest's sister and her husband, who were a part of the scheme from the start. No one could know—not my parents, not my brothers and sisters, and most of all not Sister Enough's husband's family.

I felt humiliated and as dirty as my terracotta days to tell her a lie, but too much depended on it. Sister Enough and I told no one because her mother-in-law and husband would lose face, and Enough's life, as hard as it was, could worsen with the loss of my status in our world of "guilty me, guilty you." I hoped the truth would unravel and evaporate in the air as it traveled from my school to the far-off confines of the sealed world of the brick factory.

"May I listen to your radio news? I have no radio as you know, and I yearn for news," I asked.

Sister Pretty turned on the radio, and within a few minutes of our talking of this and that, the announcer read the new rules. It was true.

We turned the radio off, and Sister Pretty asked me hesitantly, "Was the rumor true? Did the school fire you, Hong Qin?"

"No," I lied. I thought quickly and blurted out, "I quit because I am going to take the test for college entrance."

Sister Pretty looked at me and smiled.

"College? But you were already a teacher."

"I want to be a real teacher with a college degree, if I can pass."

"How is it possible, Hong Qin? It is unheard of, and I hate to see you feel the pain of failure. This is a dream too high. How can an eagle reach the sun? How can even a winged horse reach the moon?" she asked.

"A golden phoenix can be hatched from the humblest of bird's nest," I said with a feigned confidence as I turned to leave, with the lie hanging in the air.

"Wait! If you need a place to study, you may use my desk when I am not in need of it. It is clean and quiet, and there is free light. But do you really think—"

"Thank you, Sister Pretty," I gave her my answer.

I had settled my own question. Once riding on the back of the tiger, it is difficult to descend without feeling the bite of his teeth. I was trapped into studying for the test, although I had little hope of passing or going to college. My fear wrapped around my heart and choked my confidence. There was only one choice: to taste my failure or to touch my dream. I would take the test rather than reveal my loss. I needed to make them believe I was headed toward something or I would shame my family as a useless, worthless person. I needed them to believe I had dropped something good for something better. Yes, I had quit my teaching job to take the test. It was the best story to keep the shame from the family's name.

The next morning, I walked to the fields to gather my few possessions in a sack. As I looked back over the lines of weary, tilted straw hats, I picked up my sickle and threw it as far as I could possibly throw and watched it float and drop into the murky rice paddy. This time, no one would take the weeds from my basket, for I had certainly thrown the farthest.

CHAPTER 17
THE MONSTER'S GULLET

Terror and relief joined forces and left me numb, but I had no choice but to move toward the impossible. There was no retreat and no return. I turned slowly and walked to the Education Department of the commune. Dripping in sweat, I headed directly into the office and introduced myself. "I am Zhao Hong Qin. I am here to get your advice about the college entrance test."

The assistant's smile was suspicious as he reviewed my pathetic self, from the state of my tattered clothes to the red rash of mosquito bites on every exposed inch of my body. His face took on the look I knew so well.

"Is there something wrong?" I asked with a tone of innocence. I was ready to defy him. I would not let anyone block the only path I had left to keep me out of the wretched fields, if only for a while. I sat forward in the chair, preparing for the battle.

"Not at all," he said, recapturing his civility.

Then he shook his head, let out a breath, and politely explained the new test rules. He spoke with a tone that was something short of respect, but the door remained open, and I was amazed to be invited in. The representative reviewed my choices.

"You will have to pass the test in seven subjects in order to enter college," he said. My heart was still full.

"The test is given this coming July 7, 8, and 9. Before you take the test, you must choose an area of study—either science or literature. At the same time, you will choose three colleges you hope will accept you. Your results will be sent to your first choice of the three colleges. If they do not accept you, they pass your name on to the second and then the third, in turn. If you aim too high, your opportunity may be lost. If you aim too low, your fate could be a lower-valued education, which of course would limit your job assignments ahead."

There was a small emptying of my heart's joy. I read the subjects on the list he handed me: comprehension, literature, politics, geography, ancient and modern Chinese literature, and history. *These I could learn by reading*, I thought. I was skilled at that, starting with the little tiger paper. I was so grateful that I had first, second, and third grade to count on, but the science category with chemistry, math, geology, and physics would be impossible to learn in the ten months ahead, and I would have to earn my keep during those months as well.

"So I will study literature, since that is my only possibility," I said.

"A wise choice, since a literature focus will not require any science tests."

"Must I pass all seven subjects equally? No choice to eliminate the math?" I asked.

My heart let out its hope. I had been such a good math student, adding and subtracting in my early grades—even getting a problem on the chalkboard correct after two days of missing class. But, algebra, geometry, and higher math would be too much to learn in such a short amount of time, I worried.

"You do realize there is a fee to take the test and it is not refunded if you fail," he said, again reviewing my poor state. The remainder of my joy left my heart.

"I don't care if there is a fee. I need to take this test," I said.

Then he hesitated and leaned forward as if to share a secret. "Well, if you choose to study foreign language, of course, you are exempt from math, but I am sure you would not wish to take that challenge on. You would have to choose a language in that case: French, English, Japanese, or Russian," he said grinning.

Again, he reviewed my pitiful state, up and down, taking in the odor of my classless self. "I assume you do not read or speak any languages?"

I thought of my brother-in-law and his shelf of thick college scientific books in English. I would have access to books there, and perhaps he could help. I looked at the smug man for a few seconds, and his smirk ignited my answer. I interrupted his doubts, boldly saying, "English. Yes, I will major in English."

My fate was set. I could not so much as give a greeting in English, but it was my only chance to pass. I decided that I would apply for the test with a major in English, and I chose the more humble colleges for my consideration, with little hope that I would ever secure a college placement at all. All the while, I thought of this only as a way to buy time, a solution to my need to cover up my firing, with no thought that I would ever pass the test. It was my desperate means of avoiding the doom of the fields—my certain demise.

真

I took the familiar six-hour bus ride to the home of Sister Double Happiness, and this yellow-furred fledgling humbled herself to return to her employ. I resumed my daily routine: cleaning, laundry, and child care for her family of six, but this time with a purpose. Any payment I had to make in labor would be worth the gain to keep me from the fields, if only for a brief few months until I could find another unimaginable way to escape. I remembered Father's words: "An ugly toad cannot expect to eat of the swan." My daily chores of a dozen hours exhausted me, and I had little time to study, but any time was precious. I asked Sister Double's husband Da, "Arrival," who could read but could not speak English, to start me off with the English alphabet.

He drew the strange shapes on the paper for me. Upper case, lower case—ah, I saw it right away. The upper case, the capital letters, must be the language of the government. The officials, the leaders, letters tall and straight, lines formal, lines of soldiers, barriers beneath strong structures with only a few of the letters showing the weakness of a curve. And the lower case must be the language of the people, the laborers—curvy, round, rolling like acrobats, compliant, bending like contortionists performing on the square.

Letter "a": Yes, I see: two human tumblers, one curled in half, back arched, the second standing straight behind to support the first.

Letter "b": The straight one standing in front of a smaller arched one, feet at his partner's waist, head to his toes, like one cotton laborer standing straight at day's end with the rounded, heavy load of cotton tied to her waist.

Then letter "c": one solo acrobat in a back bend, legs suspended over his head.

Yes, those lower-case letters must be the language of the people, I was certain. Those were the flexible, bent-back workers—weaker, smaller, rounder, working together for the cause.

I studied the upper-case letters that led every thought, every sentence, and marked every validated person or place with a proper name. I memorized them, the upper case, the lower case, all twenty-six sounds times two, representing the rules of the government and the obedience of the people. Arrival taught me their sounds, and I memorized their angles and their bends. I learned their shapes—A, B, C—and then their sounds, "aee," "bee," and "see."

Sister Double saw the light from my room in the late hours. "How can you study at this hour, reading into the night? You cannot hold an idea in your head without sleep. You reach for the star, you burn your hand," she warned me, fearful of my potential failure, worried about my feelings. "Hong Qin, no one beyond their high school years dares to take the test. You will be the tall weed in the garden. You are six or more years older than most students who sit for this test."

"You reach for nothing, you hold only air," I answered, quoting Mother while keeping my eyes on the letters.

These were not yellow books of love poems. This was the language of the mysterious Foreign Ocean Devils that made the yellow soap and so many things we could never afford. It was enticing, alluring, dangerous.

I listened to the radio every day—one-hour lessons at 7 p.m. in English, gathering in the words, the sounds, just as Mother grasped to remember the ancient poetry in mid-air before the burning. But my learning was moving too slowly for me to reach the deadline of July, listening only once a day. Not wanting to go off my strict plan, I slept upon the softness of the words for only three hours each night and sometimes fell asleep upon the rough and folded laundry by day. Like the schedule on Principal Mu's blackboard, I wasted not a minute and planned every second, but I followed my own rules.

While I scrubbed the laundry, I recited with each rub, "Good morning, my name is Hong Qin." While I swept, I repeated each letter's sound. My math was good enough to know that I could not make it to my goal at that pace.

Brother-in-law Arrival had an idea. "Hong Qin, there is an afternoon class that was started at my Institute for employees to learn English. I will sneak you in, if you like."

I sat in the back of the class with an air of a scientist so I would not attract attention. The acrobats and contortionists began to cheer me on, began to beckon me to follow them, rolling across the page, beginning to make sense. I learned verbs and nouns. Arrival carried a big English technical book into my room for me to see. I had no textbooks to learn my English and no dictionary. I had only what I could hear on the radio and see on the blackboard in my beloved class. I could hear each error that was made by other students, and they stuck out as a detour in my plan. "Wo bu ting—I won't listen.'" I shut my ears for fear their errors would set me back or contaminate my learning. It was already January. It had been two months, and my preparation moved like I was pulling pallets of tiles on my first brick-factory day. I needed the nudge to get over the hump in the road with my heavy cart, and there was no Sister Pretty who could help me with a push.

Double Happiness was out full-time from the home. She couldn't help me; she spoke only Russian from her college days. Arrival had to work hard to earn money for his family, with a tight budget and four children; they were always riding on the edge. I could no longer keep the dream and keep the job.

Again, Spring Festival saved me. I left for the celebration with my family, and again being the ungrateful sister that I was, I never went back. I moved into Sister Enough's small apartment at the brick factory to ensure my precious time for study. But this time, instead of a bitter letter, Double Happiness sent me gold—a thick envelope filled with sample tests used for preparation by high school students. I treasured them like the little tiger paper, greedily devouring the characters from the pages.

I needed to learn English and reading comprehension. I needed to read ancient and modern Chinese literature, history, geography, world history, politics—seven years of study in ten months. I laughed, so ignorant of the distance I would need to travel. I hoped that somehow I could draw the brilliance and the knowledge from Mother's ancestors' minds into mine. This was my one chance. This time I might be the scholar she dreamed of, a city girl. I had the memory of Mother's face at the accusation meetings and my dark, bent-back days in the horrid fields to urge me on.

I lived in Sister Enough's little apartment with her husband Yun, "Cloud"; her mother-in-law; and her child in a small space with the rooms separated by hanging cloths. I was grateful. The first week, I scrubbed all of the laundry while Sister Enough loaded her bricks all day. I wanted to lift her burden and do my part.

"Zhen'er, you are here to study, not to work for me. The memories of my years with Double Happiness are still in my stomach. I will care for the laundry," she said with sympathy.

I tried to hide my dirty laundry from her the next week because I did not feel it was right for her to work so hard, but she found it.

"You make me mad with your stubbornness, insisting on helping me. You make more work for me having to hunt for your hidden dirty clothes," she said.

I looked up from my book to see my laundry folded neatly on my bed. We had the same fate—I had saved her from the fields, and she would save me from the fields.

"You are being spoken of in the factory, Sister Hong Qin," brother-in-law Cloud said. "As often as the rooster crows at the sun, and I am tiring of their questions. Why can't they leave you alone, let you just try? They are not the ones who sleep only four hours a day," he said, showing his support.

I wanted to know what disturbed them so much about my efforts. "What are they saying, Brother Cloud?"

"They say it is a foolish waste of time at your age. One of your former bosses said, 'She left a good position in our brick factory, where she should have been grateful.'"

The world was watching this ant try to lift the Iron Rice Bowl. They thought the porcupine could not be embraced without the sting. Hopelessness and helplessness lived deep in the workers' souls when it came to choosing a destiny.

真

Sister Enough carried her ration of hot water from the factory in her bucket for me. I was so yearning for a bath. I pushed aside the curtain to bathe in the family basin and ran into her blushing husband with not a single garment to grab for his protection. Cloud quickly covered his manhood with both soapy hands and barked me out of the room. When he heard Sister Enough's laughter mixed with my whispers later that evening, he was angry once again, and we giggled once again. Privacy was one commodity we could not buy with any amount of tickets.

Sister packed her thermos full of the cooked food daily to share with her "book-headed" sister. World War I, World War II—I memorized the facts for twenty hours a day, allowing four hours for sleep. I set the alarm clock next to my head in case I slept too much to avoid missing precious hours of study. Too often, my brother-in-law had to come into my sleeping area to turn the alarm off.

In this way, I covered four years of high school and three years of middle school. I had no one to ask a question of because no one I knew at the brick factory had been to high school. Beyond the test samples and some borrowed books, I was on my own with no real thought of being able to pass the test. It was like plucking down a star. No matter, I could not allow my mind to go to the dark place that was beyond the test, the dark, bloody mouth that sucked me into the monster's gullet—the haunting call of the brigades. I kept my eyes and mind only on papers and books for as long as I could.

If there was little chance of passing, I could at least cling to the little time I had left to study. I was postponing the threat of the endless days in the fields, the endless days of hopelessness. Whenever my mind drifted into that fearful place from the pessimistic words or jokes from the workers at the factory, I pulled back and buried myself in the location of some country or the dates of some world event.

The president of the brick factory passed the office where Sister Pretty worked and saw me studying at her desk.

"Do yourself a favor, don't waste your time. If someone like you can go to college, then a chicken can go to college. Come and show us your passing grade so we can all cheer. Impossible," he said and waved me off, shaking his head from side to side.

Cloud had a good friend whose mother was the principal of the number one high school in the area where Sister Double Happiness had once had the honor to work. He imposed upon this friendship to secure permission for me to sit in the back of the classroom for the most important class I would ever take. For the brightest students who would take the college entrance test, an entire semester was dedicated to learning how to take the test and preparing for the world of knowledge that I would need to know.

真

I entered the classroom on the first day, having swallowed a parade full of kites throughout my night of dreams. I was floating and hopeful again. I passed by the high school students on my way to my seat. I had grown years beyond their age, suffered pain beyond their imagining, labored far beyond their soft hands.

Folding myself into a smaller size to fit in, I sat in the back of the classroom where, from habit, I assumed the Enemy should be. Although in my twenties, as with all students of my kind, I was called a "social youth student." Being an Enemy of the State in a real high school classroom was too much for my mind to bear. I had to work to keep my feet on the floor.

The teacher called on me to answer. "Yes, you, Classmate Zhao Hong Qin." Heads twisted around in one fast motion with wide eyes to see the grown woman in their class. I answered correctly.

In May and June, I enjoyed the privileges of a student without prejudice from either student or teacher. My classification was no matter to anyone. I breathed in the knowledge and cried with gratitude at night. I was a student again. I had dropped the hoe and picked up the pen.

Each morning, I would eat a breakfast of porridge and take a bun to school in my little sack that would give up its moisture to the heat and challenge me rock-hard at lunchtime. In the evening, I uncovered the plate that Sister Enough had so lovingly saved for me and ate greedily. Students who lived at the school ate from the cafeteria, but I did not have money to eat.

Cloud bought me a watch so I could time myself and not be late, a true luxury. I looked at it often, not only to check the time but also to simply admire it riding on my own wrist. In June, I walked forty-five minutes each way to take each section of the mock test. The teacher corrected them for me as though I were an equal student. I got the geography test back and failed. I cried on the walk home, planning to keep the secret to myself, but Enough knew me too well.

"What is wrong, Zhen'er?" she asked immediately upon seeing my face.

"I failed the geography mock test. What will I do?"

"Oh, I thought it was something really worse. You worried me," she said.

I was alone with the desperation of this dream. Even those who cared about my happiness could not imagine that a person of my age, my background, and my education would ever have a chance to pass.

The day came for the test—July 7, 1979. I was nearly twenty-three years old. The test was given in our high school, the main test zone in our region. Armed with guns, the police eyed me as I approached. With my official test badge in hand, they let me in. Just as I had been promised, there was no prejudice. Each test room had two monitors who were teachers. The doctors and nurses on duty tended to the overwrought students who vomited, collapsed into uncontrollable tears, or fainted under the pressure. I watched them take their dragging feet from the room to reunite them with the sea of anxious parents waiting outside.

Three out of four candidates traditionally failed, the data said. I looked around to see which would be my three, allowing me to be the one who passed. That kind of math I knew was flawed. I could picture thousands and thousands of students in all of China sitting in a testing class like this, each taking a bite from the possibility of changing my life forever, each having the chance to put me in the fields of hopelessness forever.

I had no choice; I could not return to the factory. My classification was now openly known. I could not go to the fields, or I would surely be found mindless with my body covered in leeches in a rice-field ditch. I could not face my family and shame them back into the Enemies that they were. I could not face Mother with her broken dream, and certainly, I could not take the life that she had sacrificed to save. The future was a place too dark for me to go.

First, I filled in the spaces with my pencil when I found an answer I knew. Gratefully, I knew many answers at first sight. A smile stretched across my face when I reached the question on the Middle Earth Sea. My Ogres' arguments and my friend Spy Lake's voice were in my ears: "It is somewhere in Europe. I believe it is called the Mediterranean Sea. It is definitely not in China," the scholar had insisted. Ha! I completed the answer, "Mediterranean Sea."

Then came the Four Inventions question. So easy, there were the three from the first night's discussions around the lantern and one from the night after. What was the fourth? Ah, yes, snoring, fireworks. *Thank you, Uncle Bu.*

When I came to the optional math section, I decided to take it to see if I could add just a few points to my score. For three days and seven subjects, I watched the students drop from fear or leave with arrogance each day. Having never taken a test of that kind before, I had no idea how well I did. The weeks between the test and the posting of the results were torture, with rolling eyes and whispers behind my foolish back. The papers had to be transferred to the correction center for scoring. The results would be posted in the high school on August 17th, 18th, and 19th, for all to see.

I received a notice at the school that our district had scored the highest; therefore, the baseline standard for passing would be higher than in other areas, 360 and above. The score I had to reach was more than it would have been if I had lived in my rural region, due to the quality of our schools. For the first time in my life, fairness and equality were guaranteed. Here in this test, there was no classification issue. For this suspended moment, I was one of them.

真

On the last possible day, I went to find my scores with only the shortest straw of hope left in my hand and the blackness of my future descending. The names were listed alphabetically. I looked up my name and read the score. I ran my finger down the list and read it again to ensure I had not mixed up my name with some other fortunate student's score. I had a score of 460, one hundred points above the baseline.

As impossible as it was, the sun did rise in the west. I had passed, I was astounded, I was suspicious, and I was spent. On August 19, 1979, I, the only Enemy, the only social youth, the only uneducated one to take the test, the unteachable one, passed the test by one hundred points above the baseline requirement. It could not be true.

I had captured my one chance, but still I grew nervous. My worry spiraled down into my stomach, and I retched. What if a college didn't pick me? I checked daily at Sister Pretty's office where the mail would come with my notification because I had used Sister Enough's address for the application. From her apartment, I could see the postal delivery man ride up to the main factory office on his bicycle with saddle bags of mail at the same time every day. Sister Pretty sorted the letters and papers each day into stacks, keeping an eye out for my fate.

Every day I endured the jokes and sneers of people I passed by at the brick factory on my way to check the mail, and each day I sheepishly returned using a roundabout route when there was no letter. Curling myself up in my chair at home, I waited for my demise. With hands over my ears, I tried to still the din of the doubters' voices in my mind. *Wo bu ting, wo bu ting—I won't listen. I won't listen.*

The time was getting close. Perhaps college number three had no use for me, either. Other students had already received their acceptances. I ran to check one more time and saw my name on the outside of the folded paper. They had misspelled it, but I knew it had to be me, even though it read "Zhao Hong Qi," not "Qin." I took the letter and pressed it to my heart as though I could change the words within. Then I opened it, wanting the news, not wanting the news—college or peasant, life winner or life loser, pen or fields, hope or despair, no in between.

I was accepted to E Xi Normal College for three years with a final teaching degree as my prize, should I succeed! My face was enough to tell Sister Pretty my fate.

"I am so happy for you—amazed, but happy!"

Her boss walked by and furrowed his brow at our cheering.

"What is this celebration during work hours?"

"This foolish dusty brick worker, this clucking chicken, is going to college." I said with great satisfaction. His jaw had not yet dropped as I strutted from the room with my arms flapping like chicken wings, waving goodbye, squawking, "Bawk, bawk, bawk, bawk."

The cymbals kept on beating and roaring in my chest as I read the acceptance letter over and over. My body was too small to hold my heart. I exploded from the door of the building into the dusty air and moved down the darkening path to the riverside. I was more foolish than I had ever been in my childhood, and I fell into the joyful moment with abandon, something so rare in my wretched life. I was dancing in a New Year festival in my mind—swirling, laughing, bobbing my head like the powerful golden dragon, stretching my arms wide, then waving imaginary yards of red silk like a royal red butterfly dipping from side to side.

I had no idea how long the trance went on or who had witnessed it. I only knew when I rose from the insanity of my celebration and settled back into my narrow bed that my face ached from my smile for hours afterward, and I could not sleep for the fantasy of being a college girl, at last. The extraordinary news was trapped inside me like a mad bee seeking to explode, desperate to make the impossible flight to buzz in the ears of Mother, and my Ogres. I had reached the first of the dangling earring dreams that she had promised.

My family and friends were very happy for me. The ones who had taunted me for my stupid self said nothing at all. I could not resist walking around the area on feigned errands just to run into the doubters to tell them of my good news. It was my unseemly pride, but I confess I enjoyed the moments of sweet revenge.

真

Again, I walked the familiar hours to the aqueduct by the brigade to see Sister Complete Happiness and Mother and Father, holding the news like keeping chickens in a row, my thoughts going in a million directions, my face hurting from the joy as I walked.

"I prayed for you and promised my goddess that if you succeeded in this test, I would abstain from meat and fast for all the remaining holidays of my life," cried Mother.

"DaDa, it was your blood in my veins, your stories in my memory, your force that did it for me," I said.

CHAPTER 18
TERROR ON THE BRIDGE

The most shocking thing was yet to happen to Sister Complete Happiness, who had spent well beyond a decade laboring endlessly in the brigade, suffering the indignities of body and mind. Her husband taught in the brigade school, while each day she struggled to complete her assigned work and to care for her children, endless year after year.

As Sister Complete told the story, it happened on a hot summer evening in 1979. It was just a common night. The smoke was wafting from the cooking chimneys, and the noises of evening's busy rush were audible everywhere—the barking of the dogs and the loud calls of the parents urging their children home for dinner. The mud brick houses of the peasants were strategically located on both sides of the banks of the aqueduct that guided the water from the Yangtze River for irrigation of the crops and consumption by the people. Sister Complete's house was on the west bank, the sixth one from the main bridge that crossed the canal. The routine evening was suddenly interrupted by the striking of the brigade bell, followed by the loudspeaker announcing a meeting at the aqueduct bridge.

Another meeting of no benefit, Sister thought, but she had always reluctantly and obediently trudged her way to those meetings.

Although a bit noisier, there was some advantage to living closer to the bridge. She continued her housework to the orchestra of the swarming mosquitoes until the bridge was filled with people before she left her home.

The full moon was particularly bright that night, providing an unusual spotlight on the bridge. Some women brought their sewing work with them to catch up on a few stitches to make new shoes, while others still in the midst of eating simply took their bowls along. Sister Complete was among the last few to arrive. She stood behind everyone else in the far back.

The brigade cadre called my sister's name. "Zhao Sheng Fang, you stand here, in the middle!" he commanded.

Sister stood rigid in terror, so shocked that her body couldn't move. "What did I do wrong? In what trouble? Accusation meeting for me?" she said out loud.

"Yes, you, Zhao Sheng Fang," the cadre repeated, pointing in her direction while Sister Complete held her hand at her chest.

She dragged her feet closer to the center of the illuminated bridge.

"All of you move, let her through," he said, signaling for the nearby peasants to move to open a space for Sister.

The cadre's last name was Yang, and his first name was Bao Dong, meaning "Protect East." East often referred to Chairman Mao. Sister Complete said she would never forget that cadre, his words, and that one moment.

He stood straight with a serious face and announced, "Our government has passed down new orders...."

Sister Complete Happiness gripped the railing of the bridge. What more can they do to me, what more could they take? She could not imagine her fate. *Please, please*, she begged in her mind for mercy.

"Everyone must now live, accordingly. From this day forward," he paused and pointed at my sister. She faced the twisted necks, the glaring looks, and the cold faces of her lifelong taunters. She hung her head, not wanting to see his face or their grins when her deathly sentence came. In a loud booming voice, he added, "The

Enemy of the State Classification is abolished! Everyone, including you, Zhao Sheng Feng, is now equal, according to the law."

Sister couldn't believe that she had heard his words correctly. She saw all the heads turn to look at her. She knew that she must have heard him wrong. Awaiting the taunting laughter to begin, she was frozen with fear. She feared it wasn't true, it was a joke, it was a dream.

Then came the regretful comment from a neighbor: "Well, I guess we can't earn easy working points from accusation meetings anymore." From that single heartless comment alone, Sister knew it must be true.

After the meeting was over, Sister Complete Happiness felt as though her feet could not reach the Earth, her heart could not be still. The heavy mountain she had been carrying all those years was suddenly lifted from her back. Even though on the next day, the burden of her toiling was the same to her small body, the sun seemed softer, the soil was friendlier. For the first time, she found just enough freedom in her heart to sing softly to herself as she worked.

Her heart had new hope. From the day she was handed over to the woman peasant at fourteen, she had lived in terror every day from nearly every adult in the brigade who had power over her. While she had worked back-to-the-sky with her hoes, sickles, shovels, and her carrying pole with baskets, her peers had been in their classrooms maneuvering their pencils and crayons on their lucky papers. She was always alone. Finally, the voice of the young girl who had loved to sing but had been silenced by fear for years found its freedom, and she sang her way home with abandon.

真

Sister Complete Happiness forever lost the chance to go to school, but she took the greatest pride in my education. After I succeeded in my college entrance examinations, she took me to visit relatives, including sister-in-law Forest, who was surprisingly unkind and jealous. Perhaps she wished her own younger sister had the opportunity. I couldn't help crying after Forest turned a cold face on us and walked away.

Mother and Father had left the dilapidated borrowed home and moved from the levee to live with Sister Complete and her husband in their own household by the brigade fields. Mother's negotiations and strategies set so many years before had worked in her favor. By defying tradition, she had the right to live with her own daughter, who had never been an in-house daughter-in-law to her husband's family.

When the day came for me to travel to the far west of our province to college, Sister Complete Happiness, no longer under the thumb of the brigade leader, took one luxurious day off. Her husband, the brigade teacher, also joined us. I stood with Mother in the doorway to say our goodbyes. All of my life with her came together in that moment—the pain we suffered together, the laughter, the lessons.

"The fish has left the pond to enter the ocean," she said.

Father was the first one among the surrounding villages to own and be able to ride a bicycle before Liberation. He had taught us well. My brother-in-law rode one bicycle with Sister Complete sitting behind, while I pushed the other bike carrying my modest luggage.

I stopped to turn around, holding Mother's eyes with mine. I ran back and lowered my head to honor her, our most poignant form of intimacy. One goodbye was not enough for the woman who had prepared me for this moment. There was no look deep enough, no smile warm enough, no way to send the message from the butterflies living in my heart to hers. Nothing was really enough except to dream that my success would give her hope. I could still see her when I looked back, her arm waving until the turn in the road took her from my sight. I would fly away lifted on wings, far, far away. Even my uncontrollable joy could not rise above the deep pain of leaving Mother. I knew it could be many years before I would see her again. The sadness rode with me for quite a while.

Sister Complete decided we should take a brief detour. Instead of leaving the village from the west bank straight to the public road, she insisted we go over the bridge and wheel our bicycles along the east bank of the aqueduct, where she knew many peasants from her brigade were working on Party Secretary Qin's house. She waved at them with her news ready to burst from her smiling lips. I shivered at the memory of the audacious letter Sister Enough and I wrote that brought Father to his knees at the feet of Secretary Qin.

"Isn't it a nice day today?" Sister Complete asked lightheartedly. The people turned their heads from their precarious spots, hanging on ladders, dripping sweat from their labor in the humid, late-summer morning. These were the abusive people who had clawed at her soul daily in the fields, taunted her for her bad classification—the very peasants Sister had avoided and feared. But on that special day, she greeted them with pride, explaining, "Oh, I had to take a day off today to take my sister to the ship to leave for college. Have a good day." It was an unthinkable luxury, a day free from labor to see me off to the passenger ship that would take me to college. One day away from the filthy water that delivered the fungus that invaded her toes, one day free from the rice-paddy water that rotted the peeling skin on her feet, a single day off that in the past would never happen, no matter if she had been deathly ill. This day off, announced for all to hear, gave her immeasurable pride, immeasurable joy, immeasurable satisfaction.

Riding our bikes to the ferry, we crossed the Yangtze River and arrived at Sand City, the city where Mother had planted the seeds of my dreams. The destination of her dream was simply the point of my departure. We talked of her as we walked our bikes and stopped to take a rest. While recounting the many childhood stories Mother had told us about fairy tales, empresses, and princes and how the Great Wall was built, we shared her wise sayings and lessons.

"I know, here is one." Sister Complete Happiness remembered. "Be grateful to people who help you."

"Sister Complete," I said, "you are saying I need to show you gratitude right now for taking me to the ship?"

My sister smiled. "Or," she continued, "remember, this one? One drop of kindness should be returned with the gushing flow of a fountain."

"So, shall I push you in the fountain for your kindness of coming to see me off?" I asked.

We laughed again.

"Here's one," I added. "Always make people miss you."

We stopped and looked into each other's eyes, deflating slightly at the thought of our separation once again.

"Hold your back up straight," I added to push away the sadness.

"Observe people's facial expressions when talking to them." Again, we checked our expressions nose-to-nose.

"Don't expect too much from others because there is a saying, 'People can't be nice for a thousand times as flowers can't stay red for a hundred days.'"

"But that one is not true of you," I said.

"Never owe anything to anyone; better to let them owe you," I quoted. "I have failed in that one, for I owe Mother so much. Remember, her way of being critical of someone was to say, 'She *so* has no knowledge!'" We both said the phrase in unison and punched each other's arms.

"Or she would curse them by wishing them to be pregnant," I added. "She never used vulgar words, never called names."

"Yes, so we grew up never knowing how to curse, either. We were powerless, but it may have saved me on occasion when some of the peasants in the fields were particularly cruel," Sister said. "I had no evil words to lure their further cruelty."

"Our two sisters-in-law made up for her lack of unacceptable words, didn't they?"

"Yes, we certainly observed Mother's facial expression when talking to her about that!" We laughed at the memories.

Even with Mother's words in my mind, I knew I was short on the wisdom I would need for my unknown journey. My sister and I were not used to sharing tender words; we had the tendency to have them stick in the throat but live in the heart. "I have three words to describe you. Can you guess them?" I asked.

"Maybe unfortunate, uneducated, and unaccepted," she said thoughtfully.

"No—humble, enduring, and creative. You have always been selfless and kind to me, and on this journey, which should have been yours, you smile at my good fortune. Thank you."

真

The big ship was white with wide blue stripes wrapped around it. Little colorful strings of flags like happy little kites waved to me from the deck. The layered decks looked like a city building with balconies. Many passengers were leaning on the rail to watch; others were in line to disembark. Boarding this kind of ship was the dream of my cousin Joy, but her dream had died with her. I would go on her behalf.

I stood at the edge of the Yangtze—the river that produced the great woman emperor, Wu Ze-Tian. I stood on my toes, watching the ship approach, while playing nervously with my knee-length pigtails. Sister looked at me, then at the ship. Her eyes were shining. It was as though she herself were going to college—no jealousy, just excitement and support.

After so many years of suppression, we had all survived. We had all endured without causing much disgrace to our parents, despite my corrupt escape schemes. Good virtues were so important to them. It was all they could hope for in their limited world. Sister Complete refused to leave and wanted to watch me board. After I got on the ship, I immediately went to the back of the boat to wave to her. Sister waved back, still standing there on the dock. She said she would always remember that moment. I was wearing my only jacket—the red-checkered one that Sister Double had bought me. She watched until I became a red dot, farther and farther out of her sight, until the ship turned the bend in the river.

I was in the cheapest class, receiving only a blanket to sleep on the deck. No food was provided, but I had the beautiful flowing river and the excitement of the people all around me. It was the first time I had moved on the Yangtze, not on a ferry, but on a glorious ship. Best of all, I felt the breeze take all the Evil labels I had carried on my back my entire life and pass them off into the distance, along with the smoke from the big stack above me. When they all had left my soul, I drew in the fresh air from my perch on the deck and my chin rose—but just a bit.

The bursar kept my ticket to guarantee that I would return the blanket, but I had the freedom to roam the deck. There was much to see. I was captivated as we passed by two of the famous Three Gorges of the Yangtze River. Equally as fascinating, were the first Yang Gui-zi I had ever seen. I peered into a window and saw them—my first Ocean Devils, the people whose language had brought me to this wonderful boat on this unexpected journey away from my persecuted past. There were only a few of them, and they were in first class, dining on a feast. "You shall go to a restaurant and order anything you want." I remembered Mother's words and smiled. A tall foreign man looked up at me through the dining room window and smiled. I dropped to my knees out of sight.

I lay my blanket in an open area directly on the route that people had to take to get boiling water. I loved to watch the passengers on parade. The same smiling man from the first-class dining room walked by.

"Excuse me," he mumbled, a mere formality as he was passing by.

He was not expecting an answer, but I said, "No problem," an expression I had learned from my English class. He looked down to see me sitting on my blanket. He recognized me. There was no way to drop farther from his sight and, admittedly, I was curious. He stopped and looked at me in confusion, thinking he must have heard me wrong.

How is it that this poor Chinese girl, long pigtails and innocent smile, could possibly speak English, he must have thought. I could read his face. Anyone who could speak English would be in their cabin instead of sitting in this dirty, crowded, open walking area, wouldn't they? I was very nervous. It was my first time speaking English to a real English-speaking native, and I felt so intimidated.

"Did you just speak to me in English?" he asked.

"Not very good English. I soon shall learn it well in college," I said.

He spoke very slowly and louder. "I so seldom have a chance to speak English with a Chinese person. There is so much to learn, to understand, but I do not speak Chinese, I am afraid. May I sit down?"

We introduced ourselves. I helped him to repeat my simple name several times, helping to get his lips around the unfamiliar shapes and sounds. "Zhao, pronounced like 'how' with a 'ds' sound at the beginning, as in han(ds), and then Qin, like 'chin,'" I explained. With my English hints, he got it right away, although his Zhao sounded more like Jow than Dsow. His name was Steve, and he had a wife and family back in Canada. I understood all that he said, and I was very proud.

When I looked at him more closely, I was surprised to see how much hair he had on his chest and arms, like a bear with tickling curls growing out of his collar and his sleeves. I knew western foreigners all had big noses, but I didn't know they had such thick hair like a blanket—hair on his chest, his arms, even on the knuckles of his fingers.

If he had the same thick hair everywhere else beneath his clothes on his entire body, how did he wash himself? It was hard for me to wash my hair in the washbasin every now and then. I could not imagine if he had to wash the hair all over his body from a small washbasin, dipping one part of his body into the small basin at a time. I had no idea how the big-nose foreigners could clean themselves. How many buckets of water would they have to haul in from their pond? I had much to learn about these Foreign Devils whose language saved me from the fields, but there was little time on our one day of travel.

The Ocean Devil waved goodbye and called to me as we disembarked, "Good luck with your English."

After we arrived in the riverside town called BaDong and had rested in a motel for one night, I boarded a bus for the two-day bumpy trip to En Shi College. I never tired of it. I was going far away from my secrets; I no longer had to hide who I was.

CHAPTER 19
MARGARET THATCHER MEETS O. HENRY

My small college sat in the middle of a mountainous area in the far west of our province that bordered the far eastern side of Si Chuan Province. I saw the local people from the bus window dressed in their strange style of clothing with heavy towels wrapped around their heads. When we stopped for a meal, I heard them speaking with their unusual Si Chuan accent, and I ate their spicy food that delighted my tongue.

As my feet finally touched down from the dusty bus, my eyes caught sight of a big banner strung across the gate of the college entrance. It was red with bright white characters.

"We Cordially Welcome New Students," it said.

I kept looking at it, breathing it in, standing for a long time in silence. I was thrilled to feel so included and so wanted. The simple message from the banner might have been passed by unnoticed by others, but it was divine to me. It made up for all my lost childhood dreams, rising high above my yearning for the Young Pioneer red scarf—I was cordially welcomed.

The campus was so beautiful to me. I saw colorful sunsets dancing on the leaves of tall maple trees. I was overjoyed that Mother no longer needed to hide me from the brigade. I had brought her happiness and had escaped her most feared nightmare. Now I formally belonged to the elite class of the country that ate from the commodity grain, which forever ended my illegal city-dweller, black status.

I was grateful for the help that so many people had given me to be able to reach that moment, including someone I never had the chance to meet. He was the one responsible for the greatest change in my life, my family's lives, and the lives of all other Enemies of the State; his name was Deng Xiaoping. While I stood balanced high up on the brickyard scaffolding and heard the loud announcement of the death of Chairman Mao, I had no understanding of what it would mean to me. As I watched the weeping people all around me who were falling to the ground with grief, I had no understanding that in that moment, the hope for my life's dream had taken root. I had no idea about the impact this new leader of China would have on my small and insignificant life as an Enemy of the State. I could not imagine the changes that would take place as he unraveled the tight ropes of control that Chairman Mao had around the minds and souls of the people. I could not predict his policies of modernization and social change. How could I, an unimportant Enemy, understand the meaning of the visit of the American President Richard Nixon, or what the passing of Chairman Mao's regime would bring to my country, to my life? With the rule of this one man, Deng Xiaoping, my Enemy status was wiped clean, and Mother's hope was fulfilled—my family's name was restored.

To my great surprise, not all the newcomers were as excited as I was. Because the college was not a first-class university, many of my classmates were disappointed to enter the door of this school; they felt they were qualified for better. This was their third choice. Some of them had even grown up in the advanced provincial capital, Wuhan City. These privileged children came all the way to this little-known remote college, riding the bus on the winding mountain roads for days, only to experience rural life for the first time and to face not being cared for or pampered daily by their parents and their servants. They had surely known cotton fields only by the feel of their soft shirts; they had certainly known wheat only by the sweet taste of their meat-filled buns—rice water and weeds were something never savored by even their household staffs.

Unlike myself, a social youth, most of the classmates were current high school senior graduates, and I was the oldest of the female students. Our lead teacher, a fashionable, good-looking middle-aged lady, Teacher Cui, appointed me Chairman of the Female Students Association. I was used to being at the bottom of society, and I had no idea about how to be an officer. I never believed myself to be a qualified one, but I was always put in various leadership positions throughout my college years.

As a leader, I was once summoned to attend a meeting in town. I was even taken there among a few other school leaders by the school truck, which was such a privilege. When I arrived, I realized it was a public execution meeting. The criminals being put to death were tied up in ropes, soon to be shot. My soul was deeply disturbed. I didn't know their crime nor the reason why I had to witness this kind of scene, but I knew I had once been an Enemy, and I had once committed the crime of lying about my illegal Black Status. My father had several times narrowly avoided being shot, and my honorable grandfather starved to death under the persecution. Having the stories of Mother in my heart, I could not tolerate violence, no matter what the cause.

My name began as a plea from my mother to the sky for an end to having more children—a mother's plea that made me wonder if I had been wanted after all. With my newfound fortune, it flipped upside down like an acrobat from *being* Really Enough Complete Happiness in the desperate times in which Mother gave me life, to *having* Really Enough Complete Happiness in this life that I was building for myself.

真

I sat in my first English class, and my teacher announced, "Class, as English majors, we will all use English names while at school. Yes, and you in the front row, you will be Robert for Robert Frost;

Henry for O. Henry; and you are Emily for Emily Bronte; and you Jane, after Jane Eyre," she said to a slender tall girl with stylish short hair who was seated in the back. "And you, Mary for Queen Mary," she named my good-natured friend. The teacher made the rounds of all of the students in the class, and reaching me, she dubbed me "Margaret," for Margaret Thatcher. I had more than one name throughout my life—my baby name, Zhen You Yuan Xi, Really Enough Complete Happiness; my school name Zhao Hong Qin; and finally, my English name, Margaret.

We listened with heads cocked like roosters to understand the Voice of America and BBC broadcasts. Our minds followed slowly like a swollen lazy river while the English words like dragonflies lit upon the water, now and then. Quickly, we would catch a word, then another, but most of them escaped in between. In the midst of the string of unfamiliar words, the dragonfly lit upon my name as the voice of Margaret Thatcher filled the room.

The other students looked at me and gasped to hear the voice of my namesake and tumbled into laughter, pointing at me and covering their mouths. I stiffened, drew in, but this time the teasing wore an edge of envy and admiration. I was no longer the outcast. I was a dignified and powerful stateswoman, a British Empress like Wu Ze-Tian. It was an irony that filled my heart long void of honor.

I am often asked, "How did you get that English name? Why didn't you keep your given Chinese name? Why not change it back?" Ah, but it was both given and ironic. When I searched the meaning of the name in an old book in the English library, a magical smile came upon my face, for in English, Margaret means "Pearl." It was the very baby name I had wished that Mother had named me to show that I was cherished in her heart. So, in an unexpected and fortunate way, as often miracles tend to happen, I had finally become little precious Pearl. So the circle closed, and "Margaret" I would remain.

The eldest male student was a local resident who had been an elementary teacher who decided to quit his job to pursue higher education. Everyone regarded him highly. Henry was a quiet young man, knowledgeable and honest. When I allocated work to my fellow classmates, he would be the first to take on the job happily to support me. Until college, the only allocating I had done was to distribute the various homework papers to the Ogres for their special use, so I took my responsibilities seriously.

The class called Henry "Elder Brother," while they called me "Elder Sister," given that we were years older than the others. In this way, we were naturally paired together and were leaders in the class.

"Where do you hope you might teach someday?" Henry asked shyly. He had stayed late in the classroom as an excuse to spend more time with me.

"In the city, definitely in a city near to my family, I hope," I said. We both knew we had no choice about where we would teach; our fate was in the hands of the government.

Dating was frowned upon in college, so we used our academic prowess and dedication to spend more time after class organizing and tidying up for the next day's class together. One day, he met me nervously in the classroom. Rustling some papers, pretending to be busy with legitimate classroom business, he whispered an invitation to go to town with him on a Saturday to see a movie.

Elder Brother and I started to see each other secretly. From then on, we stayed late in the classroom and talked after everyone else left. Because he was the local, I went to town by myself, and then he met me there. On a sunny Saturday, we went to the movies. We sat looking straight ahead. In trying to share the same armrest at the same time, we found ourselves touching. Our touching led to gazing; gazing led to holding hands—daring, hot hands. I was so nervous stealing glances at him, and my heart was beating fast like a rabbit. It was against the school rules. I was in true enemy territory.

Not many boys were ever interested in me, and I wasn't interested in them, either, because my mind was on my studies, and my goal was to become eligible for the commodity grain. Mother's inspiration had a down side. The little girl she had called a star, despite the flaws and scars, had become a proud princess at heart, in love only with books. There was only one young man in my girlhood who showed interest in me, and he was back in the brick factory.

Henry didn't really take me seriously. I was someone who could laugh wildly and talk freely, paying no attention to the details of the finer ways. I was not worried about impressing any boy. He also didn't think I was his match because he grew up in the town. With my long pigtails, I looked very much like my country past without a city girl's fashion and elegance. I was very hurt when he commented on some country girls he knew who were coarse and not virtuous. He called them an ugly name, "sunflowers." I made it clear that I still owned my virtue.

"Do you think I am a sunflower just because I am from the countryside?" I asked. I felt so insulted and was so angry with him that I cut my long hair short and dressed up to show him my grace and elegance. I enrolled and participated in the school performing arts department, acting in Shakespearean plays, dressing in gorgeous dresses, and even wearing thick makeup. I was determined not to follow in the footsteps of women who fell into the traps of the remnants of the feudal system of the past. I refused to accept the rules of the day that were imposed upon women to control them, as my grandmother had to do in accepting her bound feet. I wanted to express my true extroverted nature, and I wanted to experience the new world that was wide open in front of me.

I was too much of a spicy challenge for the traditional Henry. When I went back home for summer break, he sent me a long letter naming the reasons he should break up with me, even though there wasn't much to break. I had received many rejections, but not this kind. I immediately burned the letter. I cut my vacation short and went back to college early to confront him. Even though we had not gone far beyond two innocent hands in a movie and hours of talking about school, I could not bear to have him cast me off. My pride spoke for me. "You might regret this. I am now a special blend, not found often in your life with the genuine heart of a country girl and the fashion and sophistication of an educated city girl. Perhaps you have been too quick to judge me," I said.

真

There was little time for a budding relationship amid all of our studying and activities as class leaders. My most passionate love was found in the library. When I first discovered that I was permitted to withdraw a book at any time at no cost to me, I was elated. I swooned over the shelves of books that held the classics, the masterpieces of the world's greatest authors. Bumping my fingers along their spines, I whispered: "*The Taming of the Shrew*, William Shakespeare; *Great Expectations*, Charles Dickens; *The Adventures of Tom Sawyer*, Mark Twain; and *Pride and Prejudice*, Jane Austen." I read them one after another, quenching my thirst from the dry years of my bookless days. I read far beyond the class requirements with no self-control. My English was improving, but I could devour them only slowly at first. I thanked my limitations, for there was no other way I would want to take in the beauty of their words but to carefully savor the aroma of every phrase.

When I finished the classics, I moved on to poetry. Edgar Allen Poe's poems were addictive. They raised bumps along my arms and left me unsettled. One day, I plucked another book of poetry from its proper place and dropped down to the floor to read it. It was by a poet I did not know. Flipping the thick book open to a random page, I read. It took away my breath, and I quickly cupped my hands over my mouth to hide the grin that stretched over my shocked face. I was swept back instantly to a long-forgotten feeling that invaded my heart and traveled down my body. I smiled. The poem from the yellow book, secreted from Sister's Double's husband's bookshelf in my young teen years, had found its way back to me. The author's name was Robert Burns. My face became warm, and my lips moved to let the forbidden words escape: "Oh, my love is like a red, red rose, that's newly sprung in June; my love is like a melody that's sweetly played in tune." I audaciously read the English version of the poem again out loud, creating an echoing disturbance in the quiet room that only made me laugh more with my mouth wide open. I had the freedom to read. A strange and unfamiliar feeling passed through me, a mysterious kind of knowing, as I read the final verse: "And fare thee well, my only love, and fare thee well, a while! And I will come again my love, though it were ten thousand miles."

At our final class of the Chinese literature course, Teacher Wang singled out my composition to read to the class. He even made a comment that humbled and excited me. While holding my paper in hand, he made me stand up, and he said, "This classmate of yours is extraordinary. She will achieve great things. Just mark my words." I lowered my head. Teacher Wang didn't really know how unextraordinary I was. A rumor was passed that I was the one being selected to stay to be a professor at the college. I had studied and done well in all of the subjects to catch up with my classmates, even though my starting point was so low. No one knew the truth—that I had only five years of formal schooling before my arrival.

Graduation day had two faces: one looking back with regret that my college years were over and one looking forward with the pride of capturing the dream of being a college-educated teacher. As the oldest student, I sat in a place of honor in the center of the graduation photo. After the ceremony, we were designated as teachers, and the government assigned us our teaching positions. There was no such thing as a choice for anyone. Except for the few local graduates, all of the students wanted to teach either in the city or in their own hometowns; no one was granted the wish. We were all cast far and wide. I heard the slogan recited all around me:

The Communist Party and the Country have cultivated us,
Now it is time to answer their call,
Wherever the Party is pointing us, there we will be, all.

It was not really a surprise to me when my two classmates, Edward and Bob, were selected to stay at the college as teachers, the highest award and honor, while I was sent to a far-away assignment. What great things could I achieve, if I was not good enough to be selected to teach at my college? The great expectation turned to great disappointment. I cried privately, and Henry was the one by my side.

"There is no choice. Besides, you are a teacher, now, your dream," Henry reminded me. Finally, I wiped my tears away, counted my good fortune, and accepted my assignment to teach in the county called Xuan En in the mountainous region, far away from anyone in the world who knew me or loved me. Even though the mountainous ridges were considered the backward areas compared to the cities, I still belonged to the commodity grain status and had achieved the desired prize, the Iron Rice Bowl. I would always have a designated job and government provisions, but I would have neither the freedom to move anywhere I chose nor the ability to see my family for a very long time.

真

My assigned school was called Number One Xuan En High School. Henry was assigned to another school called Ba Jiao Middle School, located three counties away. The departure brought us closer, and we committed to each other, hoping that the flower could blossom on a stem that had been cut.

The local people in the school showed great respect to me. They spoke a local dialect, while I spoke Mandarin. I was the only one with a college degree in English that had been earned by pure testing and pure study. Teaching was a joyful job for me. English was one of the main courses emphasized from middle school to high school to university. This was one governmental change that benefited me. There was a lack of English-major students because China was just opening up to the world. My plan to avoid math in the testing resulted in my being a rare commodity—an English-speaking Chinese teacher.

My students loved me. I knew how to inspire them to achieve the highest test scores. I used humor to make the learning interesting. Even though we were English majors, we didn't have any real foreigners to teach us. Chinese were teaching English to Chinese. I was the second generation of Chinese teaching English to Chinese.

In time, I began to feel lonely, and I missed my sisters and my parents. I worried that they were getting older. Henry had forgotten his stereotype of me as a sunflower since I had become an English teacher with style. He wanted to get married so he could transfer to my school and we could live our lives together. In the meantime, we shared only a few occasional weekends. I asked the mother of one of my students, who had a high position, to take me to the marriage office. I bought a marriage license by myself. I signed Henry's name for him, and he was married without even knowing it. As Mother always said, "Act now, worry later."

A short time after our marriage, I discovered I was pregnant. Getting married was simple, but being pregnant was not. I was sick and was losing every meal I ate to the back of the building or the toilet, if I was so fortunate to arrive in time. Henry had still not received his transfer to be with me, so I was alone. I became so weak that I had to stay in the hospital to receive intravenous fluids, and I even retched the IV out. The school wasn't happy with me. I was useless as a teacher with my sickness. I felt so alone. How I wished I had been closer to Mother and my sisters. They would have taken care of me because they all had upheld this family tradition time and again while pregnant with everything flowing like the Yangtze River.

I never wanted to have babies after watching Mother struggle. I had suffered such a difficult life, and I could not control my own fate, let alone the fate of a child. My life was in the hands of the government. I did not want to have a child whose fate would be in the hands of others, as mine had been. I did not want to bring a child into a world in which I could not keep the promise of a good life. When I first told Henry I did not plan to have children, he said, "Oh, I will have to talk to my family about that." Another sign that my fate was not of my own design. The subject was dropped. Within a few months, I was only skin and bones. After six months, I had somehow recovered, and my belly was protruding. Eventually, I had to wear a big men's jacket from Henry to cover myself when I stood in front of the students. When I led them to read the new words in a rhythm, the baby moved in rhythm, too. I was amazed it was still alive after months of so little nutrition. I was Mother's daughter with my invincible belly. In my misery, I appreciated and understood her choice of names for me from a different angle— *Really Enough*, for certain.

When I became pregnant, my colleague suggested that because of the bad economic conditions, I should have an abortion. I was a coward; the child was allowed to grow. I had heard too many stories from my sisters about the suffering they experienced giving birth alone in the fields. With no mother, no phone, and no one to ask about this new thing that was about to happen, I took the bus to Henry's mother's house so that I could at least be closer to a better hospital.

We had no maternity training. The horrible tales of mishaps and misery were our only initiation into the secret world of birthing. Therefore, the wetness I discovered on the bamboo chair where I sat at Henry's home was a mystery to me. I moved to the other chair and, embarrassed, I found the same outcome within minutes. We had no toilet facilities, so I had to walk to the public toilet, but the leaking would not cease. Frightened, when I returned, I finally had the courage to ask my mother-in-law about the flowing urine.

"Your water has broken. It is a sign you are ready to give birth. You need to go to the hospital right away!" she said, alarmed.

Leaving immediately, I walked one hour to reach the hospital, arriving with water soaking my shoes. I checked in at the reception desk to the sounds of women screaming. I told the nurse about the breaking of my water, and she hurried me into the labor room.

"You are lucky you didn't drop dead!" she said. She elevated my feet and told me to be grateful I was alive.

Next to me in the labor room was a very pregnant woman in tears.

"Are you all right?" I asked. "Don't worry, it won't be long you will be holding your little child," I said to comfort her.

She was in despair. "I will never hold this baby. I am not married to the father, so they will not let it live." She was emotionless by the time they carried her out into the operating room.

The pain struck me, sudden and intense. I screamed, shredding and twisting the wet sheet. There were no pain relievers and no visitors because it was too personal a thing in a woman's life. The nurse came in to check my status and impersonally inserted her fingers to measure.

"One finger," she said and walked away.

I continued my lonely, torturous night, screaming, not knowing what to expect. "Doctor, where is the doctor?" I called out, but no one came. The nurse brought in another roommate. I continued my wailing as each deep pain grabbed me.

Finally she said, "Why are you screaming? Your natural time is here—melon ripe, stem falls. Your baby is ripe and about to drop, like fruit ready to leave the vine. I am here to have my baby taken from me. I am not allowed to have it. I should be the one screaming. My husband was fixed, but it failed, and we have our quota already. I would love to keep it; it could be a boy," she said.

After she was taken from the room, I suffered through the night alone, feeling wretched, adding my painful moans to the cries of a dozen other women. Finally, when the measurement was the right number of fingers, the nurse said, "All right, get up now, it's time to go to the delivery room."

"I don't think I can walk," I answered.

"Yes, they all say that, but they all can walk. Come on, now."

She held me under my arm, and I dragged my spent body into the delivery room. On July 23, ten days after the start of the summer break, I had the baby who had held me hostage for those long months. As soon as the baby was born, I again walked to the recovery hall, where dozens of women spent a day waiting for the first sight of their babies. As the milk came in, it was good luck to press the excess milk from both breasts and throw it against the wall. The dingy wall was already marked with the smears of a thousand women's first milk.

Henry was outside in the hallway waiting for the news. He admitted to having a split second of disappointment after he heard it was a girl. It was supposed to be a full moon that night, but instead it was raining, lightning, and thundering. I gave her an English name, "Light," wishing her to be smart and full of light.

A few other birthing mates had their babies on the same day. When we received our babies, only Light was wrapped in a red-colored floral blanket; the rest were in just plain white. I found out it was because Light was the only girl. Whenever people asked, "Is it a girl or boy?" the answer was, "A girl," and the congratulations became comforting with a softer sympathetic tone, "Well, that's good, too."

真

The days repeated themselves, delivering me a life of sameness. It wasn't until Light was two years old that Henry finally got permission to transfer to teach in the same school with me. He quickly became content with his life. He was a good teacher, a good father, and a good housekeeper, as well. I was restless. Because I grew up with nothing to cook, nothing to clean but the clothes on our backs, and a dirt floor, Mother had no need to teach me much housework or cooking. Her lessons were all about books. My attention span started to diminish. I was tired of the life in the mountainous region. A storm was gathering black clouds on my mountain and deep restlessness in my heart. I had still not reached the dream of the city.

Perhaps it was the seed of Mother's dreams for me that made this gripping hunger in me, I thought as I fell into a dream. I dreamed of a night of swirling images, dark and threatening, the years of repressing hopes that made me restless, wanting more, wanting my fullest self to take off from this mountain and fly with the full feeling of the wind. When I awakened, I could not share my dreams with Henry. I had dreamed in English for the very first time.

He feared my greedy, strange self who wished to transfer to the city so we could watch TV, receive mail faster, and watch movies—all of the new things that were happening in the city. True, all of it, I wanted all of it and much more. I could not even define the "more" I sought, but the city dreams drove me. Henry was practical, and he didn't want to dream in vain. He believed we were fortunate enough to have the Iron Rice Bowl, knowing we had to go where we were told to go and work where we were told to work. I believed that "fortunate enough" was not my fortune.

My transfer requests to the local government were nothing but the wind passing through the valley; they were ignored. The failure didn't stop me. I found another escape hole from the box. I went to take another entrance examination for advanced education and passed. I was accepted by the Hua Zhong University, Central China University, which happened to be the school where Sister Double Happiness had graduated in the beautiful Wuhan City. I walked among the fragrant osmanthus trees, thanking each one, thanking the flowers and thanking the sky for my magnificent freedom. I was deliriously happy—"delirious," the daily vocabulary word I had learned just in time to give expression to my soul.

Henry and Light accompanied me to the famous Wuhan City, the capital of the province. We took pictures at the East Lake where my brother-in-law, Arrival, had taken me when I was babysitting for them. The big elephant statue was still there with his nose curled up. Perhaps my nose was curled up as well, but the remote towns were at my feet, and the city was in my mind.

It was the first time Henry and Light had seen a big city like Wuhan. We had fun until the time came for them to leave. Henry was to drop Light off in the care of Sister Enough, and he would take the ship and three-day bus trip back to Xuan En School. I held my daughter with the fierceness that I wished Mother had been able to hold me with when I left for college. So many things that were just not done in Chinese culture had become so natural to my English-speaking self. Hugging and kissing my daughter was a strange Western way I had come to love. It fit my heart, and I knew it would be many months before I would see my little girl's face again. I studied it carefully. Then I took her hand and walked her to the bus. When I placed her little hand in her father's loving hand, my heart split.

CHAPTER 20
THE OCEAN DEVIL

The campus was huge and beautiful, with so many old, tall buildings that housed the classrooms and the dormitories. I could easily get lost there. It was a fine university. I was so proud of Sister Double Happiness, who earned her degree from such an impressive school.

It seemed I was never able to escape the pattern of being the older student learning with the younger students. While other adult students were grouped into a special separate class, I was placed with the first-year students. It gave me an advantage because it challenged me to study harder to keep up with the younger students in the full curriculum.

There were two American teachers, a couple named Robert and Jean who were our English professors. This was the first time I had learned English from an English-speaking native. With a better foundation in English, I spent more time with these "Ocean Devils." We went shopping, and we spent time visiting and talking together.

One afternoon, as I was walking on the campus after class, I passed by a young blond foreigner. I remembered the first time the Ogres spoke of the important things imported from the Yang Gui-zi, the Foreign Devils, the Ocean Devils. I had thought of it my whole life as simply a label, not an insult, although it was clear the Chinese people used it both ways. This Yang Gui-zi was intensely watching the physical education teacher demonstrate Tai Chi.

"Hi," I said, casually breezing by, practicing my English, not really caring if he heard me or not.

"Hi," he said, as he caught up with me.

We introduced ourselves. He taught non-English majors. He lived in the same Foreign Guest House building as Robert and Jean. His name was Danny.

Later, when we went out shopping, Danny came along, too. Even though he was a little short for a Foreign Devil, I thought he was very handsome, with big hazel eyes and white skin. It was his second time in China, having come to teach right after he graduated from college, where he had majored in psychology. He introduced me to his Chinese teacher Min, "Nimble," an English teacher at the university. I also met a female student of his named Wan, "Curve."

Danny caught the flu. All the foreign colleagues avoided their contagious friend, but I went to keep him company. I entertained him by telling him about a movie I had just seen from beginning to end. I thought it helped him to relax, and he enjoyed it. The truth came out later; he was dying to interrupt me, but I hadn't left a breath of space. One late afternoon, we happened to encounter each other on the campus. We picked a seat under the tree at a round stone table and chatted away. I told Danny about my daughter, Light, and my husband, Henry.

Danny looked me in the eyes and said, "Your husband is so lucky to have you. You are extraordinary."

"You think so?" I asked. I was astonished to hear a compliment like that. Henry had never said anything like that to me. Did he ever appreciate me? I started to question. Why did Chinese people rarely say such things like "I love you"? Why was that considered so unattractive, so uncomfortable? Why did we stand and lower our heads as the only expression of love at the most emotional times in our lives? For all the deep love and gratitude I had for Mother, all I had was a nod to express it. I had never even heard words of love between my parents. Their relationship was simply practical, although I knew they must have loved each other in some way after all those years. I felt I was different from the other people from my culture. Did I have the heart of an Ocean Devil? I liked to hear the soft sound of Danny's words. It was as though the pages of the lovely books of poetry had come alive—the yellow books my sister had hidden from me. It was my nature to have strong affection toward people. I enjoyed expressing myself. As a Chinese woman, I was not regular; I was strange.

The first time I went home after I entered the college, I took the liberty to hug Mother with my arms tightly wrapped around her, and I kissed her on the cheek. It shocked everyone around us. They thought I had become corrupted by English and foreign ways. Secretly, Mother loved it; she didn't think I was strange. She and I were so much alike in many ways. She told me many times, "Zhi yin nan mi—a soul mate is hard to find," but I didn't quite understand what that meant, although I know she never found hers. Was Henry my soul mate? He called me sunflower; he didn't like to hear me sing; he didn't think I was good-looking with my unusual-sized chest; he accused me of behaving like a royal empress when I was suffering from the sickness of my pregnancy; and he...wasn't...Danny.

Danny had such a gentle, sweet, soft nature. He was so understanding and tolerant and kind, from the way he spoke about me to other people to the way he respected people who were different from him. We became friends, eating breakfast in the cafeteria together sometimes, or going out with others in a group. He was attentive to me, and I always had a wonderful time when he was around.

I appreciated his standard native English, and he could always answer my English questions. He appreciated me for my joyful character. All of my ways that were strange to my own people, including the outgoing, funny side that made Mother worry that no one would want to marry me, were charming to Danny. He wrote letters to his friend, Frances, back in America, telling her that I was radiant and full of life. He loved my loud laughter. He said he enjoyed hearing me sing Peking opera. *Did I unexpectedly encounter my rare and special match Mother had spoken about? Could a Foreign Devil American be my true soul mate?* I wondered.

It was on a cold, late autumn evening when we wandered into the campus botanical garden. It was quiet. We were alone. The air was chilly, and our voices made two misty clouds that suspended above us, blending into one as we talked.

"You must be cold," Danny said.

He took my chilled hand in his and buried it in the warmth of his jacket pocket. My head snapped in both directions, searching over my shoulder to make sure no one was looking. The blood drew to my face, and despite the cold air I became red, and perspiration moistened my cheeks. My fear began at my mouth; I should have said something. It moved to my hand; I should have pulled away. When it reached my heart where the memory of the red, red rose lived, the clanging cymbals quieted and I was helpless to withdraw. I left my trembling hand to warm within his pocket. It was the first time we had touched. I could not believe that the elusive yellow-book romance was happening to me. It was dreamlike. It was evil, wrong, and lovely.

I just wanted to close my eyes and blindly follow him anywhere he would take me—close my eyes to prevent me from seeing this Ocean Devil holding my hand and unthinkably touching me. He was like a dream, a fantasy. We stopped talking, and when the wisps of our conversation disappeared above us and the dream cloud cleared, I was ashamed by what I had done. I was a married woman; I was a sunflower.

A sense of guilt overshadowed the windfall of joy. It was wrong of me to do this. *I shouldn't betray my husband,* I thought. My heart was tortured, but still I didn't have the will power to withdraw my hand from his pocket. Our hands were glued with the moist heat of my fear and my passion. I felt the warmth pass from our hands to my flesh, to my soul.

Sister Double's warnings of the yellow books of poetry had merit. She understood more than her yellow-furred fledgling sister ever could have understood. For the words burst from a dangerous place in which I had kept them. As he squeezed my hand, they came tumbling from my heart, words that I never had the joy of understanding, words that overcame my senses. I could have stood there all night in the frigid cold melting from the warmth of it all, melting from the resurrected words, "Oh my love is like the melody that's sweetly played in tune."

My forbidden mouth sang a small part from the Peking Opera, there, out loud with Danny's eyes deep inside me. The melody kept reality at a safe distance, but as the song ended, it rolled in over me and took my knees. If I were caught, I would be expelled from the school. The rumors would destroy Sister Double, Mother, my family, my reputation, and Henry, for certain. It was illegal to have an affair, to even allow myself these feelings. The shame of my black status had returned by my own hand, tucked lustfully in a foreign man's pocket.

It was hard not to think of each other. The next day, we met again.

"I did not sleep all night. I cried alone in my room asking my God 'Why, why is she married?'" he said to me.

Then, he showed me his Bible, reading me a passage that said all men were brothers. He didn't want to hurt Henry because in his God's eyes, he was his brother. He was a sensitive man and a believer, like Mother. We both cried and felt miserable. Finally, I told Danny we could remain friends until I could speak with Henry about us.

"I will tell Henry my true feelings. If he forgives me, everything will stay the same. I will stay married, and you and I will only be friends, for which we should feel grateful. That would be good fortune for us considering what we have done," I told him. We would be forgiven, sinless. "If Henry does not want to forgive me, I will invite him to rid his life of me and ask for a divorce," I said. "Besides, I got the marriage license myself; I signed it for him. He didn't even know he was married. We never even lived together for years afterward, we had no wedding, we made no vows," I told Danny. I tried to justify my sins.

Danny smiled at the thought of it, but his face changed.

"Why would a man want to ever give up someone like you?" he asked.

"Why would he want a bad woman like me—an evil sunflower? He had never thought I was his match, anyway," I justified the fire-cracker I played with in my hands.

"Ours was a typical, practical Chinese marriage. We were the same age; we were the leaders of our class. In this brief time, I have connected more with you than in my entire marriage to Henry," I said.

真

The school year was ending. Sister Enough took the bus and brought Light to Wuhan to visit me. We planned to visit her house for a while before I returned to my life teaching in the mountainous region with Henry. Before I left, I took Light to meet Danny. He was so expressive, loving, and alive. He found a big brown box for Light to play hide-and-seek in with him. She was delighted with the game and felt so safe with the playful man. She was four years old already and knew to call him "Da Ni Shu Shu—Uncle Danny." "Da Ni Shu Shu," she said, giggling and plucking at the long hairs on his arms, "you grew long hair, long hair like a monkey."

When it was time for Danny to return to the USA, and for me to graduate, I felt an overwhelming sense of loss. I waited for Danny to leave first. He ordered a huge wooden crate to put all his belongings in to ship to America. He bought me a dark green purse that unfolded into a large satchel to carry my few things home. He was so thoughtful. I treasured that bag very much for a long time. I used it until, like me, it fell apart.

I accompanied him to the airport with his student, Curve. She was graduating and was assigned to work as a teacher in Guangzhou, her hometown, which was the most desirable fancy city for any graduate. She was a modern young woman, living the modern lifestyle. She carried fine tissue in her purse, which I considered a luxury, and she had a boyfriend.

It was at the airport that Danny and I disclosed to her that we were in love with each other. It was so rewarding and exciting to share this secret with our closest friends and receive their understanding and support, which we desperately needed. We told only a few trusted friends: Curve; Danny's Chinese teacher, Nimble; and my best friend and roommate, Celine.

"Why can't we married women have a choice anymore?" she said in support of my relationship with Danny.

"What we are doing, it goes against all tradition," I said. "I wish things were different. I wish I had a choice."

As I watched Danny evaporate from my days, I felt a loss beyond all losses, beyond my understanding, with little hope that our oceans could be crossed.

CHAPTER 21
RESCUING THE YELLOW YOLK

I was not eager for my journey back to the remote mountainous region at all, not after my two years in the most modern, biggest city in the province. The only comfort was Light, who wouldn't leave my sight after living without me at Sister Enough's house for two years. She was able to read children's books already. I had ached for her, missing her so much. As we left for our home, I ached for her, for what I had done.

It was the same return route, but everything seemed rougher. The big ship wasn't as exciting as before, and the winding, long bus ride was bumpy and stiff. It was so frightening to look down at the bottomless cliffs as the bus crawled to the top of the mountains, and it was equally unnerving when it snaked down the sharp curves on the edges of the road. The motel was filthy. The white quilt had turned a dark gray from the body grease and sweat of travelers passing through.

Finally, we arrived. Henry was happy to see Light and to have me back home. We were a united family again after the long separation. We were living on the fourth floor in the school apartments provided to the teachers. Nothing had changed much. We had our first color TV, but we never had steady reception. Light loved to watch the Disney cartoons such as Mickey Mouse and Donald

Duck. She always cried when the TV screen changed into snowy dots. Then we would go to the balcony to watch the tower on the top of the hill far from the school. Not until the red tower light came on would the picture come back. Sometimes the red light did appear from the tower, but it was too late for the TV programs.

It took me a little while to adjust to the old lifestyle. I didn't feel it was necessary to tell Henry about the episode between Danny and me. On the bus ride home, I made the decision to be a good wife, to keep my simple, faraway life safe from my own uncontrollable emotions. I didn't want to cause any drama, chaos, or have any "news" pass, which would lead to a huge explosion in our close-knit community. I pushed the mountainous red-hot ball of feelings down inside me, certain that, in time, I could bury it deep enough to quiet its screams, deep enough to prevent its eruption.

After the summer break, it was Henry's turn to go to receive an advanced education. He was accepted at a different school from mine but in the same city, Wuhan. As for me, two of the high school senior classes were assigned to me to teach. It was an honor. I would be responsible for their high scores in English. The primary goal of the senior year was the success of the National Entrance Examination, just like the one I had taken. Unlike my own fears around taking the test myself years before, I had the confidence to make it happen for my students. I was so proud that the average score of my classes ranked number two in our large regional district. Because native English-speaking professors had trained me, the expectations were even higher. Parents were thrilled when they heard their children belonged to my class.

The new term was approaching. As I was preparing to teach, Light was ready to go to first grade, and Henry was preparing for his move to Wuhan. I believed that with Henry gone, I would more easily become skilled in my practice of exorcising my love for Danny. Little by little, I would release the pressure from the smoldering passion within me that was threatening my peace daily.

The school office was open with mail service and new-student registration. One afternoon, Henry came home from the office with Light's favorite children's magazine and a blue envelope with foreign stamps.

"There is a letter from the USA for you," Henry told me with a smile. "Must be your professors."

I felt the hot blood rush to my face, and my head slammed like I was struck by lightning. I snatched the letter from Henry's hand and darted to the balcony. Danny remembered me, and he even wrote my address and name in Chinese with a child-like handwriting, so cute. I felt the two sides of a chasm separating in me, an earthquake of feelings threatening to release an explosion of buried emotions. I stood holding on to the railing, not daring to open the letter. I was desperate to be alone with the violence of my feelings, to prevent the overflow of scorching, hot lava into my sweet, simple life. There was no privacy in my little apartment. There was no need for privacy where there was no need for secrets.

"How much fun!" Henry said, following me to the balcony, wanting to read the English letter to see if he could understand the words of a foreigner, a native speaker.

"No!" I held the envelope tightly in my hands. He looked at me, confused. In a family between husband and wife with no concept of having something of your own, my reaction was very strange to Henry. It was telling.

I waited impatiently, nervously, until the next day when Henry was away at the market. When I opened the letter, a picture of Danny fell out. I stared at his sweet smile, and his big, hopeful eyes stared back at me. He was so soft, peaceful, patient, and trusting. I knew I was disappointing him. I had to disappoint someone, no matter what I did. I wept without control.

His letter was simply informing me that he was back in the USA safe and sound, and everything was "organized." The word "organize" was a secret code for us, derived from a sound-alike Chinese word. It meant "I love you more." We found opportunities to use that word when we were with other people. We would look at each other smiling, sharing our secret interpretations whenever others stumbled on the topic of organizing. "We need to organize the students," someone would say. We agreed, saying, "Yes, we should organize" with a wink. It was our secret message of love.

With me in the far-flung mountains of China in my assignment of no choice, and Danny in California in the west of America, we had this huge ocean between us, and it seemed fantasy to think I would ever be able to cross it. I couldn't even save a little money to visit my parents on the other side of the province. Tears kept running wild. Just then, Light's TV show stopped playing again, and she rushed in, whining. She stopped when she saw my tears and Danny's picture.

"You miss Da Ni Shu Shu, Mama?"

The doorknob turned, and Henry came home. Light thought she could help to cheer me up by running to Henry, saying, "BaBa, Mama is crying because she misses Da Ni Shu Shu!"

"So, Marggie, you have anything to tell me about your professor from America?" Henry asked with a calm voice but with eyes that burned through me.

"No." I refused to discuss it. "He is not *my* professor," I continued. "Please leave me alone. I will be fine."

Henry took Light to play at the Green River close to the school. I was by myself. Finally, I had a chance to cry out. I felt deep fear. I could feel it erupting, the uncontrollable voice of the truth demanding to be told. I rushed down the stairs from the fourth floor with one breath. I ran toward the river. It was at the bank of the river as Light played nearby, with winded breath that I told Henry about Danny. He had the right to know, and I would let him decide our fate. He said nothing but looked out over the water, called to Light, and walked her home. My news was whisked away like an annoying fly that had no chance of returning. I was left by the bank of the river feeling the crushing weight of guilt fill in the empty hole I had opened up inside me with my truth.

真

The time came for Henry to leave for Wuhan for school. Light and I saw him off. He hadn't mentioned my admission. He had made no clear decision, and I didn't dare to ask. Just as the bus was moving, Henry stuck his head out of the window and said, "Out of sight, out of mind. I am sure you will forget about that professor." He left with hope, and I remained with a heavy heart. The irony of his words hung around my heart, for he, too, was "out of sight, out of mind," and I was left to wonder.

Light and I were together starting our new life's routine on our own. Either I took her to school in the morning or she would go with her little friend, Ying, "Clear." I prepared our lunch at midday. In the afternoon, I was busy teaching two classes. In the evenings, I prepared dinner, corrected papers, and went to teacher meetings. Every day was the same schedule, the same routine. Light had the same hard time with the TV, and the washer couldn't wash anything clean, so I still washed our laundry by hand, and I moved through it all slowly with the solid weight of guilt that filled my soul.

Light was a big help. She went to the cafeteria to bring up food and sometimes stopped at the school office after school to bring home her own children's magazine. She was my independent one. Then one day she came home with another letter from Danny. I opened it up eagerly. There were beautiful stickers for Light in the fold of the letter.

"Look what came!" I said, and Light tried to grab them from my hand.

"Shi ni de ma—Are they yours?" she asked. In a return letter, I told Danny what Light had said and how she loved the stickers. Danny was so happy and forever remembered Light's remark. It became a favorite phrase for him that he could say so well in Chinese, "Shi ni de ma?"

The most exciting thing for Light was when she received a parcel from Danny. It was a Mickey Mouse puppet. Light was the only child perhaps in all of China who had a real Disney toy. It was heaven on Earth compared to that rabbit I had made.

真

During spring break, Henry made an unexpected visit home. When he arrived, Light and I were eating dinner. He looked at our food. "So, you both live on food like that?" He felt pity for us because I couldn't cook a decent meal. Every meal still seemed a scramble. He was so much better at cooking and house cleaning. His purpose in coming back was to have the heart to finally talk of the future. He was hoping to salvage our marriage, and I was convinced to try, too. There were so many reasons to try. There was too much to fear, too many people to lose through the fraying, broken bottom of our woven basket—colleagues at the school, my students by the hundreds, our friends, and our families.

I thought of Sister Complete Happiness telling me that she was afraid of foreigners because they looked scary. Then there was Henry's mother, a very industrious, kind woman who raised all of her children by herself because she was widowed as a young woman. She loved Light very much. How could I take her away? She took a bus to bring a gift for Light's first birthday even though she had to suffer from motion sickness for days. I didn't want to hurt the feelings of those who loved me. My reputation would be ruined; rumors would run their teeth off. I would be regarded as a sunflower woman, an unworthy wife who was selfish and unfaithful, abandoning her own motherland in seeking the luxury of the Ocean Devil's land. I couldn't just live for my selfish self; I had to live for others.

My status as a high school teacher was a rare dream that had come true. It was like heaven walking into the classroom, being respected, honored, and even worshiped by my students. I could walk out on the street with my head held high and no fear of being called a Landlord hog, no worry about rice for the next meal. I was eating the commodity grain. I was living a life beyond my childhood dreams—certainly not a life of the wealthy few, but well above the bottom from where I had come. Yes, I had a hundred reasons to enjoy what I had and to live just happy to be alive. But my efforts to be satisfied fell short. I was racked miserably with the torture of my inexplicable depth of desire.

真

Loudspeakers overtook a normal, peaceful Saturday morning. They were having a public execution meeting in our school's large central square. I had heard the horrific details of the mother who was put on the stage for public viewing before she was shot. She was guilty of using a sickle to injure a neighbor who had spread rumors about her husband's infidelity. She stood guarded by female police. She pleaded, worried that her children would not remember her. The police postponed her fate only long enough to snap a picture to satisfy her last wish.

Another execution was held, right there in my school and in my space. I was feeling dreadful about the primitive practice, while others found it electrifying. It was contaminating the school, which was meant only for learning. I continued teaching in my classroom, trying to hide myself from the loudspeaker, trying to escape it. I stepped out into the concrete toilet room to escape, but I could still hear it. I ran to my apartment and closed all the doors, but I could hear it. I buried my head in the pillows, but I could still hear it, both the accusation over the loudspeaker and the sound that I knew was about to split the air.

Finally, I decided to run to the Green River. I grabbed Light, and like a tornado, we swept down the stairs. There in the court-yard that we had to cross, I encountered the tied-up criminal. My eyes met his. He was my former student. He looked at me plead-ingly, and I froze. I covered Light's eyes and ran with her until the sound was just an echoing pop. His look haunted me for years. It was the final cruelty of the government's ways that made me real-ize I simply could not remain.

Later, Henry was very disturbed when he saw me putting dish soap into the cooking pan instead of oil and keeping the shells but throwing away the eggs. He started to worry about my mental state.

"I don't know how your Ocean Devil really feels about you. We all know the westerners don't take love seriously. If he makes a promise to me that he will never mistreat you, never leave you, I will be willing to apply for a divorce."

I did not turn around from the sink where I was desperately trying to rescue the yellow yolks from slipping down the drain. I trembled, knowing the unthinkable and devastating storm I had created. I feared the terrible words that would break into my world like thunder and the lightning that would strike each heart as I took my daughter and walked away. The thousands of fallen leaves that would explode in the air around the selfish decision I would make would be devastating. I would destroy everything I knew and had strived for, and I would break the Iron Rice Bowl forever if I chose to live on the other side of the Earth amid the Ocean Devils. I had to choose. I chose the complete unknown; I chose the Devils.

CHAPTER 22
THE CURVE IN THE ROAD

I was in a daze, but Danny was thrilled to hear the news, and he said he would make the trip to China to make the promise to Henry, in person. I took a trip to Guangzhou, my first time out of my province, to meet Danny at the airport. My nephew, Sister Double Happiness's son Bo, "Vigor," was with me.

Guangzhou was an even bigger city than Wuhan. For the first time, to my great astonishment, I saw disposable plastic spoons and forks being swept away in a dustpan. I wished to pick them up and save them for later, to send them to my family for a special gift, but I restrained myself.

When Danny arrived, he had a very special gift for me—a personal, embarrassing, but touching gift that made me realize that he saw me and understood my suffering; he brought me my first bra. Not a fancy, alluring thing, but simply a sports bra that would allow me to be myself. I had confided in him about my lifelong embarrassment in China from the overgenerosity of the gods when it came to my chest. I had no freedom to run, and I was hindered when playing sports without any support to keep the mocking eyes of the men or the discomfort away. I spent much time hunched over or moving with one arm across the embarrassment. It was such a hindrance. This was not something I would speak of to my

Chinese husband, but the cultural barriers seemed to evaporate with my cross-cultural love. His thoughtfulness touched me.

Danny, Vigor, and I took the long-distance train from Guangzhou to Wuhan, where Henry was waiting to meet Danny at his hotel. Their meeting was cordial, and I thought the communication went well. Danny wrote a promise contract accepting all of Henry's terms. The conversation then turned to the fact that Henry was still in love with me. Danny threw his hands in the air as if he were surrendering.

"If you can change into a more communicative person so you can make Margaret happy, I will be willing to back off," Danny said.

"I do not feel I have anything to change," Henry said. "But I do wish to try to make her happy as my wife."

Danny emphasized that all he wanted was my happiness. I got so mad at both of them. I wasn't a commodity for anyone to negotiate over. It was late evening. Unable to listen to another bartering word, I took off into the darkness to take a bus to sleep with Light at my friend Victoria's house.

真

The year 1989 was eventful. The students had a massive uprising demanding democracy in Beijing's Tiananmen Square, which attracted the attention of the outside world. Danny was closely watching the events from the other side of the Pacific. He was so anxious about Light and me, urging us not to go into the streets. He wished we were with him in America during this dangerous and unpredictable time and made me call him collect so he knew we were safe.

The demonstrations echoed nationwide, and the waves of uproar swept far, reaching all corners of China, as far away as the remote mountains, where I remained teaching. The students were within inches of receiving recognition from the government, and a victory of democracy was near. With both excitement and chaos, a pulsating country was anticipating a new era, thanks to the scholars who gave voice to the unheard and the demonstrated bravery of the martyrs. The student leader, Wu'er Kai Xi, was able to show heightened power by rudely accusing Premier Li Peng of arriving at the negotiation meeting late. I shivered when I saw that on TV. I thought the students shouldn't lose their fundamental courtesy and manners toward people, so as not to lose the delicate respect of their supporters, not to mention the fact that they were on television with the Premier. I felt they needed dignity to reach the people on the fringe.

The voice of democracy sounded louder and louder in the streets, filling the news from the twenty-four-hour radio news broadcast to the newspapers to the national official TV media. On June 4th, the dark sky fell. The massive tanks silenced all the voices to ready them for condemnation, to trump up a charge against the young activists. The intellectual leaders of the students who were once called heroes were labeled criminals. People were thrown into a state of panic and despair, fearing what to say, not knowing whom to believe. The crackdown on the demonstrators was in the spotlight, but the shock and fear people felt could be shared only in whispers.

In my small corner of the remote mountainous region, things were calmer. College students were released from school early so they would return home to avoid more trouble in the cities. They brought home rumors, news, and tragic stories that I could not fully catch between the breaks on my snow-dotted screen. Henry was among the students who left the university early. He returned home with a heavy heart.

One and a half months after the Tiananmen Square turmoil, we had something to cheer us up. Light was turning six years old. She loved holidays and birthdays. We bought a big watermelon, cut it open, and put six candles on it. Birthday cakes were not a Chinese custom, but I had fallen in love with the tradition while at university. Her best friend, Clear, dressed up in a beautiful dress and celebrated with us. We sang "happy birthday to you" in Chinese. She blew out the candles just like the little Foreign Ocean Devils would do.

The promise was silently carried forward. Henry went to our school leader to request a letter to apply for the divorce, but he was flatly refused.

"No such thing, Teacher. You and Teacher Zhao are like a model couple in the school. She is a wonderful person. Are you 'feng la,' losing your mind, to divorce her? I am doing you a favor by my refusal. No, sorry," he said.

It was a citizen's legal right to marry or divorce at that time, but locals once more had control. "Mountain high, Emperor far," as Mother would say. Henry felt no one should deny him his rights. So he tried to convince the leader with his demands, starting a heated argument.

"Even the wisest judge can't marshal family affairs," Henry quoted.

Not only could he not get the letter, but he also offended the leader. The bridge was burned. At this point, it was a matter of his pride and power. Henry was on a mission to fight for his rights, and I was to be the beneficiary of his ire.

Instead of following the system rules, he was forced to use the old "guan xi," corrupt connections. In the same snake-like way that I got our marriage license on my own through an influential woman in the city, Henry looked for the right student's parent who had the right power to secure our divorce.

真

Summer was going by fast. It was September, and the school year was about to start. It was on a miserable rainy day when Henry climbed up our stairs dripping wet, pulled out an envelope from under his shirt, opened it, and handed me a piece of paper with a full, round, official red seal—our divorce. My eyes were riveted on the mark. It was the same color seal I remembered seeing on the diploma of Sister Double Happiness that burst open my parents' joy, making their eyes hold that unusual gaze—the confusing gaze that I finally understood. They were looking back and looking forward at the yin and the yang—the sacrifices of my siblings in the fields, the pain, and the losses—all traded for the accomplishments and the chance for future dreams. All of these thoughts battled and blended into that one look. I shared that same conflicted gaze as I stared at the official divorce paper shaking in my hand.

My body sank onto the hard wooden couch with the paper that Henry had kept dry.

"I hope it makes you happy," Henry said.

No thoughts could escape my muddled brain. Joy and shame, hope and fear battled in my heart, and in their standoff my throat closed to any passing. I said nothing. Light tiptoed to wipe off my tears and then went to tidy up the room by picking up her toys and books. She knew that was always a way to make me happy. Through my blurred eyes, I looked around the apartment at the furniture, the beautiful desk, Light's artwork and pictures on the wall, her marks of height at the doorway, the squeaky clean floor that Henry had mopped, and the bookshelves with our favorite Chinese and English books and diaries kept over the years. My eyes turned to Henry. "What are you going to do?" I asked him.

"Don't worry about me. I just want you and Light happy," he said.

"I want you happy, too," I said.

My heart knew Henry would have a hard time facing our disrupted and stirred-up little world. He would be questioned, sympathized with, and scorned by many. How could I just brush the dust off my dirty hands and take off, leaving him like that? Why couldn't I be satisfied with my life? Why was I so selfish? I was overwhelmed by guilt, and I couldn't help sobbing. Light was worried and started to cry, too. Henry held Light tightly in his arms; I sat alone with my guilt.

There was much to be done before school began. I didn't want to face the faculty, the students, or my shame. Escaping was the focus. I turned in my resignation and packed up only some personal necessities. I knew how to make my unworthy self disappear. I made sure to take Light to say goodbye to her friend Clear, but they were not home. I left them a note with a can of juice at the door. Beyond those few people, not even my family received my farewell. I simply slinked off like a guilty wolf taking the only chicken from a poor man's coop in my mouth, a silent departure with screaming guilt.

真

Danny was so happy that we made it to Wuhan. I stationed in Sister Double's home, which was located in an exclusive complex for the high-ranking cadres. They had a security reception office at the gate with a telephone, too. I could receive my mail there, as well. My college classmate, Victoria who lived nearby in Wuhan, was taking care of Light while I was busy preparing my ID documents. The complexity of the system held me hostage, delaying my escape into Danny's arms.

He sent me a card with a beautiful message on marriage. That same day, Curve, Danny's former student, got in touch with me. She was among the first to know of our love, two years before when she went with me to see Danny off to America. I told her the exciting news that Danny was coming to marry me. She congratulated me as any friend would, asking if Danny would like to visit her on his way through Guangzhou, where she was teaching near the international airport. Of course I wanted Danny to have someone to show him around while he was in Guangzhou before his connecting flight to Wuhan. So I gave Danny Curve's information, and I gave Curve Danny's flight-arrival information.

He called me from Guangzhou when he arrived. He told me that he had spent time with Curve and that they had hugged. He said he was so happy to see his former student, but I felt he didn't have to report that to me. I reminded myself that to Americans, hugging was just like our nodding of the head. I was truly happy that they could see each other again.

Three days later, Danny flew to Wuhan, and I went to meet him at the airport. He looked tired and told me the flight was very bumpy. I was so happy to be with him. After we arrived at his hotel, he dropped down on one knee next to me as I was sitting in a chair.

"Will you marry me?" he asked.

I laughed. "Why would you ask that? Haven't we talked about marrying already?" I asked, confused.

I had no idea about the "on one knee" American tradition for a proposal. He gave me the diamond ring that he sold his truck to buy. I didn't know how special that was. Later, I was so ashamed of myself as an incompetent English major. All I had learned in school was literature, grammar, tests, listening, writing, and speaking, but I was ignorant of the basic customs and the culture of the place I had chosen as my future home.

Danny was my true love. I wrote him a poem:

You are the sun; I am the moon,
You shine with my radiance; I glow with your light.

It took us one month to prepare the application for a marriage license because marrying a foreigner was still rare. The procedures were very complicated. Even the basic document, the birth certificate, was a huge problem; I didn't have one. Birthdays were unimportant to unimportant people. Mother didn't have the luxury of giving birth in a hospital. By lunar calendar, I was born on May 8th, but I never figured out the right date for the solar calendar. Every time I completed the long chain of paperwork, I forgot the solar-calendar date I had used earlier. As a result, I had many different birth dates that some well-meaning clerks and I had randomly selected. Somehow, I was assigned the birth date August 12th as my final solar calendar birthday with a two-year difference from my lunar Chinese calendar. I was instantly two years younger.

In the end, all the papers had to be unraveled, unified, and narrowed into one birthday, and that was the one I had to stick with for all documents. Before I could take a breath of relief, a new problem surfaced with my last name, Zhao, which against tradition and at Mother's choice didn't match my father's name, Tsai. I was required to go back to my birthplace to get a letter to explain and to prove he was my father. It proved challenging because he had passed away the previous winter. Seeing the official write the name "Tsai" on the forms saddened me. Father's death had been so difficult.

In the midst of my previous winter of chaos with Henry and Danny, just after Henry agreed to the divorce, the news arrived that Father was very ill. With the burden of my divorce and my secret transgressions weighing heavily on me, I left teaching for one month to return home to care for Father. I felt the hopelessness again as I watched him suffering with his cancer in a countryside clinic for those who had no money to pay for better. He had for his comfort an intravenous line with some unknown substance and a blanket in an otherwise bare room. Having used nearly every Yuan for the trip, I had only a small amount of money, and I pressed it into his hand.

"Thank you, Zhen'er, your mother and I can use this when I get better," he said.

"Yes, Father, you will enjoy spending it together," I said. I only wished that he could.

With my guilt filling me, I suffered the punishment of my freezing feet willingly and stayed with him until he left us, holding his blue hand. This was the ending he was given after a lifetime of being a criminal, after a lifetime as an Enemy of the State who had made no mistake except being born into success. Despite my achievement and my elevated status as a teacher, money was something I had little access to; food, yes, housing, yes, but there was no way to trade my labor for a little comfort for Father's last days, nothing to give but my cold hand in his.

My sisters arrived, and we all helped to do whatever we could. My brothers never came. In the middle of the winter just before the New Year Spring Festival, Father no longer had to run from his debtors or think about his children's suffering. He received the only true liberation he had ever had in his adult life—his own death.

I told no one of my situation or the plans for my departure with Danny. I held the shame of it in my heart as I said goodbye to Mother, my sisters, and my brothers who had arrived only in time for the funeral. I knew this would be the last time in a very long time that I would be able look into their eyes. The funeral service was simple; my life was not.

真

The trip back through the twisted mountain roads matched the treachery with which I was living. I continued the arduous paperwork process, going to the notary with the document verifying my Father's paternity. I had to travel to a specific law office to secure the notary stamp. The official English translations of the documents had to be done, then notarized and translated again, followed by more translations and more notaries. The bag that I used to carry all the documents in was wearing out.

Meanwhile, Victoria continued to take care of Light. One night, she was putting Light's socks on, but Light didn't want her to. She said to Victoria, "I don't want the socks, you little prostitute!" It was such a shocking, laughable episode to all of us that Light had used those words at her young age. After Danny heard it, he was so amused that he imitated her in Chinese, "I don't want the socks, xiao biao zi!" Later, we learned that Light had been watching TV. Since Wuhan had better reception and more channel selection, she had learned the adult words from a Chinese soap opera. Things were changing fast, and Light was learning very fast—too fast!

Finally, I had all of the documents in order. It was on October 9 that Danny and I went to apply for the marriage license. We paid the money and turned in the thick stack of papers. We were told to return in ten days to find out whether we were approved. On the tenth day, we returned and we got the license, two little red books—one for me, one for Danny—red books of a very different kind. These two little books certified that we were legally married, a Chinese woman and an Ocean Devil. We even received a box of candy. We were grateful. Danny's long travels and my exhausting trips had all paid off. When we looked at the date of the license, we realized we had been married earlier than we had known. They had used the date we applied for the marriage rather than the date we received the license.

With the required proof of marriage in hand, we were able to spend the night together. The hotel management entered our room in the middle of the night to check to make sure no extra people were staying in the room, interrupting the first relaxed night of our forbidden romance. There was no privacy. Before we could catch enough sleep, the early cleaning man just opened the door, walked in, and started his cleaning. There was no such thing as locking your own door or having your own key in China, either; the hall monitor handled that. Danny was very angry. He yelled at him in English while I hid under the blanket, not wanting him to see me, a Chinese woman, sleeping with a foreigner.

By the end of October, with my new Chinese passport and Light's documents in order, we were eager to go to Guangzhou to apply for the American visa. Danny was anxious to go back to work. He worked as a clerk in a record store, which to me sounded like a peddler selling chestnuts on the roadside.

"Pulled eyelid, pulled eyelid, selling chestnuts," I teased him with my little childhood song.

I had decided to marry Danny, even though he was at the true peasant level in his country. I remembered Louise, the little street girl who was my image of all American children from my third-grade textbook—poor Danny, my love. Danny said he would need to start a business to support our family.

"So we would both be small-business classification? Do you have a lesser Landlord status?" I teased. Danny laughed. "Good thing Mother doesn't know about my being an in-house daughter-in-law to an Ocean Devil family," I continued, only half kidding. Danny encouraged me that with hard work, we could change our lives in America.

"I can't imagine—hard work in China only gets you more of the same," I said, laughing.

Although I had finally escaped my own classification, it was a freedom I could not begin to understand. I wondered what glorious things Light might choose to be. I decided that I did not have a single concern about marrying a peddler, for I knew how to rise.

Henry saw us off at the train station.

"Henry," I pleaded, "let me help. I can ask Sister Double's husband, Arrival. Maybe he can help you transfer to Wuhan so you can have a fresh start, get away from wagging tongues." I looked at his defeated face, and I suffered regret that my happiness required his sacrifice. "I just want to do whatever I can to make your life better, to compensate you in any way possible," I said.

"Never mind me. Nothing can compensate me even if I was extolled as an emperor. I have something important to tell you. There was a letter that arrived at the home of Sister Double Happiness addressed to Danny. Sister heard the mistake you made by letting Danny stay in Guangzhou with that woman, Curve. She must be eager to steal Danny from you. Do you want the letter? I have it here with me."

My heart sank. Danny had spoken of her constantly with much affection. I was suspicious, but I could not admit this to Henry, who had just sacrificed so much to let me go.

"No, I do not want the letter. Please, just keep it for me, Henry." I didn't have the strength to know what was happening between them. I could not face the mystery of the Ocean Devil's ways. I clung to the words in the poem on marriage that Danny had given me; I clung to love.

The train was moving, and Henry had one last second to hold his only daughter, Light, at the door. I watched his receding figure from the window. I felt I owed him so much. He loved me so much to have set me free; he loved me so much to try to protect me from another woman; he loved me without saying love. I was trading wordless love for loving words.

From the last glance at Henry, my eyes turned to Danny, who was sitting next to me with Light. He had fascinated me. He had burnt me alive with his passionate pursuit and flaming love. He had traveled so far to capture my love. One of his letters to me was nothing but a page full of the word LOVE. The more I thought about the letter from Curve, the more I became suspicious. He had often mentioned Curve in our conversations. He adored her. Did he want her? Could three days with the modern woman in Guangzhou replace three years of our earth-shaking love? *How powerful was the forbidden fruit?* I wondered. Was I the mere sunflower?

My jealousy rose up caustic in my throat, latching on to my soul like the double-mouthed leeches, impossible to pull free. My heart became heavier as the train reached closer to Guangzhou. I suspected that Curve was not an innocent sweet friend of ours anymore. What other motive could she have had in writing a letter to Danny and not to both of us? My imagination went wild. I feared the evil glare of her eyes were full of tricks; I feared I was walking into the monster's gullet.

CHAPTER 23
READY FOR WAR

It was the last week of November. The weather was much warmer in Guangzhou than in Wuhan. My head was still vibrating with the clunking of the rails after I got off the train. We dragged our luggage and carried Light to the Bai Yun Hotel, "White Cloud Hotel." We chose the room with two beds, one for Light and one for us. "One for us." I could not say it so easily, this unheard-of phrase, "one for us." We were "us."

Light was a very good girl, knowing how to entertain herself by playing with her Mickey Mouse puppet and drawing. Even though she knew no English, she called Danny "Daddy." They both shared a great natural bond as father and daughter without any pretention. But the bond between Danny and me was breached, weakened, and damaged. I was like an anxious cat waiting at the hole of a fat rat, positioned to charge and catch. If the word "Curve" came out of his mouth, it would give me all the fuel I needed to pounce. I feared that his love, his written promises to Henry, were all purely a game. Did he deserve to act as a father to Light? I dropped everything—my career, my reputation, my free health care—in pursuit of love; I feared it would all evaporate like dew in the sun.

I had dropped the Iron Rice Bowl forever. Once the bowl was broken, there could be no repair. It would be all in vain if it were true that westerners had no lasting love, as Henry had warned me. Jealous thoughts were like foreigners who moved in uninvited like a gang of Evil Ogres, taking up all the space in my mind, but these Ogres were not kind. Envy was the price I paid for passion. I spoke to the imaginary traitor's face out loud, my hot-lava thoughts boiling up, gathering heat, ready to erupt. "Curve, how tricky you are, disguised as my friend, urging me to telegraph you his arrival plans so you could seduce him. You thought you were clever to use my trust to satisfy your plot; you thought chasing him with your letter would somehow allow you to catch him?"

The night with Danny was peaceful, with no mention of the unmentionable woman. The next day, we were occupied with schedules, having physicals, shots, and preparations to apply for the visa. While waiting for the results, we had some free time on our hands, so we went out to play in the park, but my mind wasn't free. I was still obsessed with fear, anger, and confusion.

I sat on the long bench in the park as Danny and Light's playful, laughing voices faded away. In the soft rays of the winter sun, exhaustion invaded me. My mind and body became heavier, and I felt myself drift off. I dreamed of Mulan and my Empress protecting me from the woman who wished to destroy my happiness. I heard the comforting voice of DaDa. She wore an Empress headdress with delicate tassels of pearls and jade. Her gold imperial robe was alive with a dragon, a phoenix, and blossoms of peonies. She opened her arms and wrapped me in her long, flowing sleeves. We sat on our golden chair, and I felt so loved again. My tears stained her silk sleeves. "She looks like a monster with a wide-open fierce mouth and poisonous claws, and she is going to tear me into pieces," I said to DaDa. I felt a soft feather brush my cheek. When I opened my eyes, Light was tickling my sleeping face with a wild flower.

It was dinnertime. Danny said to me, "Let's go invite Curve to have dinner with us."

I violently shook the dream from my head. The irony of his words pushed me back against the bench. I had the urge to scream, to explode, to interrogate and spit the pent-up anger right in his face, but I shuffled back my sharp arrows and quivered. Only one word came out of my mouth as I rose from the bench and looked at Danny: "Why?"

"What do you mean, why? She is our friend, isn't she?" An innocent blanket wrapped his words. Was this the snake tongue of the Ocean Devil I was warned about, or was my loving Danny the person I dreamed he would be? I could not tell. I was so unaccustomed to the subtleties of life, so innocent and confused by matters of romance and emotion. I knew only the black of burning books or the joy of pure white rice. "Yes or no?" I screamed in my head. I dug the sharp-ended bamboo pole into the earthen floor, ready to confront him. I answered the question myself before the truth could destroy my faith and my high-cost love for Danny.

"Oh, yes, you are so right…she is a friend," I said with a venomous and sarcastic edge that traveled from my words and hung on the corner of my mouth. I took a deep breath, trying hard to calm myself. He was not the Party Representative coming to take Mother to the accusation meeting; he was my gentle Danny. I breathed, but I couldn't keep the lid on the boiling pot; I had to let it out. I was afraid to ask the question. I took the coward's path. "She is your friend—yours, not mine!" I said. "Go ahead, have dinner with her yourself."

It was the first time Danny had seen my rare and furious Mulan side—my rude and rebellious nature when someone I loved was threatened. This time it was my own self and my daughter I was protecting. He should have seen my shredded cotton worker's fingers; he should have seen me violently pulling double-mouthed leeches from my leg; he should have met the taunted Landlord hog; he should have known the little girl who used her haunted voice to curse an evil man's son to protect her mother. He should have seen it all. *He should have felt my soul's ache while he still had a chance to change his mind*, I thought. But two wide brown eyes were looking up with fear. For Light, and only for her, I could not let the rushing violent waters break the dam.

The evening at the White Cloud Hotel wasn't peaceful. I eagerly waited for Light to go to bed and then pressed Danny to tell me what happened between him and Curve when he stayed in Guangzhou. I was ready to confront him calmly with my daughter sleeping sweetly on the far side of the room.

"What was the hug you reported to me? Was it like shaking hands? If not, like what? Do you want her instead of me? A modern woman not burdening you with a child?"

I looked toward the little lump under the blanket. I had taken her from all that she had ever known. Was I taking her little hand into the fields of another kind? I left no space for him to answer. "You can take your Curve," I said with resignation. I hadn't had many choices in my life, so I gave this one to him, as well.

"Can I speak now?" he asked. I smiled but only slightly, only briefly, for even in my seething I could see the humor in my long ranting. I could see my tirade had left no space for Danny's words.

"There was nothing. She came to visit me. I admit the hug was long. We talked about our childhoods and fun things about the differences. She brought me ice cream in her backpack but forgot to give it to me, and it melted on the floor. We laughed, and that was it," he said.

"Then what was it that distracted her so much that she let the precious ice cream melt?" I asked. I understood how powerful love could be. That was what had brought me there to that confusing mess. I was willing to surrender to the karma. He only needed to admit that he was in love with her, and I was ready to drop everything, take Light with me, and flee into the underground that had been my darkest early years.

Danny was exhausted, and he held his head with his hands. It was late, and I was still demanding an answer when there was none.

"Just say it! You love her!"

"I don't f—— love her!" he said. For the first time I saw him hysterical, matching my insanity with his own. This word I had only heard rarely and never in reference to love. I did not understand the full use of the word, but I knew Danny was either desperately guilty or falsely accused. He went to take a shower and came out. And then he went to take another shower. He started to scream. I became frightened, not understanding the explosion of the migraine in his head. He was tortured, thrashing around the room to escape the prison of his own mind. He was in uncontrollable pain. I became so worried. I begged him to relax. He told me he needed aspirin. I ran to the hotel reception asking for aspirin; they didn't have it. I came back to let him know that I was going to take a taxi to go somewhere to buy aspirin, but he dismissed the idea.

"Never mind, it will pass," he said.

I became calmer, and he became calmer. I reached out like a cautious kitten, drawing back my hand two times before I touched him. I comforted his raging head with loving fingers. We sat in silence while the storm subsided, letting the smell of the fresh rain cool us, calm us down, soothe us both. I felt unlike myself. Floating in the quiet, I listened to his heartbeat and the breathing of little Light.

Finally, he was feeling better. With tears in his eyes and a soft voice, he asked, "Do you think she would take care of me like this? Do you think anyone else is you? I love you!"

I wrapped his words around me. I knew that as much as I might absorb the Ocean Devil ways, I would never change one certain thing about my Chinese self; I may have liked hearing the unfamiliar "tell me love" of words, but I would only truly trust the "show me love" of actions. I would never trust meaningless words, only meaningful actions.

The next day, for the first time in my life, I received one beautiful red rose from Danny, his way of reassuring me of his love. I put it to my nose. It smelled so sweet. Although I had never held one, I loved roses, the symbol of love. I remembered the yellow books Sister had pried from my hands—the beautiful books with romantic poems that always spoke of roses, so foreign in my life devoid of such things. I put the rose in the glass from the hotel and added water to keep it alive.

We had the physical records and all the forms ready for the visa. The officer was a nice man. He asked where Danny was from originally. Danny told him Charlotte, Michigan.

"Oh, I am from there too. That's amazing," the officer said.

This was a good start. The man who held the final stamp for us to build our lives together was from the same village as Danny. At least in China, that would be a very good start, but fellow villagers had betrayed me before. Then he turned to Light. I stiffened. Once again I sat in fear in front of someone who held my fate in his hands. He asked Light, "Who is he?" pointing at Danny.

"He is Daddy." Light's little voice was so confident.

Danny and I were both shocked. She was able to say the only English she knew, the right English at the right time. He looked at me and then at Danny, and I saw the movement. I saw the flicker in his eyes before it traveled to his mouth. He smiled and extended his hand to mine. Our visa was granted with a stamp on our passport. That stamp gave me wings to fly free into the welcoming sky.

When you are in trust and love, you are more forgiving; I was forgiving. We invited Curve to visit us in the hotel after we had dinner together. She didn't change much from three previous years. I was surprised at how I had created her in my jealous mind. She was actually much shorter than I remembered, nearsighted with glasses framing her cunning, foxlike, slanted eyes. Her upper body stretched down a long way before it met the stubbiness of her legs. She did look athletic and strong, so on that account, my memory was correct. Because it was late when we finished dinner, I encouraged her to spend the night if she didn't mind sleeping with Light in her bed. I was concerned about her safety, taking the bus at such an hour.

The next day, we said goodbye to Curve, and we three took the famous Star Ferry to Hong Kong. It was marvelous, amazing, with too many things to see. Danny left us at customs because he could go through easier as a foreigner than Mainland Chinese citizens could. The male guard at customs treated me very rudely. I didn't care. Freedom and democracy were beckoning me in America, where all were treated equally, so the statue goddess with the lantern said. Finally, Danny was united with us, and off we went to the famous city of Hong Kong.

Instead of spending a night in the hotel, we spent a night in our friend Gary's apartment at Hong Kong University. He was a foreign English professor at the university where Danny and had I met. I was so happy to see him again. Gary's passion was poetry. He had translated famous ancient Chinese poems into English. He wrote many poems himself, too. I thought perhaps I would impress him with a poem that Mother had taught me as a child, one that she had plucked from the fire and sealed in her memory, a poem that I was sure he didn't know. I shared the ancient verse with him, writing character by character. The verse was about snow, using a dog as the image with no mention of the word "snow" at all:

The world is a blur
The icy well has a hole
The yellow dog turns white
Then the white dog swells.

The images brought me back to the bucket of water stuck in the frozen hole of our pond.

Gary laughed. "I didn't realize how educated you were about ancient poetry. You are something. What are you going to do in America?"

I looked at Danny, and I realized that I had no idea what I would do. Danny nodded his head and answered with a positive tone, "We'll see, we'll see."

I couldn't see. I did not have a single image to cling to, except the many times I had dreamed of my new life while looking at pictures of the scenery or the skyline of America. I had not had the audacity to dream beyond my fantasies to the life I would actually lead in America; I had only clung to the dream itself as the most fulfilling and hopeful life I could ever have imagined.

Gary took us out to dinner, and I was amazed at the high buildings, standing so close to one another like massive redwood trees in the photos of the California forest. Gary put money in the telescope for me to see the many different views of Hong Kong. It was so beautiful when evening came alive, with more lights than I had ever seen.

"This must be like the lights of America." I said.

The dark shadows of the mountains that protected the hidden harbor faded into the blackening sky. The outlines of the sails on the drifting Junks, the traditional Chinese trading ships, remained in sight, but just for moments before millions of colored lights lit the skyline. It was a perpetual Spring Celebration, the fireworks of a fantasy fairyland, and I felt it was a celebration just for us. There were lights, glorious electrical lights for one purpose only—to light my heart on fire. I was in the world-famous city of Hong Kong.

"DaDa!" I called out loud to the wind, "I have gone beyond your dream; I have reached the city. I wish you were here to see the dangling earrings in the sky! Thank you, DaDa." Danny pulled me closer. This was Mother's fantasy; this was her child's destiny.

CHAPTER 24
LIBERTY GODDESS

Tuesday, December 5, 1989, was a date that I would never forget. I lived that date twice, yin and yang. It was on that date that I boarded an American Airlines flight from the Hong Kong airport, stunned with the awareness that I had left everything I knew behind, everything I understood; and it was on that date that I arrived with pure joy in America right into the arms of the City of Angels, leaving all of the feelings in between to dissipate somewhere in the expansive sky.

I had forgotten about the international dateline until the announcement came over the loudspeaker.

"Light, you get an extra day when you go to America. We will leave China and arrive in America on the same day. Today will become tomorrow but still be today," I said.

She looked at me with confusion. "This week you will have two Tuesdays as a gift from America," I said, trying again while smiling down at her excited little face. She held Danny's hand tightly. I realized for the first time in all the excitement that I understood about the changes in the time as we moved around the globe, but I did not at all understand the changes in my life to come. I had not said goodbye to anyone before I left, so ashamed of the mess I had left behind. I knew they would not understand my actions toward sweet Henry or my love for this American stranger. I hoped that someday when I saved enough money, I would return to see them again. I decided to flee first, confess later.

As we crossed the International Date Line, my excitement grew calculating the hours left to reach the blue sky of America. When the pilot announced that we were flying over the city of San Francisco, I couldn't open my eyes wide enough to take in the full expanse of my new home. I searched desperately for the first sight of the golden bridge.

"Oh, I saw the Liberty Goddess!" I exclaimed to Danny as I looked down through the window.

Danny laughed. "Sorry, Margaret, that's all the way on the other coast in New York. It's called the Statue of Liberty."

"Really? We call it Liberty Goddess in Chinese." I didn't want to believe him. "You should be able to at least see her from this high in the air don't you think?"

There was no logic to my thinking; these were the images I had held in my heart for years. My eyes were glued to the window. I squeezed his hand so tightly that he laughed.

Light leaned her little head toward the window, unable to see. In my hopeful imaginings, I saw the Liberty Goddess on every mountaintop, holding the torch high with her loving arm, welcoming me.

"Danny, I have memorized her message. I *have* to see her," I insisted.

"Speak Chinese Mama, please," Light said.

I recited, "Liberty Goddess Statue says, 'Bring me your tired, your poor.'"

"I am tired, Mama."

"Yes, we are tired, Light." *And we are very poor again, and with no Iron Rice Bowl*, I thought. "Your huddled masses yearning to breathe free." I had ached for that freedom every day of my repressed life.

"She knows me. I was restless," I said, gazing out of the window. I was so restless, having given up all of my passionately captured dreams to come to a strange and unknown country. I did not understand at all what I would do in America stripped of my teacher's title, starting all over like a newly hatched chick. I had the freedom to do whatever I wanted, go anywhere I wanted, no papers, no permission, and that was enough for the unteachable one, the tempest tossed, the illegal, paperless peasant, the funny outcast who never belonged.

Even with the changes that allowed me to become my brand in China, I still had to teach where I was told, far away from my home, no choices, no family, no Mother or Father to visit. I took out my passport and opened it to my American visa just to see it once again, and I pressed my hands together in gratitude for the golden door. Like Mother, I had my goddess; unlike Mother, it was a goddess to whom I could freely pray.

I watched every move of our plane above the clouds and below the clouds, over the farmlands, over the waters. I saw so many houses, small like matchboxes in organized order. I saw the long roads moving with cars like ants. The soft, charming voice came on again, announcing our arrival at the Los Angeles airport in fifteen minutes, then the weather and the temperature. I knew Los Angeles was a big city, but where were the big buildings like the forest? I was confused.

"Are you sure we have arrived at Los Angeles? This must be a mistake."

"No mistake," Danny said with another meaning in his tone. We locked liquid eyes, my Foreign Devil and I, my love. I played with my little square napkin printed with the words "American Airlines." My hard leaving had a soft landing as the wheels touched down in my unknown future.

真

The L.A. airport was amazing, electrifying, with sights pulling my mind and eyes in a thousand directions with so many foreign-looking people all in one place. What did I expect? We rode down the escalator watching the yellow, brown, red, bald, and even pink and purple heads of hair drifting down below us. The English announcements, the masses of people, the big noses, so many shapes of noses—that's what I noticed the most. A

Chinese family passed by me going up the other side, and I waved to their familiar flat noses, slanting eyes, yellow skin, and dark hair. They looked behind themselves, confused to see if I was waving to another friend and not them. I waved again to reassure them, but they looked straight ahead as they passed me by.

Light and I stopped at the ladies' room. It was amazingly clean. It took us a while to figure out what to do with the toilet paper. It had a cutout section in the shape of a head. I pulled it down, and it looked like a tongue hanging out. Then I saw that the shape seemed to fit the shape of the toilet bowl seat. Aha! I put it down over the immaculate toilet. What a waste to flush it away down the toilet. It could be wonderful drawing paper for Light to trace a picture from a magazine. Oh, that was the perfect kind of paper for making a small kite, too.

Then we got the softest toilet paper on a thick roll. We could drag it as long as we wanted, but we didn't. We didn't want to waste any. Was there a limit? Was it being counted? Should I take a few squares for later? While watching others, I saw they even used another kind of nice paper to dry their hands, and then they threw it into the trash.

I followed and dried my hands with the one sheet, but instead of throwing it away, I folded it carefully and put it in my bag. I wanted to keep it for future needs. There were so many things, details I had never thought to ask. When we left the lovely ladies' room, I realized that Light would never know the tortures of my early days of the night-shift and day-shift guards who patrolled my childhood toilet shed. I smiled.

Danny lived with his parents in Redondo Beach. They all came to meet us at the airport—his father, Jonathan; his stepmother, Nancy; and his stepsister, Jennifer. She had beautiful blond hair like a movie star, and she would be my sister. They were all white with high noses and hazel or blue eyes. They spoke English very fast, and I couldn't understand much of what they said when their engines got moving. I had no chance to listen again a second time, like rewinding the tape recordings in my college language lab, but I was so happy to meet them.

I could see the big WELCOME banner that Danny's father had hung across the door of the house for our arrival, so thoughtful, like the sign at my college. I felt grateful. It was an auspicious beginning.

An elaborate dinner was prepared for our arrival. I had to translate everything for Light. We learned by watching, putting the napkins on our laps and picking up the fork and resting the knife across the edge of the plate. They passed each item of food around on platters, and we scooped a small portion onto our own plates, no poking chopsticks in the same dish all at once like at home. *This is my home*, I thought.

Most of the time, Light did so well, except when it came to eating. She did fine with the sumptuous and delicious meal—chicken with vegetables and potatoes whipped high with a lovely puddle of brown sauce. When she was served a round piece of meat in a white bun, an American tradition, she couldn't swallow the big chunk of cow meat very well. Suddenly, she was gagging hard, and I knew she was going to throw up. Everyone at the table was looking at each other, surprised. I was able to catch her just in time to reach the bathroom, and she vomited there in a very clean toilet. I could imagine no unmentionable creatures could ever grow there. I learned there was plenty of free paper, too. No need to bring our own.

When we came back to the table, everyone continued the meal. I turned my eyes to watch Danny. Carefully, each adult, one by one, removed the precious, luscious skin from the chicken and reserved it on the sides of their plates—the best for the last, I assumed. At the end of the meal, the skin remained. Ah, I see, it was to be saved for another meal, or soup, perhaps. I had so much to learn. Stepmother took her plate and walked into the kitchen, stepped on a pedal, and slid the skin into the trash, scraping the extra vegetables into the same shameful hole. She was not eating it. She was not even saving it for a soup. I was confused. Was it for the animals, fertilizer, or was it waste, like the paper in the airport? Every part of the chicken was a delicacy—the head, the liver, the intestines, the gizzard, the skin, the feet, all so delicious.

"May I eat your chicken fat and skin, please?" I asked Danny's father very politely.

I could not bear to see another morsel follow the fate of Stepmother Nancy's meal. Danny's eyes were begging me; my eyes were begging him for the luscious skin. His begging, I later learned, was to have me stop my begging.

Stepmother Nancy was startled. "Jonathan, don't give her that!"

I must have looked like a punished dog. She stopped and asked, "Oh, do your people do that? No, no, no, I can't let you do that. You may not know, it's not healthy for you, dear."

Before I could accept the tempting fatty skin, she took her husband's plate away and dumped it in the trash with the heavenly potatoes sliding right behind. I hid my shock.

While she was busy in the kitchen with dessert, I looked at Danny's plate, eyeing his pile of unhealthy fat. I reached my hand to his plate with pleading eyes. He was more generous with his stepmother gone. He let me have it, and I ate everything. I even sucked the bones dry, making up for every meatless meal I had ever had.

Danny, Light, and I shared the same room. Danny had a futon, which was quite low to the floor. The room was small but cozy. It was not cold like in China. A noise came on in the middle of the night, not bats, just a warming breeze from a slotted hole in the ceiling; how wonderful.

The next day, Danny brought me to the backyard to show me his car.

"This is my car. Oh, I mean *our* car," he said smiling with a touch of guilt because the car according to him was a very old cheap car, "a piece of junk." Since he sold his Toyota pickup truck to buy me the engagement ring, he later bought this car from the roadside for three hundred dollars. It was called a Datsun. "No one could beat that price," he said.

"Let's all go out and drive around."

"Yes, let's." I agreed.

It was my first time riding in a sedan car. As we backed out of the driveway, I once more admired the welcome sign that honored

Light's and my arrival. I felt touched. What a luxury a car was. Light sat in the back seat; I sat in the front. We all had seat belts, too. In China, we only rode in buses. There weren't any seat belts. The roads were so bumpy, it felt like your head could shake loose from your shoulders and hit the roof of the bus, and often it did.

The car ran well, except when it stopped breathing when we stopped at the crossroads. Danny quickly turned the key and pushed his foot many times on the foot pedal, growling. Sometimes, our car hesitated, and the cars behind us honked. Honking in China was constant and common. It was part of the exciting city life. This was the first similarity I had found so far in my new home, the only thing that made me feel a little more at home.

We lived with Danny's father and stepmother for the first few weeks until we could get our own apartment. I called his stepmother "Mom," with the Chinese style respect of a daughter-in-law.

"Margaret, please do not call me that. I am not your mother, dear," she said.

"Sorry, Mom," I said, slipping again. And then I returned to my room. I had become Mother's greatest fear, a daughter-in-law in a household that did not want me. They tried to be kind, but I still felt I was a burden to them, and I couldn't blame them.

The excitement of the newness turned from light to heavy with every single daily thing I had to do. Even the simplest thing exploded into a hundred pieces like having to memorizing each petal of a rose, its shape, its color, its placement on the bloom; it felt overwhelming and impossible. Eating became which utensil, where to put the fork, how to use the fork, where to put it at the end, napkins on your lap, what is this food, how do you eat it, how does this faucet work? I simply want to wash my hands! Opening a door, showering, telephoning, and the machinery—washers, dryers—were all a mystery to be solved. My mind could not stop the incessant scanning of the world around me. The automatic dryer made me feel sad that the sun had no purpose. It made no sense to use up electricity in sunny California, to not to hang the clothes to enjoy the benefits of the free sun. There was no fear of frozen standing pants in this delightful place. Soon, the threads of every common thing in my new life wove themselves into a dense and heavy blanket that day by day dropped down upon my happy spirit, suffocating me, making my limbs feel so heavy, weighing down my soul, wrapping me in self-pity.

I took to staying in our room to avoid adding to the mistakes I constantly made, to avoid having to learn another thing in my so-called cultural adjustment. My joy waned with each hour, and I was drawn down into a dark place as I spent the passing days alone. I could not find myself, and I feared the same near insanity I had flirted with when working in the fields. When in my life had I lost my passion for learning? Without money to buy clothing, I wore Danny's sweatshirt every day, keeping my one dress for a future job. The proud and educated teacher was someone no one ever saw, disguised as the confused and stumbling woman in their son's little room.

I was both grateful that I didn't have to work and suffering because I didn't have work. For the first time since I was a little girl, I was useless. And I was so very hungry, not daring to go out of my room until Danny came home. One night, I finally admitted to him I had been so very hungry since I came to America. It was late.

"In America, we just call and they bring the food. Watch!"

He picked up the phone and ordered a pepperoni pizza. It came in 30 minutes, amazing. I loved the spicy sauce and meat, but the yellow stretchy rubber on the top I had never had before. He made me try it. It stayed with me for such a long time and gurgled and rolled inside. My Chinese stomach was finally full.

真

I came to life again when we moved to our own apartment in Anaheim where I could make my mistakes in the privacy of our own space. It was nothing like the nice place that Henry and I had, but it was better than the open-to-the-sky abandoned house of my early years. A large cockroach walked out onto the table. I was quite surprised that it looked the same as the ones we had in China, but this luckier cockroach lived in the abundance of America.

We expected that the Datsun was close to taking its last breath, and it did. We had to buy a new car. I knew nothing of cars, going only by the color and the sleek lines. I chose a Lexus; Danny laughed and chose a Ford Festiva. We were able to drive Light to her first day of school in style. She would take the bus from then on—a treat she so enjoyed. We passed an advertisement for nearby Disneyland on the way, and I quickly distracted her with questions. As much as she loved *anything* "Disney," I knew the budget would not allow a visit. We managed to keep her from knowing that we were living right in the backyard of the most alluring thing she knew about America, until we could afford to go. Although it pained me to deny her such a joy, I refused to add to our debt.

I was grateful our shiny new car would never lose its breath while at an intersection, but my mind was on one thing: the large white sticker on the side window—the price, the loan, the payment, the interest, and the debt. It frightened me to drive home with the guilt of our debt advertised on the window for all to see. Was Danny my father's son, too comfortable with owing? The fear settled into my stomach and would not move.

Our days together were peppered with arguments and misunderstandings. My delusion that I would understand American culture by virtue of speaking English alone was naïve and was again dispelled. When I cooked dinner and served it to Danny, he refused to eat it. He left in the car to buy a hamburger, and I was left staring at the food in disbelief. Food was not to be wasted. I felt he should eat it even if it wasn't his favorite, even if I had no cooking skills. He did not want to have Chinese food at every meal, but it was all I knew, and I was too overwhelmed to learn anything different. I had no respect for his taste in food. Having little experience with choice, I was inflexible about it. *You should be grateful to have a full plate in front of you,* I thought.

Wanting to take advantage of the bright California sun, and frustrated with trying to figure out the washing machine dials, I washed the laundry by hand in the tub with our free-flowing clean water. It was difficult to do, bent over the tub for hours washing piece-by-piece, rinsing and rinsing. My little childhood song came to mind:

Xi ya xi, xi ya xi
Rub, rub, rub
Wring, wring, wring.

When I finished wringing them, I draped each piece proudly over the railings outside the apartment to smile at the sun—a vibrant sun that wicked the wetness so quickly. I was delighted. Danny was not happy when he came home to my "decorations." "The neighbors!" he said, "They won't like it."

"Why?" I asked.

"Because it looks like a tenement."

"It is a waste of the sun and electricity," I said.

"That is what the machine is for," he explained. This was one of many things that confused and frustrated me.

I hurt his feelings when he so thoughtfully bought me a birthday present. I had no gift giving in my past, either. I had no understanding of the tradition and its importance to him. I took every gift back to get a refund, insulting him. As much as I thought I was a romantic, I did not know how to be romantic in my new culture. My practicality trumped my passion, and coldness seeped into our days.

I was beginning to understand the stack of bills on the kitchen table. Even my poor math told me Danny's income was not nearly enough to keep ahead of those numbers and the new car payment. Besides, it wasn't right to pass a day without some work to do. I had to find a job. I had no car, and the thought of learning to drive was beyond my dreams. Danny needed our new car to go to work and besides, walking had been such a given in my life. Walking I knew how to do. I walked Light to the school bus stop and held her hand as she stepped up happily to go to a place where she knew nothing of what was being said. She still seemed delightfully enthusiastic about it all. I was relieved to see her brave little waving hand through the window of the bus. I worried for her safety in this less-than-honorable neighborhood. I worried about our debt, and I still worried about Curve.

At home the next morning, I searched the job ads in the *Penny Saver* newspaper for the door to my new self. The little newspaper had been my only source of reading since I arrived. I saw an ad for a job nearby. I needed to wear something better than the sweatshirt and sweatpants I had taken to wearing while hiding out in Danny's room. Sister Enough had given me a silver floral silk dress, a good and lucky color. I opened Danny's dresser drawer and found the perfect socks to keep me warm in the brisk morning. The thick white soccer socks covered my legs all the way up to meet the silk dress. I looked in the mirror, "Tai hao le—perfect!" I slipped on my heavy walking sandals and Danny's cozy Lakers sweatshirt, and I was ready.

It was so sunny and beautiful in southern California, the sky so vibrant even in the colder winter months. As I breathed in the cool air and followed the map Danny had given me, I discovered that walking made me find myself a bit. I had to find a job nearby, so that set my limits. I could look within an hour's walk or so. I did not have to register with a brigade or tell anyone where I was going or living. I floated down the street without my strings, smiling. I could do this. After a brief twenty-minute walk, I saw the address. I read the sign, "Receptionist Wanted." I needed to be wanted. It took a very long time to complete the application. I hit one question I could not answer. *What is "HS?"* I wondered.

When the large gentleman reviewed the application, he said, "Why didn't you fill in this part of the education section?"

"I wasn't sure what HS was. Can you help?" I asked.

He dropped the paper on his desk. "I am sorry, the position was just filled."

I may not have been a speaker of perfect English, and I did not know the subtleties of American ways, but I knew it was a lie as it peeled so instantly from his lips. My mind was searching for options. I thought I spoke English. When I was in China, I was admired for my fluency, but in America, I may have *known* and could read English, but from the looks on people's faces and our awkward exchanges, I didn't *speak* English. My heavy singsong accent confused the listener, and the rapid-fire delivery of their words like fireworks dispersed in my mind before I could capture them.

I continued walking a brief fifteen minutes to the next job, for a bookkeeper, which interested me the most. With my love of books and as a descendant of The Book Fragrance Family, I would be just the right person to care for the books. It was my heritage. I looked for the bookstore but found only an office building. I told them, "Yes, of course I could do bookkeeping." They sent me home with an application.

That evening, Danny said, "You can't do bookkeeping. You don't have the skills."

I started to cry at his negativity. "I am a teacher and college graduate and a lover of books; I am from the Book Fragrance Family. Just until I find a way to teach again," I pleaded. He explained what bookkeeping was. I looked at the growing pile of debts and wished I had the skill.

真

I started out again each day with hope to continue searching. Walking down the street with my folded newspaper one day, I found a food place that was bright and looked quite inviting named Taco Bell. Standing at the big glass windows, I watched the people in the restaurant eating everything with their hands. America was so casual, so relaxed. I remembered Mother's words in Sand City: "You will eat in a restaurant and order anything you want." Not yet, I thought. I was hungry, but I had just a few dollars in my small purse, and there was plenty of food at home.

I walked in and sat down, but no one paid attention. As a good observer, I saw that you had to place your order with the person at the counter. Then they called the customers back to get their food—very efficient. You cleaned up your table yourself—good teamwork. *America loves to make you independent*, I thought. Then you put everything in a wooden "Thank You" box through a swinging door on a hinge—very polite. I approached the counter and stared up at the huge menu of items overhead. Then I saw the sign, "Help Wanted." I felt that way myself.

"Excuse me and good morning. I would like to apply to work here."

"Just a minute." The counter person twisted her neck around and yelled, "Shirley!" and the manager appeared.

I didn't know that kind of food, but I needed work, and I could do what the people in the back were doing—simply rolling, filling, stuffing, and wrapping lots of colorful things, no hauling buckets of water for cooking from a pond. It looked like fun from my viewpoint with eighty-four-hour dusty brick weeks in my past. I could see a few workers on their break eating from the commodity grain, food handed to them from the person at the grill. Easy. I just wanted a job.

The next day, I returned with the completed application, having enlisted Danny's help. Listening to the Spanish being spoken by the staff, I knew I was in trouble. I didn't know I would need Spanish and English in America.

"OK, so you know Mexican food, right?" the manager asked, standing over me as I tried to memorize the menu.

I was a Chinese woman in a Mexican restaurant who spoke English that no one understood. I realized that I did not understand a single thing on the menu—taco, tortilla, salsa, and guacamole. The list was long, and I mispronounced them all. The manager was a white woman. She sat down across from me to interview me.

"So, what are you?"

"Uh, I am not sure." I hesitated. I did not want my first answer to be wrong.

"Are you Chinese?" she asked.

"Oh, yes, Chinese." I smiled.

"Yeah, my husband cheated on me with a Chinese woman," she said, staring me in the eyes.

"Oh, I promise it was not me; I am married."

She laughed, "So was he."

I was lost.

"So, you went to college, huh?"

"Yes, I was a teacher in China."

"OK, we could use some brains around here. Come back with me and get your uniform. You start tomorrow. One more thing—you're not a cheater, are you?"

I thought of Henry, asked for forgiveness, and lied, "Of course not." *I am no sunflower*, I thought. And I would certainly never cheat with her husband with my Danny in my life. So I felt it was fine to tell the small lie.

I tried on the beautiful uniform, burgundy and grey with a hat. I had Danny take my photograph. I admired myself in the mirror. It had taken one month of walking and interviewing every day. It was February, and I had my first job. I straightened my hat in the mirror. This would do fine. It was beyond my dreams to be accepted, to have a paycheck, to have a job in America. I did not have the luxury to even think about finding my way back to my brand, to be a teacher again.

I had never seen a cash register. They showed me quickly, and I smiled at the customers, but I couldn't understand any names of the food items or drinks. All the people working there were Mexican, except two African Americans and Shirley. Many customers were unhappy to have to point to everything as they ordered from me. I watched as people in line switched to other lines. When the store manager handed me the dustpan and broom and told me to go out to clean the parking lot, I was shocked. This time there was no pagoda, and there was no humor in the task. It took me a few questions to understand that he actually wanted me to do that. When I walked out of the store, I felt ashamed. I was a college graduate and an honored teacher in China, but I was cleaning the parking lot in America. Holding the broom and the dustpan, I looked around me at the moving traffic and the busy streets, but no one noticed me. One good thing about knowing no one and being invisible is that no one pays attention when you are humbled publicly.

I took the menu home. I knew how to study for a test. I read the menu items aloud for Danny to make sure I got them right.

"Tor-tee-ya, not tor-tilla like Godzilla," Danny said, laughing.

I was able to start taking orders the next day with Chinese–Mexican flair. On my break, I heard the manager screaming at some of the workers. I thought that must have been how Sister Complete felt in the fields, constantly abused in her helpless position. For some reason, he was always polite to me and shook his head, laughing. I didn't mind his laughing, although I hadn't done it myself in quite a while. One time there was a twenty-dollar loss from my register, and the shift manager told me that the store manager said not to tell me. I was very grateful and humbled. He didn't short my pay, either.

Danny had made me put a big glass bottle of coins in paper tubes, which gave me a chance to become familiar with them. It was helpful later when I had to run the register as the cashier in Taco Bell. It was easy to know one penny or to say "ten cents," but not easy to learn the nicknames of the coins—dime, quarter, and nickel.

By watching and studying very hard, I soon learned everything I needed to know. The manager said I was doing wonderfully. In fact, he said the customers loved my smile. They said they felt good seeing my smiling face and hearing my strange, warm greeting after a long, hard day's work.

The store manager wanted to promote me to a shift manager, but the shift manager said it was better for the store to put me in the front because customers liked to see me there, smiling and caring about each little pack of salsa.

"She is driving business to us," the shift manager said. "They love her Chinglish."

I had not heard the expression before. I was an educated Chinese woman speaking Chinglish, selling Mexican food. When the store manager again wanted to promote me to shift manager, Danny rejected the idea, saying it was too much responsibility for me. After two months, I received a raise, five cents an hour; I had never earned a raise. I was making $4.30 for one hour, nearly the same money I made hauling dusty bricks for seventy-two hours at the factory.

I gave every paycheck to Danny so we could pay off the debt and pay for the rent. Dealing with money made me nervous. I had no experience with American money, and money was not the focus of my life in China, either, where the government took care of all our needs. Danny told me he would take care of everything. I was so grateful that there was no need for me to add one more complication to my life like having a checkbook. I truly felt I did not need money because I did not drive, and my only stops were home and work where food was plentiful. I was thrilled that I was able to contribute to the family. I had made fast progress with fast food.

真

When I left Taco Bell to go home each day, I passed a beautiful building right across the street that attracted me. I wandered into the fancy building—University of California at Irvine, UCI Medical Building. Being at a university made me feel right at home. I thought this would be the perfect place for a teacher of my status to begin. After taking a free class in the community on how to interview, my confidence was high. I applied at the MRI facility and got the job as intake receptionist. I answered phone calls, made appointments, completed paperwork for patients, and did patient intake for their procedures. I liked that word "procedures." I was proceeding, or so I hoped. Again my language tripped me up. I could not understand the names of patients, nor could I spell them.

"I am sorry, can you spell that please?" I said over and over, all day.

"Beverly, as in Beverly Hills," the patient said.

"Oh, I see, can you spell Beverly Hills, B, yes, E, uh huh, V... oh, Beverly, yes, I have it. Now, let's do your last name. That was Hills?" She hung up.

It was painful to wait until the letters came together to make some sense to me; sometimes they never did. I never knew which names were male or female. If Jim was male, why was Kim female? I did much worse on symptoms. I tried to schedule a hysterectomy for a male patient who had called on his wife's behalf. "Yes, what procedure? Did you say history economy?" I asked. The patient asked to speak to my manager. It was my last chance. After two weeks of torture on both sides, I was fired.

I went home exhausted and so discouraged. I took Light in my arms and cried a long, overdue cry. Thinking the mail might cheer me, I went out to the mailbox. Yes, there was a letter stamped from China. Any word from family so far away was like a thousand ounces of gold. I ripped it open, excited to hear the news, until I realized it was from Curve. How did she have our new address? I wondered. Then I noticed the letter was addressed to Danny only, not to us. There was no mention of Light or me. I had still never asked Henry for the letter she had sent Danny, not wanting to distrust him. I read the letter, and in it, Curve used the words "future," "us," and "we." I waited for Danny to return, and I approached him with fire in my eyes.

"There is no 'us' between Curve and me," he assured me.

I was furious, exhausted from the disappointing day.

"I will write to her and tell her not to write again. There is no "us." Are you happy now?" he yelled.

No, I wasn't happy. I could never let it go from that day on. "Do you want to be with her?" I badgered him.

"No, I told you there is nothing. Whatever, it is, it's in her head, not mine," he said, reassuring me.

"Then why did she write to just you?" I probed. I dreamed of him with other women, and I told him so. He laughed. "Don't be silly," he said. I sank into a kind of insanity—searching the mail daily, haunted, jealous, obsessed, waiting for his admission to what I was sure was the truth.

Carrying the heaviness of my fears like a basket of stones, I went to take free evening government classes to learn medical terminology, just in case I needed it for my next job. I learned that an orthopedic doctor was a bone doctor, a pediatrician treated children, and I finally learned the term "hysterectomy." I returned to UCI and applied for yet another position as an office clerk, feeling more confident. I was relieved to get the job. With the harsh wind of debt and fear blowing at my back, I added a second job distributing nutritional products and a third doing telephone surveys at night.

真

With no sisters and no Mother to soothe my weariness, I needed somewhere to belong. Having been raised in a country that forbade religion, I had only the spirituality Mother provided in secret to sustain me. I knew how much the temple meant to her. I passed a Christian church with signs in Chinese, and in my desperation, I attended the Sunday service. I listened to the message of hope and forgiveness and was welcomed by the community. The Chinese words echoed around me, and I drew them into every cell. After the service, I lingered in my seat. A girl came and sat next to me. Her kind words broke into my private pain. I told her about my life with Danny and the threat of Curve to my soul and sanity.

"Maybe you should choose happiness for your daughter's sake and your own. God will take the load from your shoulders," she said.

I made a plan to bring us together as a happy family again. I decided to choose happiness. After we all went to the church and were baptized, I had hope.

"So where are you working tonight?" Danny asked one night.

"Nowhere. I am taking time off to be with you and Light. I am choosing happiness with my family," I said.

The three of us went to the park and played with a Frisbee, and I embraced my newly-found happiness. I put my mind to being a good wife, resurrecting my smile and even my laughter.

That night, he poked his head inside the bedroom door with something on his mind. I was anticipating that he would be uplifted with the new hope that our life would turn around, that our love would thrive again.

"Do you want to say something?" I asked.

"You won't want to hear it. I am afraid it will hurt you."

"Is it about the debt?" I asked.

"No, I, uh, I want to bring Curve to the US," he said.

"Do you mean to find her a husband? I don't know how she will adjust here with so little knowledge of English. It has been difficult for me, and I have the language," I suggested.

"I thought you said you weren't happy. I thought you would eventually want a divorce," Danny said.

I had realized there was a change in Danny for a long time, but I was too busy surviving my schedule to notice. My happiness seemed to have the opposite effect on him. I realized he didn't really want me happy. He really didn't want me to cut back on work so we could rebuild our lives. He wanted me gone, but he wanted *me* to do the deed. My choosing happiness made him realize his game would no longer work. He was criticizing me for going to work, making me the person to blame for our failing marriage, making my obsession to repay the debt through hard work the entire cause of all of our problems. It seemed my new happiness no longer gave him power over me.

He finally told me the truth, and it was almost a relief. I was extremely calm. I surprised myself. I told him I was willing to let him go, understanding how powerful love was. Henry had freed me to follow the passion of my love, even giving me his daughter to carry away to a foreign land. Until that moment, I had not fully understood how painful that had been for him. My hand was too weak to hold up the sky. I had to give in. Mother's words came back to me: "People can't be nice a thousand times, and flowers can't stay red a hundred days."

He was surprised for a second, but then his face lit up, and he seemed thrilled. He came to the bedside and picked up the phone. The cold face I had come to know turned warm and vibrant like the day he put my cold hand into his pocket years before. He told me I was noble, and he and Curve were grateful. He treated me with loving kindness in gratitude for freeing him. The sweetness and affection of our early years had evaporated in the hours of our working life, and my happy, cheerful self was long buried in my fear. I realized he still had the capacity to love, but he would simply shift his love from me to Curve.

His excitement was so uncontrollable that he had to make a phone call to China immediately to report the wonderful news to Curve. He even had her ten-digit phone number memorized. After he finished talking to her with tenderness, passion, and love, he handed me the phone—after all, she was our friend.

When we broke the news to Light, she took his side, asking to live with them. At only nine years old, how could I blame her? My absence while working meant that Light had been in Danny's daily care. The jealousy tore my heart into pieces, the fire of anger smoldered, and I spiraled down, down, until the vultures had me as their prey, picking at all that remained of my defeated self. Then Mulan pulled me up from my demise, and I grabbed the phone. I surprised myself, surprised Curve, and surprised Danny.

"Forget about Danny," I told her. "He is my husband, not yours."

"If it is meant to be, he will be mine. You make him crazy like a Chinese evil witch, and I love him!" she exclaimed.

"I love him, too," I said.

I dropped the phone and ran out to the street in the dark. I called my friend, Rachel, from the church, and she picked me up and took me to her house. She called Danny. He came to get me. Seeing the state I was in, he reluctantly told me that he would give in, give up his true love, and be willing to stay married to me.

真

I painfully endured every day, dragging my heavy body to work. I was determined that Danny would never belong to Curve. My mind was scattered, torn between love for him and hatred for her. Danny resumed his cold face. He shouted at me in front of his parents. I had no self-esteem left. I still brought him every check I was earning from my jobs, as usual. I tried to keep things as they were, buying time, hoping I could earn back his love.

There was no talk of Curve, and I knew he had no money to bring her to America or to support her. The money brought in by my work would stay with me if I should go. There was a small light of hope. The people at the church urged me to fight for my marriage. I lived in a silent scream, unable to tell my family; it was too mortifying.

CHAPTER 25
ELIMINATING THE ALIEN

T hree years had passed since I had set foot on this land of freedom as a legal alien resident. I had experienced such a whiplash of highs and lows: the joy of being hired, the dismay of being fired; the chance of buying without money, the sting of paying with interest; the freedom to reach for a star or to dream of simply nothing at all.

Despite the pain of all the choices, I loved the equality, the democracy, and the freedom to change. I wondered where I might be in my life had Mother given birth to me in this land. *Maybe it is not too late*, I thought.

I filled out the application in a legal office to become a real citizen of the United States. There was a test to take. To me, taking this test was a profound privilege. I prepared for it with joy in my heart. I learned the principles of American democracy and the system of government, and I memorized the rights and responsibilities.

"What is the name of the national anthem?" I asked myself. "The Star-Spangled Banner," I answered, looking in the mirror as I dressed for work. The entire office knew I was studying for the citizenship test. One day, a co-worker asked me, "Margaret, how many states are there in the United States?"

"Fifty," I answered. I appreciated her testing me.

"Are you sure it's not fifty-one?" she questioned. Then a voice from the next cubicle suggested, "Just go count the stars on the flag. Each star means a state."

The day of my naturalization ceremony in Los Angeles was the most beautiful day. Danny and Light both took the day off to accompany me. I had a little American flag in my hand, and Danny and Light had theirs, too. They were standing at the back of the hall. I was seated in the center among hundreds of other immigrants, eager to rid myself of the label "alien." Even though I was a legal alien, it was a word that always made me cringe.

I was intoxicated by the welcoming ambiance, touched by the music, inspired by the speaker. I felt so included. I was never to be an Enemy of this State. Standing with my back straight, as Mother had taught me, with my right hand on my heart, I said my oath clearly, and I understood every word: "I hereby declare, on oath, that I absolutely and entirely renounce and abjure all allegiance and fidelity to any foreign prince, potentate, state, or sovereignty of whom or which I have heretofore been a subject or citizen; that I will support and defend the Constitution and laws of the United States of America against all enemies, foreign and domestic; that I will bear true faith and allegiance to the same...."

Then came the one phrase that I was grateful I would never have to act on, since I did not have the stomach for it: "that I will bear arms on behalf of the United States when required by the law; that I will perform noncombatant service in the Armed Forces of the United States when required by the law; that I will perform work of national importance under civilian direction when required by the law; and that I take this obligation freely without any mental reservation or purpose of evasion; so help me God."

Tears of joy warmed my eyes. The national anthem touched me. I was a proud citizen of the United States of America. I laughed to myself at the thought of me as an official Ocean Devil. Feeling joyful and honored, I stood on my toes and passed my eyes over the sea of little flags and waved to Danny and Light, who were smiling at me proudly.

The next day I went to work, not as an alien, but as an American citizen. I thought of Sister Complete Happiness and the cadre's announcement at the meeting by the bridge. I regretted that this was a joy I couldn't share with my distant family, who had not seen me for so many years and who knew nothing of my journey. This was one of the few truths about my years in America that there was no shame in telling.

I couldn't wait to tell everyone how exciting it was for me. When I arrived at our office, my supervisor and my co-workers all lined up to surprise me. My cubicle was beautifully decorated with ribbons. On my desk sat a big bouquet of red, white, and blue fresh flowers and a big cake that read "Congratulations." Strung across my cubicle was a sign that read "PROUD TO BE AN AMERICAN." I smiled and cried, and I was so grateful to my co-workers. How could I have deserved this blessing?

真

The only thing left to do to be a real American was to get my driver's license. I had wanted to do that for some time. Danny had discouraged it. He had willingly driven me uncomplainingly everywhere so that I would have no need to get behind the wheel of the car. He was not fond of being a passenger in the hands of an inexperienced driver. We bought a used Ford Granada for me to learn to drive.

First I would take the written test; that would be easy, just memorization. I had watched Danny drive a thousand times. I knew I could pass the driving test, too; after all, I was an American. I was wrong, but I did learn the entire Orange County area. The first time I took the test, I went to Fullerton DMV. The instructor made me go through the hand gestures, and it was easy to do. Then he took the passenger seat. He was wearing a short-sleeved uniform and had a clipboard in his hand. I got the OK to go. I thought I was doing well, following his requests: turn right, turn left, stop, etc. With each stop, I saw his body jerking back and forth against the seat, but amazingly, it didn't prevent him from writing on his board. Upon the near impact of the man's head on my dashboard,

I knew I needed more practice. He rudely scribbled on the paper "F" and nearly jumped out of the car before I could park. I was not even allowed to finish the test.

"See you next time. You need practice," he said. But there was to be no next time for me to see that unfair man. I searched for my better-luck DMV in the next town over, then the next, and then the next. The first man was not patient, but the second man made me so nervous. Suddenly, he screamed, "Watch out. You are on the wrong side of the road!"

"I don't see any yellow line on the street. What score are you giving me? I can see you are writing something," I chattered. I was so anxious to pass.

"What are you watching me for? Don't you see the cars coming toward you?" he yelled.

"But don't the cars see they are coming toward me?" I asked.

I should never have argued with the instructor. He made me drive back to the DMV parking lot, scratched a fat "F" on his clipboard, and handed it to me.

"You need a lot more practice," he said.

The next three better-luck DMVs were no different, even though I practiced hard. Finally, Danny was tired of taking me all over the county in hours of traffic to find more DMVs because I never wanted to face someone who had already seen me as a failure. I was mad at myself, mad at the mean instructors, mad at my big old Granada, and mad at the whole idea of driving.

"Forget driving," I said to Danny, "just forget it!" I was sure he was relieved. Later, a friend of mine agreed to take me for one more try. I was determined. I saw that my instructor was a pregnant woman. *Maybe this is my better-luck DMV after all*, I thought. *Or maybe I am doomed again because she might be so nervous about her baby that she may not even let me finish my test.* I figured she would probably order me back to the parking lot and give me the conspired, horrid "F."

I took a quick glance at her. She was in her early thirties with her hair tied back in a ponytail. Her uniform was unbuttoned from the swelling of her belly. Instead of holding her clipboard with her hands, she simply rested it on her platform belly. Suddenly, the clipboard flipped off her lap. She held her lower belly with her hands. I saw lumps moving like waves. I was worried. *Please don't go into labor in my car*, I pleaded in my mind. The only memory I had of delivering babies was the pain of my one drugless childbirth. I knew I could not take my driving test and worry about her water breaking at the same time. What if her baby popped out? I didn't know where the hospital was. It was supposed to be my better-luck DMV, and I was having the worst luck. "Is this your first baby?" I asked, hoping she knew what she was doing. She picked up the clipboard. "When is the baby due?" I continued.

Instead of answering my questions, she commanded, "OK, if you are ready, I am ready. Go!"

"What?" I let out a string of Chinese words. I held my breath. I had tried to be kind, asking her questions about her baby, but she didn't say a word. She was worse than all the other evil instructors I had suffered through. I turned on the engine and backed out of the parking lot.

"Good, you did well!" she said.

That was a first. I followed her instructions, making sure I turned very carefully. I had always run directly over holes, bumps, or whatever appeared on the road, so I could concentrate on the driving part. On that day, though, I was very careful to avoid all the hazards.

No baby, no baby, please don't have your baby, I chanted to myself in Chinese. When I stopped, I was sure not to make her jerk back and forth like the other instructors. On the way back to the DMV, I made sure I went over the speed bumps very carefully. *Please don't let me bump her baby out.* I didn't care if I failed the test again.

After the car stopped and the engine was off, I couldn't look at her as she scratched on her clipboard. I decided to just accept this sixth failure. I was used to the letter "F" by then. She handed me the paper. I watched her make a great effort to slowly get out of the car.

Just before she closed the door, she said to me, "This is my first baby. I am due tomorrow. Today is my last day at work. You did great. Thanks for driving so carefully, Congratulations!"

I looked at my paper. I was shocked to see the letter "P" with a circle around it. The score was not seventy, eighty, or ninety but a full-swollen, pregnant one hundred!

I rolled down the window of my Granada, yelling out loud toward my instructor's back, "Congratulations, congratulations, congratulations!" Then she said something I remember to this day: "Drive carefully." And to everyone's regret, I always did.

真

Months later, I dragged my exhausted self to my bedroom, having come home earlier than usual. My heavy work schedule was wearing me down. Danny and Light were out. On the dresser was the mail. I found the bounced checks, the bank statement I had never seen. The pay I earned from my hours and hours of work had not all been used to pay the bills as I had thought. Under the bills was an envelope addressed to Danny at an unfamiliar local post office box. I thumbed through the stack of photos that were nestled in the letter. They were a fast-forward sequence of one person—darling photos of a baby, a little girl, a sexy woman in a swimsuit, and a grown smiling woman, all with the same face—Curve's. She had sent photos of herself to Danny. I tried to tear the photos in half, to shred the flirtatious face of my enemy, but the clever girl had encased herself in laminate, anticipating my angry hands. There were letters filled with plans and a hand-drawn train station map for Danny's trip to China. Then, the ax fell. I saw the phone bill: eight hundred dollars in calls to China to a familiar number at forty cents a minute, the purchase price of my car. So much precious money for some evaporating minutes to send his words off into the air for her to catch and rock in her betraying heart on the other side of the world. How many hours of working at UCI, how many nutritional products did I sell for the luxury of those calls?

I was grateful that they were not home. I was afraid to stay, afraid I would fall prey to my twisted, damaged mind, lashing out at Danny in front of my child, or self-immolate in my flaring anger before her innocent eyes, or fall down sobbing to hear her choice of where she wished to live. So I walked out of the apartment in a trance before they could return.

My feet had no plan but to move in any direction, just to walk with some hope of letting go of the guilt and pain. For all my trying, I had failed to recapture Danny's love; I had been beaten, and Curve had taken the prize. I ran from my insanity, and the foolishness of my life and karma chased me. I deserved it all; it was the perfect resolution. The suffering I had given to Henry came flooding back to me.

I walked toward the next town, Fullerton, where a friend lived, dragging my body as far as I could go. An hour or more later, I had burned the char off of my fury and fell sobbing at the roots of a tree in front of a church. It was getting dark. A shadowy figure approached. Some momentary sense of danger came to mind, but I didn't have the strength to move. I curled up small against the side of the tree, hoping not to be noticed. The man came closer; he headed right for the tree.

Startled, he nearly tripped over me. "Who the—?"

"Sorry, it's just me," I said.

"You scared me to death. What on earth are you doing here at this hour?" He studied my face. "Are you OK?"

"No, I am not OK," I said.

"I am sorry to hear that. What happened? I am Brian," he said, looking down at the hollow of the tree root next to me, clearly his usual spot.

"I'm Margaret."

"You can talk to me," he said with a kindness that drew my trust.

In staccato sobs, I poured out my story of betrayal, Curve, and the loss of Danny. He listened. With no pride left, I showed him the envelope; I offered him the proof.

"I hate to see a woman cry, and I can't stand to see a woman hurt."

I was shivering from the cool evening air.

"You're cold. Here," he said offering a sweater that he pulled from the bowels of his cluttered things. "Don't worry, it's clean. I just washed it in the Laundromat, really. Here, take it."

I put the heavy, oversized sweater on and wrapped myself in his kindness.

"I had a son and a woman in my life. I lost them, too. I am not allowed to see him."

Unlikely kindred souls, we shared our sympathies under the tree for long hours until my heavy eyes closed. I awoke and saw him sleeping by the wall of the church, a polite distance away.

He quickly rose and said, "Got to go now." I could hear the tension in his voice.

"Wait, why? What about your sweater?" I asked, still half asleep.

"Just keep it as long as you need it and then leave it at the church office. They know me, but they'll be mad if they see me sleeping here again."

He put his hand on my shoulder and promised me I would be OK. Then he was gone, my angel under the tree.

I walked the remaining distance to my friend's house and knocked on the door. I must have been a frightening sight.

"What happened?" she asked me, staring at my ill-fitted sweater. "Where have you been?"

She called Danny on her phone. "Margaret is here with me, and I'll make sure she leaves you." She defended me without my asking, taking the stance of a friend who truly didn't know my crimes, my karma.

"Is she crazy? She disappeared last night! I called the police!" Danny ranted.

I had no thought about what would happen. I apologized to my co-workers and my boss the next day when I found out they had been frantically searching for me. I did not apologize to Danny. My friend was my strength until I could gather my own. She helped me find an apartment. Displaced, the enemy of myself, I tried to start again.

For the next month, I struggled to get a new routine in place in my poor, ground-floor apartment. I still had not mastered the art of cleaning, and the state of the place reflected my state of mind:

chaos. Danny and I had settled into a routine of cooperation, sharing time with Light. One sunny Sunday morning, Light went to play at a friend's house. As usual, I could hear neighbors talking in the stairway in front of my apartment, their loud voices invading my small space. As I grabbed my old purse and opened the door to leave for church, I saw Danny coming up the walkway with a laundry basket of Light's clothes, followed close behind by a man I had never met before. Assuming it was his friend, I smiled and backed in from the door to invite them in, but Danny's companion didn't enter. He stood by the door. Then he pulled his shirt to one side and placed his hand on the gun that was tucked in his pants.

"This is a robbery! Give me your money now. Hurry!" he demanded.

I looked at him, shocked. Everything had been taken from me that could be taken. I let loose my pent-up ire from years of trying, years of rising up and falling down. No more!

"Are you stupid?" I screamed. "Why would you come here to these cheap apartments to rob someone? You want to rob, go rob the rich!"

"Shut up! Do you want to get hurt?" He had an ugly, red, rough face like the demons of my Chinese fairytales. My instinct was to just attack him, grab his gun, and kick him.

Danny urged me desperately, "Give him your money, Margaret! Give him your money," he pleaded with me as he handed his wallet to the criminal. I wasn't finished spewing out the anger compressed in my soul for decades.

"Get out of here! Go after the rich!" I yelled. I was hoping the people who were talking in the stairway in front of the apartment could hear me.

"Do you want to die?" the robber growled, threatening me with his gun.

I laughed, the forgotten sound a stranger to my own ears. "Kill me, I don't care. Just get out of here. There is no money," I screamed.

"Give me the money!" he repeated.

"Give him the money, Margaret!" Danny tried again to wake me from my insanity.

I opened up the zipper of my purse, dumped out all the contents, and threw the purse across the floor.

"So there! No money, no money, always, no money!" I was foolishly, fearlessly caught up in my wrath.

The robber looked at me and then at the open purse on the floor, not daring to cross my fierce path to retrieve the unknown.

"If you call the police, I will come back for you!" he threatened as he ran away, stuffing Danny's wallet in his pants.

"If you come back, *I'll* be here for *you!*" I yelled after him.

Danny stood motionless.

"Call the police right now!" I ordered.

"The police are coming," Danny said as he hung up the phone and came to the door where I was standing. He took me back to the living room by the arm, opened his arms, and hugged me tight.

He whispered in my ear just as he had in the life we lived before, "I am so sorry."

For a moment, my heart softened. This was the Danny I loved so passionately. I hadn't been a fool. The lost soul was found. Touched by his tenderness, I cried inconsolably, and he held me. I would forgive him. He was sorry. The reality of the past ignited my anger as fast as his words had melted my heart. He had hurt me enough. I stepped back, consumed with resurrected fury. This was not the first robber he had drawn into my life.

"Sorry? Do you even know sorry? Sorry for what?" I asked.

"Sorry I couldn't protect you," he said with regret and gentleness.

"Protect me? Like you protected me in our marriage from that other robber? Don't worry," I said, "this robbery was nothing compared to what you and our so-called friend took from me. That man only wanted to rob me of my money. You both robbed me of everything of true value—my trust, my heart, my soul."

I slumped down amid the scattered contents of my worn-out purse. Slowly, I swept my arms wide to retrieve and return each thing back into the disorder that was my life, checking for the forty dollars in the secret zipper. What had I done to Light? How could I gather in my arms the scattered pieces of my own self, my little Zhen'er, my school child, Qin, my Teacher Zhao? I couldn't call on childish things like an Empress or Mulan; they existed only in the fairy tales of the past. I needed someone who could truly help me, someone strong, someone who could take them all in safe arms and rock them, take them where they needed to go, make them what they needed to be, bring the lost and aching pieces of myself to live together once again.

Through all the pain, through all the disappointment, there was still Margaret. Rocking my selves together, wrapped tightly in my own arms, I turned to the one person I had left to turn to, my Margaret, my American self. The last item on the floor was a small red journal that I had bought to track new vocabulary words I had learned. I needed it for something else far more important. I detached the little pen, opened to a clean white page, and listed the gifts that I would give to each of them when I rose:

1. For Light, the safety of our own home, no robbers, no roaches
2. For Zhen'er, a return to China to put her arms around Mother
3. For Hong Qin, to learn to laugh again
4. For Teacher Zhao, to be my brand again

I would start with goal number one. With Danny in his own apartment and my new checkbook in my hands, I took over my own family business—I was my mother's daughter. I saved every dollar I earned that was not needed for only the most basic of things. Slowly, I dragged through my depression and discouragement to work every day. The numbers rose in the account. Within a year of working at UCI, with my extra jobs and with the help of a dear friend who understood real estate, I managed to save enough to make a down payment on a home.

I quaked at the idea of a mortgage, but that was the way in America, my friend assured me. He insisted that I could never have afforded a home without some debt. I could not tolerate the thought of being a borrower, but the idea of the down payment and the concept of the asset gave me the confidence to sign the long and incomprehensible papers. Goal number one was checked—safe neighborhood, nice house, and I was an American homeowner with a house that no one had the right to take away by changing a rule or changing my class. I ran from room to room, spinning with wide arms. I thanked my Margaret; I thanked my new home country.

The second goal had a yin and yang to it for certain. I had left China, sneaking out to prevent the spread of shame upon my family. To be honest, I am sure I was afraid that they would try to talk some sense into my impassioned heart. Without anyone knowing except Sister Double Happiness, with whom I stayed before our escape, I had slid out of the government-imposed life I had known and into a mystery of my own making. Only false letters about my happiness and progress to Mother and my sisters and brothers preceded my return to China after six years in America.

My health was failing. Severe back pain, fatigue, and painful carpal tunnel from my jobs plagued me. Emotionally I was spent, deflated. Yet when I went to doctors for help, they saw nothing in the many tests to explain my condition. It took me one full year more to save the fare to fulfill my promise to my little Zhen'er. I decided Light and I would visit China. I went to the airport to buy the ticket and stopped to place a checkmark next to goal number two: For Zhen'er, to put her arms around Mother, once again.

CHAPTER 26
CHANGING AURAS

In May 1996, China saw me return for the first time. Along with a huge amount of luggage, I took with me my very westernized thirteen-year-old daughter, an aching body, and a burdened heart. We arrived at Shanghai and took another flight to Wuhan. My twin nephews and their older brother, Vigor, met us at the airport. I was surprised to see they had become young adults already. The twins didn't wear matching clothes anymore. One of them was dressed very nicely in a suit and tie, standing up straight and tall, full of confidence. I was pleased and impressed. The other twin was quite the opposite, dressed in casual and ordinary clothing. I was curious about the contrast.

I took the casual one to the side and asked, "Why didn't you dress up better like your brother?"

"Who would carry your luggage, then?" he joked. I laughed, feeling that all of my early babysitting years had paid off.

My oldest nephew, Vigor, a young, successful businessman, drove us home in his new car. He pulled out into the traffic with my daughter, his twin brothers, a trunk full of luggage, and me crammed into the vehicle. So much had changed. The buildings were taller, and the streets were hectic, overflowing with cars. It was as if a million mice had been let loose all at once on the road, scattering, squealing, colliding on their way to any hole they could find. Bikes and cars competed for the narrow lanes, and the horns blared in a cacophony of craziness. Traditional bikers, balancing families and furniture alike, fought to maintain their rightful place on the road.

I followed each of my nephew's maneuvers with a string of commentary: "Oops, look out, slow down, will you look at that guy, stay left, look out for the guy behind you; he is tailgating," I said, all the while slamming the imaginary brake down on my passenger side of the car.

"Yao Yao," he said, addressing me as his youngest aunt, "relax, you are acting like an Ocean Devil," he said as a car pulled into our lane and headed right for us.

"Don't you see that car coming right toward us?"

"Don't you think he can see us?" Vigor answered, smiling.

Then I stopped. It seemed I had heard that very exchange before—yes, from my DMV inspector, the second one I had on my continued attempts at passing my driver's test.

"Look out!" I continued my litany, and my nephews smiled, undisturbed by neither my rants nor the crazy drivers on the road.

English signs were everywhere. I couldn't absorb it all. The familiar landmarks were buried in a million advertisements. My nephew veered off toward Sister Double's house, and suddenly I gasped. Despite the modern changes, the dialect and the lovely way the early sun lit the skies felt so endearing to me. I had finally made it back. It had been so long. The mixture of the excitement and the sentiment of the homecoming brought tears to my eyes.

Sister Double Happiness was happy to receive me. She had retired from her regular teaching job and over the years had become a highly respected Master teacher of the ancient healing arts called Qigong, from "Chi Kung Kungfu," the natural healing energy.

Mother was living with Sister Enough. As soon as I walked through Sister Double Happiness's door, I ran to telephone her. Concealing my excitement, I asked, "DaDa, do you know what date I am arriving?" She said she had heard the exciting news and was counting the days until my arrival.

"Where do you think I am now, DaDa?"

"You are in America. I can even hear the ocean," she said.

"Yes, but I am so sorry I cannot come home. I couldn't get permission to leave work."

There was a long pause.

"Of course, yes, no permission." This, she understood.

"Ha ha," I laughed, open-mouthed, "I am in Wuhan, in Sister's house right now, DaDa!" I surprised her as I had done back in my childhood days, and she laughed.

"You have not changed one hair on your head. You are still full of mischief," she said.

"Of course, DaDa, I am still your daughter," I answered.

Henry and his new wife were among the relatives who came to Sister Double's house to welcome us.

"Light, look who is here!"

"Yes, it's BaBa." She stepped forward, they both hesitated, and they hugged. It was an emotional moment for me to return the little chick that I had taken from the nest. I felt an overwhelming need to cry, but crying would unleash a thousand apologies and a deep well of guilt. I felt the familiar restriction of my own culture, freeing in some ways but at the same time so distancing, so unsatisfying.

I was relieved that the reunion went so well. Henry and his wife took Light to stay with them in their home. I knew this experience could be every bit as difficult for her as the adjustment we had faced when we arrived in America six years before. I feared she would resent me if she discovered the details of my departure from her father. I wondered if I would receive my well-earned punishment from this child whom I adored when she returned from her stay with Henry.

真

The long ride in the airplane exhausted me, and I developed a severe sore throat. With many words to say and much emotion to share, my throat was failing me. The herbal pills gave no relief, and my voice went from speaking with a low voice to a harsh voice to no voice at all. Sister Double Happiness brought me upstairs with my niece Ya Tou, "Girly," daughter of Sister Complete Happiness.

"Will you heal YaoYao's sore throat with Qigong?" she asked Girly. Girly was a college student and had learned Qigong under the guidance of Sister Double Happiness up to the third level, a very impressive level for such a young girl. I knew little of the ancient arts myself. I was a little puzzled that Sister, as a Master, wouldn't have given me the treatment, herself.

I had no voice to raise questions but sat still as required with my eyes closed. Soon I felt a breezy coolness penetrating my throat. The fire that was burning there started to recede. Within a few minutes, I opened my eyes, and incredibly, I was able to swallow without much difficulty. By the time I walked downstairs to rejoin the waiting crowd, I was able to speak and laugh out loud. Amazingly, my sore throat was already healed with no western medicine, no Chinese herbs, just the healing energy. Sister Double had put me in good hands and had opened my eyes to the possibility of learning this skill. I felt a pressing need to understand this miracle.

"Would you teach me everything you know about Qigong, Sister?" I asked.

I was so eager to learn; the unteachable one was always yearning. Sister Double Happiness had no idea that I still clung to this hurtful label she had once bestowed on me. After hinting at the unteachable incident from my childhood, I was certain that she had no recollection at all of having even said the word that had driven so deeply into my heart.

While Light happily spent time with her father, Sister Double took me to her Qigong school and brought all the textbooks for me. I registered as a formal student. I wanted to be taken as seriously as her other trainees. To accelerate my learning, she provided me with intensive private training. She was my respected Master, and I was willingly her humble disciple.

Sister Double Happiness decided to accompany Light and me to visit Mother. She continued my training along the way on the long-distance bus ride to Sister Enough's home where Mother lived. During the entire journey, she shared her knowledge. Fascinated, embracing learning once again, I drew it into me like clean, fresh air.

Hours into our trip, Sister shared the sad news that Uncle Lao Kong had passed away. He died, as Father had, with little dignity or comfort. I was so saddened. I had not made the connection until that moment when a memory reached inside me and found my promise to my Uncle. His parting words returned: "Promise you will learn Qigong someday, little Zhen," he had said. I smiled. I was finally keeping my promise to the man, the Ogre who inspired me so much, the quiet man who taught me the lesson of soft that I was about to learn in a deeper way to honor his memory. I stared out of the bus window, caught up in the beautiful harshness of life, the seeds planted, the hints from above that had been whispered in my young ears, both whispered and shouted from the mouths of my lovely Ogres.

"We must return with the family to visit Mother's sister while I am here, to honor Uncle Lao Kong," I said to Sister Double.

"Mother would love to see her sister Abundance again. Yes, we shall," Sister Double said, not knowing my powerful history with our uncle.

"And Father's grave, too. I cannot leave China without honoring him, as well," I said.

"Of course, of course, we will," she agreed.

After seven hours, we arrived. Sister Enough and her husband had moved out of the brick-factory residences and had bought an apartment in the same city where Sister Double Happiness had once taught and where I had taken the college entrance examination. Many memories of both oppression and elation lived within that city for me.

As soon as my entourage heralded my arrival, two large rounds of fireworks exploded loudly. All the peddlers quickly moved their tables and tents to avoid the colorful explosions. Children and neighbors all stopped to enjoy the unexpected treat, not knowing the reason for the celebration. They were buzzing, asking each other, "What do you know about this?" "What is the occasion?" "Must be a wedding," one woman said with confidence, "or the birth of a precious newborn." "Perhaps an honor for someone who died?" another guessed.

Sister Enough's husband was in charge of the fireworks. They asked him, "Brother, what sparks the celebration?"

"My sister-in-law has come back from America to visit."

The word spread through the crowd, and I could hear people talking.

"Aiyaa! The Yang Gui-zi, Sister Ocean Devil has come home."

When I came into the center of the crowd, they spotted me and pointed. I smiled, nodded, held my breath, and ran through the sparks and smoke parting the crowd, which caused much laughter among the people. I took the stairs two at a time up to the sixth floor where Mother was waiting for me. I dropped everything that I had in my hands at the door and encircled her in my arms. Our hearts beating together again, I kissed her L.A. style on both cheeks to the surprised looks of my reserved family. It was a rare moment to touch the woman who had saved me, taught me, and loved me totally with so little touching, loved me with so few loving words but with such powerful strength. She smiled and enjoyed it. I knew she would. A woman who fought for equal rights for her daughters could surely enjoy a little difference, I thought. She was different; she was DaDa.

I was so happy, and I felt so guilty. A daughter's duty was to take care of her aging parents, not to leave them behind. I owed Mother everything. She held back her tears, saving them only for sadness; I did the same. We were together again. Mother looked me up and down, and I consciously straightened my back to bring a smile to her face, but she was captivated by what had become my ever-present long earrings, and she smiled as she gently ran them through her fingers.

"You have been well in the other country." It was a statement, not a question.

I wished to pour out all the bitter water from my pot: my failed marriage, the heavy debt I had nearly sacrificed my health and life to pay for, the threat to my life at gunpoint, and the insanity of all of the horrors that I harbored in my mind and body. "Yes, I have been very well, DaDa," I said. For Mother, that was the only answer that I knew she wished to hear. I had been well.

"How long can you stay?" Mother asked. She was already worried about me leaving, and I had just arrived. All of my siblings surrounded her, the center of our universe.

Light had forgotten almost all of her Chinese. I had to translate everything for her so that she would know who was who and what was happening. I introduced her to my siblings. "This is Uncle Complete and Uncle Double and Uncle Enough and Uncle Repeat and Uncle Ox." I did not try to explain why my sisters were called by the honorable title, "Uncle." Mother's determined desire to bring equality and power to her daughters was a long story and one we always found difficult to explain to our neighbors and friends, let alone to my American daughter.

More than twenty people from three generations celebrated for many days at our reunion. Sister Enough was in charge of cooking and housing us all. Some were sleeping in beds, some on the floor, and some were hanging on the wall, as we liked to joke. Each night the magic happened. The family listened to my tales of America and watched my elegant chopsticks touch my lips with admiration as I ate my yellow egg atop my snow-white rice.

Every day, early in the morning, Sister Double Happiness would take me to the top of the building to practice Qigong. She brought her books and teaching materials. Taking her teaching seriously, she was strict with no leniency for her sister, for which I was grateful. I sat still with my hands on my knees in the required respectful position. The Master teacher explained Qi, the natural energy force of the universe. I learned that everything is made up of energy and therefore, the energy exists both inside and outside of our bodies. She demonstrated how to see the external Qi by quiet observation of the relaxed fingers of our hands against the darkness of our colored pants. Slowly, I moved my fingers back and forth with patience, and in time I began to see that every finger has a glow of white light around it. When I first saw this aura of energy emanating from my fingertips, I was astounded and excited.

I continued practicing, observing the energy around me. I focused on my sister, and I could see the light, the aura of energy around her head. This time the energy was a crown, a colored version of the white light that I saw flashing around my fingers—yellow, green, purple, red, and blue, a rainbow encasing her head and shoulders. I couldn't speak. I had to take some time to process the experience. I hesitantly told Sister of the energy I saw surrounding her.

"Do *I* have an aura?" I asked her.

"Yes, of course, everyone is energy. Everyone has an aura."

"Can you see my aura, Sister?" I was afraid of the answer. I feared she would see the hidden pain behind my well-concealed damaged heart and soul. I was afraid that she would see through my darkness and corner me into revealing my shame.

She continued the lesson.

"When a person is healthy, one has a bright white aura of energy. When someone is sick or stressed, the illumination is weak and grey, muted and colorless. As you practice Qigong, you will develop a more colorful aura from the more powerful Qi you invite into your body," she said, avoiding my question.

I had to know, despite my fear of inviting the exposure of my current state of mind and body. "Tell me what my aura is like," I said.

Sister looked at me with saddened eyes and hesitated. "I am sorry. It is gray. Why is it weak, Sister? What has happened to you these past years in America?" she asked.

I did not answer.

"Let me help you," she said.

While I was still sitting in the respectful position, she put her hands on top of my head, and I immediately felt the most unique sensation I had ever experienced, far exceeding the feeling I had when Danny put my cold hand in his warm pocket. It felt like a warm spring flushing through me, a joyful exhilaration hydrating me, calming me, soothing me, filling me up.

For weeks, she taught me the theory of Qigong, and she let me feel her commanding power of Qi, the vital force from her hands. To my amazement, she stood behind me, rocking me on my feet without touching me. I was nearly knocked over by the gushing Qi she directed toward me. I was fascinated. I mastered the theory, the movements, the acupressure points, the meditations, the recharging of Qi, and the natural energy healing techniques. She gave me the knowledge to heal myself and to guide others to heal. With our intensive round-the-clock study, I immersed myself and earned the rank of a fourth level of the Master Teacher of Qigong. Sister Double Happiness also taught me many secrets that only the highest ranked Master teachers possessed.

The month passed by quickly, and my metamorphosis from arrival to departure was beyond my understanding. At the end of our time together, Sister Double Happiness, my Master teacher, said the words that freed me: "You are quite the teachable one, Hong Qin." I caught my breath at her words. "You have learned well in the short time we have had together. I am proud of you. You have our ancestors' passion, a natural scholar."

"Can you tell me something?" I asked.

"I have taught you everything I know. What is it?" she asked.

"Can you tell me what you see…I mean, my energy?"

"Colors, only colors, surrounding you," she said.

When Light returned from staying with her father, I was relieved to see that she had enjoyed her time with him.

"Mom, he is so nice," she said, "and we both love poetry and history, and we both like to read. He's the most handsome Chinese man I have ever seen…and of course, I look like him, don't you think?" She held her joke behind her lips for a few seconds, and then we laughed together, just as Mother and I had always done.

"A funny thing happened when I was alone with my stepmother, when Baba wasn't there to translate," she said.

"What happened?" I asked.

"I woke up one morning, and she started pointing to my pajamas, like she wanted me to take them off. I thought she wanted to do the laundry or something. She could see I was confused, so she got two cucumbers and signaled something else with the cucumbers. I thought maybe she wanted me to eat them for breakfast, but then she pointed them toward the door like she was going to toss them out."

"So, what was she trying to say?" I asked, laughing.

"I had no clue. She just kept pointing to the door and the cucumbers and chattering in Chinese and pointing to each of us. I finally figured out she wanted me to get dressed to take me out to breakfast and the market."

"That brings me back to when we first arrived in L.A. There were so many funny things that happened to us before our English was better," I said. We laughed together. I could see she had no problem loving Henry as her father and Danny as her dad.

I was so grateful to be able to bid farewell properly to everyone on that second departure. I gave Mother one more embrace and whispered in her ear, "You come to see me in America, OK? I live in the city, just like you wished for me—a world-famous city."

She smiled.

CHAPTER 27
ASCENDING THE GLORIOUS STAIRS

I returned from my visit to China reinvigorated and revitalized. I had been given precious gifts—good health, a healed soul, and the perhaps the key to the final two goals on my list. I opened my red journal and read my two remaining goals—number three: *For Hong Qin, to learn to laugh again*, and number four: *For Teacher Zhao, to be my brand again.*

Danny was so helpful with Light, coordinating work, school, and child-care schedules with me. He was such a good father. In my new enlightenment about myself, I understood that it was my culture shock and the harshness of my past that drove me and had transformed me into someone he did not recognize. I was not the person he fantasized me to be. He could not have known the full me, having missed so much of the show, only coming in at the very end, the romantic ending, the carefree teacher at the university, full of laughter, self-confidence, and love. I could not have known how hard it would be to fully understand love and life with a man in another culture. I knew too much about hard, relentless work as the path to survival and too little about play. We had been swallowed up by a perfect storm of roses and regrets. I forgave him; I forgave myself.

My experience with Qigong and my own healing was something so life changing. My luggage was full of Qigong books and cassette tapes of the Grand Master's voice leading guided meditations, sharing messages of energy, and teaching self-healing and the methods for helping others to heal. The books, recordings, and meridian and acupressure point charts were my treasures. My passion to embrace more knowledge grew, and I continued to study on my own.

I returned to my job at UCI the day after I came back from China. My head was still swimming with jet lag, but my heart was singing. There were no remnants of my carpel tunnel syndrome as I resumed my stack of backed-up tasks that had always caused the pain. My back pain was no longer there. Amazing!

The healing skill I had learned from my Master, Sister Double Happiness, was compelling. It was burning inside me; I had to share it. I knew as hard as it was for me at first to believe in the natural healing powers of Qi coming from old China, in young America it would be even harder to believe because it was still virtually unheard of.

I began explaining my own wonderful results to anyone who would listen. Some were fascinated and interested; most people said it was strange and weird. "New age" and "flaky" were words I often heard. I began to use humor to lighten the subject, to take down the barriers, to make it less threatening. I poked fun at the serious subject, and the doors began to open. I was in California, where acceptance of things outside the norm comes more easily than it does in other places. I simply waited for my invitation to help someone, knowing that with patience it would come.

My first candidate was one of my co-workers who had severe right shoulder pain for which she had to receive injections every six months.

"What do you have to lose if you let me give you a Qi healing?" I asked, having watched her suffer for years. She was open-minded, and I worked on her during our breaks. It was my passion and my joy. I didn't really know if it would work for the modern American with little understanding of such ancient things, but it worked. She told me a few months later that she was still pain-free. I was thrilled.

I would grab anyone who would let me practice. I pressed their hands or arms to show them where the headache points, back-pain points, or neck-pain pressure points were. It was so much fun for me to see how everyone felt the difference after I applied simple acupressure. Soon I was known for my skill. Even a doctor in the pain clinic asked if I could show his patient how to help himself with the acupressure points for his constant migraines.

One day, while I was taking a break, my new boss called me into her office. She told me to close the door. My heart sank. From the pained look on her face, either I did something very wrong or I was going to be fired. I had been there before in other jobs, but I had worked so hard at that job for years. As soon as I closed the door, she lowered her head into her hands. Elbows propped on her desk, she prepared to give me the bad news. I knew I was in big trouble.

Instead, she said, "I have such a massive headache right now. Could you help me?" I let out a cleansing breath and laughed.

"Of course," I said. It was such an honor to relieve the pain for her. She was grateful, I was grateful, and I was hooked.

The next year, I sponsored Mother and Sister Double Happiness to come to the United States. I was so excited to have Mother with me again. I knew that her presence would bring even more laughter back into my life. Having Sister Double Happiness live in my home would also restore our balance. I owed her my gratitude; she had shown me the path back to my health and myself.

I had one specific goal in mind. When Mother's jet lag settled, we went out to a Chinese restaurant. We climbed the stairs to the top level and were seated in the window at a table with the whitest linens. The tall menu was presented, and I said the words I had wanted to say to Mother since our special trip to Sand City when I was a young girl: "Order anything you want, DaDa. Tonight we will do more than just watch," I said.

She ran her hand slowly over the tablecloth as she read the menu. Then I received my gift: her laughter at the thought of it, at the memory of it, at the joy of it all. The three of us ordered three times what we could eat, the number three being such good luck. We groaned with fullness as we walked to my car, the little white boxes with the red dragon designs dangling like happy purses from our grateful hands.

真

"So now you have so many pretty clothes, you can find a nice man," Mother said unexpectedly as she sat on my bed watching me try on every piece of clothing in my closet.

It was a kind of self-soothing, a habit I developed for times when I needed to reconnect with my gratitude. It never failed to change my mood; it never failed to amaze me that I had many sets of clothes. She had hit the target on center. Even after all the time spent apart and the blurring of my Chinese self from years of life in America, she could still read me well. I was overjoyed with my work life but overcome by loss in my personal life. The loss of my marriages still weighed heavily on my spirit.

"I don't buy clothes with that in mind, DaDa," I answered.

"Still, there is no point in wasting them, eh?" she said.

"A soul mate is hard to find." I threw her old quote back in her court. Grabbing a red sweater, I pulled it over my head to hide from the discussion.

"One tree is not a forest; one person is not a family," she persisted.

"DaDa, I have Light to raise, and we *are* a family," I countered from beneath the cashmere cave, reluctant to poke my head out into the fray.

"I am dating, DaDa. I am seeing men."

"That's American English for not married. You are seeing them, but are they seeing you?" she asked, not expecting an answer to her cleverness.

"We Chinese, we don't date, we marry. Then he always sees you," she said.

"You are only thinking the Chinese way," I complained.

"What other way would I be able to think?" she asked. I peeked out to see her smiling.

"Besides, I need to wait until I get Light through college. Light wants to go to some Ivy college," I muffled back.

"All the more you need another tree to grow this ivy," she said.

"In your new country, you are free to try again, and a good man would love to have a beautiful daughter. Light is fine, smart, beautiful like her grandmother," she joked.

"I need to be here for her, save the money, focus," I insisted.

"You will be pushing fifty by the time she graduates, too old to find a man," Mother said.

I thrust my head out. "There will be many men pushing fifty, as well, DaDa. Do you think I am the only one who ages in this universe? America is wonderful, it guarantees equality." We started to laugh. I reached over and slipped a pair of long chain earrings onto her ears to change the conversation. She smiled. I took advantage; I did my redirect.

"What about you? Father is long gone, and Uncle Village's wife has passed away, too, so, your handsome prince is available now. How about you and your soul mate, finally, DaDa? How about you lift your embroidered red veil and look into his longing eyes?" I was certain my teasing would end the discussion.

She looked out far into the distance through the window. "He was not my destiny," she said. We locked eyes for a moment, both in shock at the frankness, the intimacy that was so rare, and then it broke. "And shame on you," she said. "You still remember that? Don't you have better things to occupy your mind, silly thing? He wasn't my destiny or he would be sitting here with us today."

"Then who is your destiny, if not the man who captivated you so?" I asked, trying to keep her in the eye of the conversation. "Who is your secret destiny that you hold in your heart?" I asked, trying to lure her back into the intimacy that I sensed was slipping away.

"My destiny is…you. I am happy and content with all of you, my children, my true Happinesses."

I was touched, moved, silent. Finally, I left the warmth of her statement.

"Then I am happy with Light, too. She is my happiness," I said.

"No, you need to find a man. You can do it. You are so stubborn; you always get what you want. Look," she said, sweeping her arm around at the pile of clothes. She smiled. Then, very hesitantly, she again left the safety and the boundaries of her proper, reserved self.

"You are...so lovable, Zhen'er, so sweet in here." She touched her heart. "For you it should be easy. Now that you have the power of Qi, would it be so bad to use a little for the attraction? That's part of healing, too, right?" She moved her head slowly back and forth and smiled as I watched the dangling earrings swaying. I sat down next to her, mesmerized by the memory on the levee.

"If you can get these impossible things," she flipped the gold chain earrings, "then maybe it's not so hard for you to find a soul mate, eh? You let yourself have that, OK, Zhen Zhen?"

I nodded my head and smiled at her, "OK, DaDa," I agreed.

Sadly, after five months, Mother wanted to return to China. She worried about burdening me should she get sick. She missed her home. It was a place she knew she would be well cared for by her extended family in her old age. I understood that America could be very difficult for the elderly. In May 1998, I saw them off at the L.A. airport.

"DaDa, I am a teacher in the city just like you said," I whispered to her as I hugged her goodbye.

"See, we went to a restaurant and watched the people eat," she teased.

"Yes, but this time we ordered anything we wanted," I answered.

I dropped my car keys and bent over to pick them up, feeling her eyes on me. Smiling, I stood up and straightened my back to dip down to pick them up with great formality and we tittered, hands over our mouths, touching our upper lips—"Hmm hmm hmm." Then we laughed through our tears.

"Remember, your promise, Zhen'er."

"Yes, DaDa, I know. I will find another tree for my forest," I answered.

She walked slowly down the hallway to the plane, twisting her arm to reach back to me. I reached my arm out to her, watching until she was out of sight. Eyes to eyes, no more hiding our hearts, no more laughter, for we knew it would be a long while before we could see each other again.

As Mother aged, it was hard to be so far away, and I realized if I could not be there to serve her as a dutiful and caring daughter, I would at least save the money so that her ending, should she become ill, could be made easier than Father's had been. I could never bear to have that happen again. I could never let my DaDa suffer. My goal was five thousand dollars, which would ensure her good care.

真

Two years later, as I approached my savings goal, I received the shocking call that she had died in her sleep. Suddenly, with no illness, DaDa was gone. I could not absorb the reality of her death. By the time I was able to get my visa and take the two flights to Wuhan, I had missed being by her side, and I had missed the beautiful funeral. The most auspicious day that was appointed for her burial had to be observed.

Sister Complete held the funeral, a role the sons would normally take. She prepared everything, working hard to observe every detail and videotaping the funeral for me. When I arrived, it was the third day, the day on which, by tradition, we would bring Mother the "forgetting soup" to help her to pass on to the other side. According to her wishes, detailed long before her death, she was buried across the river from Sand City.

We walked through bitter rain and wind to carry the "forgetting soup" we had prepared for Mother. It was the coldest time of winter, the time of the Ogres, the time of the accusation meetings, the time of scraping empty pots. When I stood before the rounded fresh mound, I stood in the vastness of the snow-white fields as a child again, and I cried, my frozen fingers, red like carrots, too stiff to wipe away my tears. My small voice was lost in the wind: "If DaDa dies, I want to die, too! I always want to be with DaDa!" The sound of my wishful plea went far out over the foodless fields, but there was no call of the rising phoenix, and no voice of Mother's blew to my ears. I would never hear her call me again, "Zhen'er, Zhen'er!"

I had not been at her side when she left us. The emptiness stretched out before me, and I could not find her in my blinding guilt. I could not reach her. Dazed, I watched my sisters stretch the round of fireworks to encircle the small hill that was my mother. We huddled together against the wind to light the match. The lights flashed and danced around her memory, popping and crackling, and I saw her face lit by the blaze that had taken her precious books. In my deep regret, I reached out over the flames, stretching, reaching, my face melting in despair, my hands fanning the smoke in waves toward my face as if to breathe in the disappearing knowledge from the past.

Then we struggled to light the traditional paper money. Singe, then flame, I watched them burst into rage and then flutter, sending the required ashes of respect to the sky. The wind scattered the red embers, swirling the black bits skyward to honor the woman who had saved us all. She would be forever overlooking the city, finally, forever in the city of her dreams.

She had chosen a special gravesite far from the mass cemetery near her home with few neighbors to be concerned with and plenty of space around her to breathe. I could see the city in the distance where we ate our charred rice, where I first tasted the dream she had for me. I kowtowed and bowed, the biting chill punishing my deserving face. A million burning ashes of paper money, a thousand bows to Mother could never be enough.

I watched the video and found some comfort in the three-day procession of so many neighbors and our entire family with paper flags, paper houses, wreaths, ribbons, and the crying—the wailing that I had never learned to do. Sister Complete, a lifelong woman of the peasant culture, was the only one who could be called on to cry properly in the traditional way on our behalf with wrenching words called out loud, words encased in wails, and tears to show the world our grief. The village would know that Upright Justice was upheld. They would know from the howling tears that she was loved.

When the video was over, I felt some peace invade my soul. I held her photo, and I saw her smile. Perhaps it was her wisdom that made her leave us before I could be there to suffer her ending with her. I was grateful she had not suffered any pain; she had simply willed herself away when it was time. Forever, I would hold my DaDa in my heart, if I could not have held her in my arms.

真

For three years after DaDa's passing, I charged no fee for my healing energy work except the simple reward of helping others in her honor. I felt so grateful because Qigong had been banned in China, so Sister Double could no longer teach. The government had felt the threat of the power of a movement that was forming. But, back in the United States, I was free to teach. I built a dedicated following. I was invited to speak to juveniles at the Santa Ana jail, police officers at the Santa Ana police station, doctors at Kaiser, and on a huge stage with hundreds of people in the audience for a conference. I demonstrated acupressure for instant pain relief in line at the grocery store, on the elevator, for the mailman; I was obsessed with spreading the word about natural healing methods that people could use to improve their health and relieve their stress.

I sat at home with my new red journal, the old one having overflowed with notes and jokes and schedules, and I made a plan to become my brand full-time. I had worked for six years at UC Irvine Medical Center with gratitude and fondness, but I was so drawn to my mission, I had to take flight. It meant the loss of security again from my paycheck and the loss of health insurance. I would be suspended, out on my own, but I had been there before. The unknown path was scary, but I took it. I had been hungry before—of that I had little fear—but never had I been so hungry to teach again as I was at that moment. I gave my notice.

I wasn't alone for long. I soon had many students in my house every week. We practiced Qigong movements in the park, and we did Qigong guided meditation in my living room. The energy of my house was high and harmonious.

Word spread like flowing water, and to my absolute pleasure, I became a welcomed speaker on natural self-healing in Orange County. My Qigong classes were in demand in many nearby cities and churches. To my delight, Santiago Canyon College also discovered my classes. I remembered how disappointed I was when I had failed to get the position to teach at my college in the remote mountains of China. It brought me great satisfaction to be invited to teach at an American college—an impossible dream came true!

Humor and laughter were the keys that opened people's minds to the mysterious subject. I created a Qigong and acupressure curriculum for both the Lincoln Institute and the Macy Institute, two therapy training schools. I also designed and created a program called "Non-Surgical Facelift" based on the potent power of acupressure points and the route of Qi flow to the face through the energy channels called meridians. Everyone wanted to look beautiful and feel younger!

Just as I had hoped, people were studying energy healing, and the scientific basis that was revealed was making it more acceptable. I had the opportunity and honor to know a respected university professor, scientist, researcher, and master of Kung Fu. I admired his devotion to Qigong research. As an American biologist, he enlightened me about the scientific explanation of Qi as light, heat, and electricity. I participated in studies with advanced research equipment in his lab. His equipment was able to record the level of energy, the Qi, with special measurements. It showed the difference before and after the Qigong movements. I so very much appreciated the significance of his pioneering research field of complementary medicine. I am his devoted admirer to this day.

Senior residence communities in Laguna Woods and Seal Beach were my favorite places to share Qigong. The seniors were so open and eager to learn. One of my clients and neighbors became one of the most passionate believers in my work. He voluntarily advocated for my classes everywhere, and they grew, yet again. It was he who arranged the workshops for the Seal Beach senior residential community that still meets every Tuesday led by one of my most brilliant students. There, I made a critical change; I performed my first routine of stand-up comedy at the beginning of the workshop, trying out my timing and punch lines on the crowd of attentive seniors.

On a subsequent day, as I led the familiar group of seniors down the hallway to lead a class, a very elderly male student asked me, "May I ask you a personal question?"

"No," I answered without turning around. The women behind me laughed.

"Why do you say 'no'? You don't even know what I am going to ask." he continued.

"That is why I said no," I quipped.

He chuckled. "OK, may I ask a question about your culture then?" He didn't wait for a response. "I thought Chinese women walked *behind* the man to show respect."

The line of seniors laughed. "Do you walk behind your man to show respect?" he asked me.

My humor went on hold for a moment. I was so painfully aware that I did not have a man to walk behind or in front of, a sensitive issue since my divorce. I had not yet kept my promise to Mother to find another tree for my forest. Everyone was poised for my response.

"Not me. I don't walk behind to show respect," I said, pausing. "I walk behind a man to enjoy the view."

"Ohhh! That's what I get for being naughty. You had me there. Can I ask you another question?" he asked, leaning forward on his cane.

"Sure," I answered.

"Do Chinese women like kissing?" All of the people in line let out an "Ohhh, Edgar!"

"No," I said, "but they like following...."

The entire line stopped to laugh. I so enjoyed seeing the faces light up with Qi before the class had even started.

"You should be at the Improv, you're so funny. Seriously," one of the men said with a wink.

It was meant as a light comment, but I took it as no joke. That night, I asked some friends to show me this kind of improv comedy club, something I had never seen. Two of my friends took me to see the show, and I was fascinated. The next day, with my teacher Li Wen and the circle of chalk in mind, I called the manager.

"I would like to audition for your improv," I said.

"Any experience?" he asked.

"Oh yes, laughter is my specialty. I did comedy in school…ask my mother."

He laughed, and to my delight, he invited me to audition.

真

I stood in the wings waiting in the dark, drowning in the banging cymbals of my own heartbeat. I would just tell the manager a few jokes, and then I could flee. At least he would be the only critic, and I would have the chance to actually stand on a real stage in America.

"Excuse me, what are you doing here?" an official-looking man with headphones asked me.

"I am just here to see the manager, he told me to come at—"

"First-timer, huh? You're not supposed to be here, Miss, please follow me, please. This way, hurry."

The man guided me by my arm through a full house of chattering people, toward the back of the club, past the sound booth and deposited me in a darkened corner by an emergency exit door. Necks twisted and strained. I was sure it was to get a look at the undeserving one who would be thrown from the club without even a chance.

Why was I being fired before I even had a chance to bomb? *I have been fired unfairly before but certainly not so rudely*, I thought.

Seconds later, the man in charge returned. "Your name?"

"Margaret Zhao," I answered hesitantly. Would he announce my demise?

He ran his finger down the list on his flip chart.

"OK, Miss, your lucky day, you're on first," he whispered hoarsely and winked.

"What?" Before I could protest, he placed me in the front of the line of nervous performers.

"Everyone listen up! When your name is called, just walk down the aisle quickly and take the stage like you own it," he said.

I turned to see my fellow victims, a line of shaking dogs waiting behind me along the back wall. A sopping-wet, thin, blond man, lips moving, paced back and forth in the narrow space. A very heavy woman with many sheets of paper murmured to herself. A nearly bald man shuffled a small stack of cards with one hand while relentlessly combing his few strands in greasy rows across his shiny head with the other. Behind them were half a dozen others equally strained, equally strange.

The English I had so arduously studied and practiced for years suddenly evaporated into laments of Chinese self-doubt: "Wo feng la, feng la—crazy me, crazy me!" I murmured out loud. Every word I knew left me like the birds that wisely passed over our family field once they knew we had not the sense to grow a plant or sow a seed.

I hoped my timing was better on this stage than it had been in my life. Suddenly, I was reduced to the odd little girl who created humor to survive in a regimented world, a world in which memories of my grandfather dying of starvation were my bedtime stories. Like a miracle, I stood proudly in a comedy club in Southern California, staring at six-foot-high letters on the stage wall that read "Improv." Improv? I could do improv; I had done it all my life.

The warm-up music triggered a round of applause, and the manager strutted onto the stage.

"Welcome, ladies and gentlemen...." The announcer in the sound booth caught my eye and pointed to the stage, signaling it was my time.

"Oh, God, I am glad I'm not the first one on," the heavy woman behind me said.

I summoned all my bravery and followed the demanding finger of the announcer and walked the long walk to the stage. The beautiful and free illumination lured me like a charmer's snake.

Then the manager stretched out his hand and pointed the mike at me.

"Give a loud round of applause and a warm welcome to Miss Margaret Zhaoooooo," the unseen announcer's voice urged with an echo.

I ascended the glorious stairs. Before I could savor the sweet sound of my name, take in the joy of the applause, or revel in my self-congratulations, *vroom*, the spotlight hit me, and my limbs turned to stone. I suddenly went blind, and I could see nothing except the black space in front of me. All of my confidence as a healing-arts instructor could not help me face that challenge. I sidestepped like a punished monkey to avoid the circle of heat, but it followed me. The blazing lights shot directly through my head, radiating into my body like too much powerful Qi energy short-circuiting me. I made myself small in the middle of the stage. Maybe I, too, could evaporate like the words off my dry tongue.

I shuffled through the inventory of jokes in my mind...nothing. Sounds of impatience came from the darkness. I wanted to tell them that the seniors, everyone, said I was funny. I glared at the mike in disbelief. The microphone was no longer a microphone; it was the gun of the red-banded men pointing at my parents, questioning their Landlord classification...dusty shoes, dirty boots. There was no retreating. I could not let anyone take anything from me again. I had to plunge.

Habit rose up. Adult finger touched childhood scar on my deformed eyelid, and it switched on the remembered chants of my older siblings:

Che yan pi, che yan pi,
Mai ban li, mai ban li.

Pulled eyelid, pulled eyelid,
Selling chestnuts, selling chestnuts.

Sweat poured from my inexperienced hands, and I could feel it slipping, slipping through my shaking fingers. Slow motion, the heavy-headed black stick turned its direction and nose-dived onto the floor. Screeching feedback. The announcer in the booth desperately grasped to tear his headphones off. Bouncing back behind me, the mike let out one more painful bellow.

Shoulders up and covered ears, the entire audience paid for my fear. I turned around to pick up the mike, bending rear end to the audience. Then I stopped, remembering Mother's lesson, "No bending like a peasant in the fields planting rice, your rear end sticking up to the sky. You must be ladylike, back straight, like this." I quickly straightened my back up and dramatically dipped politely to retrieve the escapee, just as she had taught me. They burst into laughter and loud applause, and I came alive.

"Margaret Zhao, ladies and gentlemen!" The announcer compassionately gave me my second chance to start. I recovered.

The audience thought it was my act—my dropping the mike, acting dumb and confused, as if I were lost, and obviously the act was funny to them. The Chinese have a saying: "A new-born calf doesn't know to fear a tiger." I was the newborn calf, and the Irvine Improv was the tiger. Awakened from my stupor by this unexpected response, I was transformed; I became the tiger. I remembered the many long, torturous walks to the school office as a child to be punished for my humor. This audience's reaction was certainly not how my strict teachers felt about my being funny. *Teacher Ni Wen, look at me now! No punishing circle of chalk needed for this stage!*

After a few hard blinks to get my eyes unstuck, I could see some of the audience in the front rows, with their eager eyes fixated on me, anticipating. I tried to balance myself and then staggered to the front edge of the stage.

Another round of laughs.

Even though my mind was still blank, I knew I must open my mouth and utter something. I had to act as if I were totally in control. I had faced much bigger threats in my life. Then I asked a question just like the real deal comedians would.

"Good evening, everybody! Are we having fun yet?" My limbs were shaking as my own disembodied voice echoed back to me, gratefully in English, not Chinese.

The answer was a unified "Yes!"

Maybe I could introduce myself, I thought, to buy time for my elusive jokes to return. I knew it could save me even if it only gave me a few seconds. I held the mike so close to my mouth that the clicks of my nervous teeth were audible in the room. More small giggles came back. I felt the scorching heat from the lights toasting me alive. *I need to survive here*, I thought. I cleared my throat and welcomed good Qi, strong energy, to enter my frightened self.

"My name is Margaret Zhao. I come from China...so, I am, uh...Chinese."

It aroused a loud wave of laughter. The audience once more found my obvious statement of truth to be funny. This was getting easier. I was more encouraged, pretending to look cool, allowing the laughter to last, while my brain frantically computed to avoid another sudden shutdown. I had no idea how much harder this would be than adding humor to my lessons.

"Yes, my name is Margaret...and, uh, I have many other names too..." Ding! Suddenly, a spark reignited my stalled brain cells. A killer joke jumped to the tip of my tongue, which had never failed me in making people laugh.

"One of my other names is The Asian Driver!"

The audience roared. I took off.

"Yes, it's true...what? You don't recognize me? Yes, that was me! You waved to me, American style with the one finger, remember? I like this American way. In China, we use the thumbs to say 'You're number one.'" I raised two thumbs and smiled wide-eyed, gazing into the crowd. "It's hard to do that and drive, too!"

I practiced my timing, pause...then, punch. I had peeled back the shame and spoken the truth. I knew that almost all of them, somewhere, somehow, sometime in their driving life, had fallen victim to an inexperienced Asian driver on the road in the L.A. area. Nobody dared use this nickname in front of our faces, but I could. If they only knew how hard it was to drive in a foreign country. Again, state the truth, get a laugh. They burst into agreement with me, laughing, punching and elbowing each other.

"Thank you, thank you," I acknowledged the audience and continued. "When I drive, I seldom get lost. It's just that I often don't know where I am.... I like to drive slow...."

"No kidding!" a guy's loud remark came from the crowd.

"When the road's marked sixty, I drive forty."

Laughter.

"When it is forty, I drive twenty. When it's marked twenty, I drive like a snail with my emergency lights on. I want to be respectful of the other drivers just to keep them safe."

Big laugh.

"When I come to a stop sign, I park there for a while, just a little rest!"

"Ha ha!" The audience was with me.

"I get confused when others honk at me, so I wave them to pass by me to be polite. When they do pass me, instead of being grateful, they either shoot a dirty look at me, or give me the special finger wave. I smile, to be friendly; I give it back. I know the American ways now!"

A roar of laughter.

"What can I say? There are many crazy American drivers on the road...."

"Ha ha ha ha ha." My repeated thank-yous were buried in their applause and laughter.

"I am doing a lot better at parking my car now," I continued. "I don't have to get out of the car to measure the space any more. I just drive in. I know the space is too small when I bang into the other car."

This killed them.

"Yes, you know driving is a huge luxury for me. I like to get the most out of it. That's why I go slowly. I want to savor it...Everything in America is a luxury...precious to me... I was a starving child in China. You remember me? Your mother told you about me when you didn't want to eat your vegetables. Yes, that was me, and look, the food you told your mother to send me...it worked!" I turned around to show my ample figure.

Roar.

Were my four minutes up? I turned red like a pomegranate. Had I broken any rules? Comedy had rules. Stand-up should be line…. line…. buh dum bum, punch line. Had I broken the pattern? I knew I should not tell long stories. I hoped this would not be my first and last performance. I crept off the stage. I was no longer an Enemy of the State, but was I an enemy of the stage?

No. The audience loved me…they told me as they reached toward me to shake my hand. "You are a riot!" Tiananmen Square came into my mind, the riot, the shots, the violence, 1989, the year I came to America…but this kind of riot I was happy to start. I knew it meant the start of something very good.

The Improv manager was pleased with me, too; he told me I could be "a regular."

"A regular?" I had never been a regular in anything. Yes, I was the little strange one who made jokes, the foolish girl who dared to question, the child with the drooping eyelid, the late-to-learn adult in a young student's classroom, the one who followed a foreigner far from home—but never a regular, never a fit.

I learned that "a regular" meant I was invited to perform regularly at their Tuesday open-mike night. It was a big deal for this new calf, this new first-time amateur. In my naïve sense of America and my belief in all of the possibilities and freedom it offered, I thought I had received a pass to enter the gates of Hollywood. I was so thrilled! I was funny! I made people laugh!

CHAPTER 28
THE DANGLING EARRINGS

I stepped into the spotlight with a feigned posture of awkwardness and fear. Honestly, any fear that still lingered from my first stage experience many weeks before melted in the familiar faces of the people who had shown up to hear me again. Word had spread, and the place was full. I had a following.

The heat of the glowing light hit me, and I instantly hatched in its warmth. This was where I was meant to be. This is where I could breathe, sharing my past and making them laugh with wide-mouthed heads tossed back, releasing their worries to the sky. This was my gift to myself, to finally step into the circle of chalk to the applause of the people. This was my red scarf. This was where I was my mother's daughter; this was my America.

"You know, it's sad," I began. They had no idea how sad, but I had truly learned the lesson in the old saying that tragedy plus time equals comedy.

"I was born in the wrong place at the wrong time," I continued. I heard the sympathetic "uh huhs" followed by silence. Everybody was listening intensely, wondering why.

"In old China, having children was considered good fortune and happiness. Naming kids was a big deal reflecting the hopes, ambitions, and status of the family. When their first child was born, my parents named her Double Happiness, even though with regret, it was a girl."

I heard laughs and "aaaawwwws."

"Soon after that, the second child was born, a son, too. He got the name Repeat Happiness, much better, our first little heir; my mother could relax."

Little ripples, one "Ha."

"Birth control wasn't in existence then. Before my parents knew it, there were too many mouths to feed. Communists had taken everything. The rich became poor quickly, like your instant coffee. Measures had to be taken. When the fourth child was born, she was given the name Complete Happiness, which meant the happiness of having children was complete. Hinting to the gods above didn't work—a fifth child was born. 'Did you not get the message?' my mother cried to the sky." I looked heavenward pleading, for effect. Then, I waited like the comedians I had studied so carefully; I worked the timing.

"So she got the name Enough Complete Happiness." Lots of laughter, and I added quickly as an aside, "Obviously, Enough wasn't enough as they had wished, since I came along, unexpectedly. So, I got the name *Really* Enough Complete Happiness!"

The audience turned from curious concentration, while listening to the sequence of names, to explosive laughter when they realized how each of the additional children got their special name. My words were muffled in the silk of their applause.

"Are you getting this down?" I pointed to a man who was writing on his cocktail napkin and handing it to a girl next to him.

He laughed, "Got it! *Really* Enough Complete Happiness," he called out.

"So, now you know all about Chinese birth control, but sometimes it worked, really it did! Just not, let's see? One billion, two hundred twenty-six million, four hundred and sixty thousand times, oh sorry, four hundred sixty thousand and thirty-four times—oops, wrong, four hundred and sixty thousand and sixty-eight times," I said, out of breath. "I have to hurry to finish my joke because thirty-four children are born in China every second. Now, that's a loooot of *really, really* enough complete happiness!"

The voice of the announcer broke through the crowd's laughter and hoots. "Margaret Zhao, everybody, give her another round of applause!"

They did willingly. I was finally my own bird landing, a comic standing.

真

I didn't have just one Tuesday, or two Tuesdays like I had when I arrived in America, but *every* Tuesday to make people laugh and to complete another pledge to myself—my promise number three to Hong Qin. I made her laugh again, and I made an entire room full of people laugh along with her with no punishment.

My Campaign of the Four Promises was a success; I checked off each one in my book.

1. For Light, our own home, no robbers, no roaches—*Check!*
2. For Zhen'er, to put her arms around Mother—*Check!*
3. For Hong Qin, to learn to laugh again—*Check!*
4. For Teacher Zhao, to be my brand again—*Check!*

I had done many things in my lifetime, but more than anything I have always valued being these two most important things: the daughter of my Chinese DaDa and the mother of my beautiful American daughter, Light. What my mother gave to me, I hoped to give to my sweet daughter, who had survived it all along with me. I knew, watching her use her brilliant little mind to do her homework under the limitless light above, that she would far exceed Mother's dreams for me. She would rise up in a country where her chosen path was in her own hands, where her dreams were in her reach.

I sat alone on Newport Beach with my feet tucked in the warm sand, a perfect place to compose. I had to focus on my routine for the next Tuesday. I opened my treasured little red book with the sayings of Margaret Zhao. Tucked inside was an unopened letter and my bookmark, the photo of my DaDa and me that was taken the last time I had seen her. I overlaid my grief with her love, touching her smiling face. It was impossible—Mother and me living together in the land of Ocean Devils.

Running my fingers from my earlobe down the long chain of gold to my shoulder, I struggled to disengage my mind from the delicate moment shared with DaDa. The memory of her brushing whining mosquitoes from my face on that long-ago steamy night lingered. I remembered my fascination with the way the moonlight danced on Mother's face and the rare and profound moment spent alone with her that I did not want to end. For all the stories she told me when she hid me from the brigade and the fate of the commune fields, it was the only time I remembered my DaDa allowing herself to be vulnerable, alluding to her fortunate past. It had soaked through my thin, patched shirt, deep into my heart and gave me the hope that had brought me to this place. If it was the only gift she had to give me, it was enough to dream of a someday pair of dangling earrings to inspire a girl who had so little vision of her fate. For those few moments suspended high above the rawness of our daily lives, I would give all the golden earrings in the world to feel the tenderness of that one exchange again— shared with the survivor, the tigress, who was my mother.

Her words stayed to keep an ache in my heart, and I picked up my pen to find some humor in my pain. She was gone, so I hummed her little song to which I knew no lyrics to draw me to her side. I had kept all but one promise to Mother. She understood that the loss of love weighed on my heart. I could not give up on my hope for true love, to find a man who could love all of me, my 'Zhen,' my 'Hong Qin,' my 'Teacher Zhao,' my 'Margaret,' and give each of them a red, red rose. I cannot say I have the understanding of my soft after all my suffering and mistakes, but I had used up all my hard. I was soft, only soft. I ached to love and be loved and to add another tree to the forest of my life.

If I were to keep this promise to Mother, I had to hope. It was always hope that mattered—the hope you give yourself and the hope you give to others. I rocked and cradled the memory of the hope that I had returned to Mother as she stirred my stolen vegetables in the boiling water feigning anger with her hidden secret smile about to erupt. It was my only childhood memory of the pot being full. I thanked her for the hope she had given to me a hundred thousand times in my own travels from unbearable low to unimaginable high. Like Mother, I had known the taking of my rightful place many times too many in my years, but I still had hope.

"Maybe it's not so hard for you to find a soul mate, eh? You let yourself have that, OK, Zhen Zhen?" Mother's words returned. I nodded my head to honor her memory and smiled. "OK, I promise, DaDa," I whispered. I would use my Qi and an open heart to draw the love to me that I had always sought. I would use the power of my soft; I would have my brand, my love, and myself—all three.

With no need for any scarf to feel my worthiness, I sent a message to my Ogres, who had given me the powerful nudge I needed to push my cart over the many bumps that stood between my brand and me. I stood up straight, and I saluted. Taking a deep breath, I let go as I had seen Uncle Lao Kong do many times, and I opened the letter. I was invited to teach my Chinese healing arts at a conference of American doctors. Me, teaching healing to a hall full of brilliant, white-coated American doctors? "Wo feng le—am I crazy?" It is like reaching for a star—you will burn your hand, I was once warned. I remembered Mother's lesson: "If you reach for nothing, all you get is air." Yes, maybe I would just do it. Healing? I could do healing. I had done it all my life.

With the foul scent of burning books in my memory, my body vibrated with the names of my ancestors. They moved through me, flowing like Qi energy. In honor of the scholars whose blood was in mine, I would teach. I would not stop until I fulfilled my dreams—until I reached my own name, Really Enough Complete Happiness.

The ancient wisdom of Lao Tzu shared by the Ogres around the lantern filled my mind: "Way, no ordinary way," Rightist Bu had translated the profound words. "We are all on an extraordinary journey." The lessons lived on in my heart. Hidden in our

AUTHOR BIOGRAPHY

Kathleen L. Martens

Kathleen Langmaack Martens is a San Francisco Bay Area-based author and former "Jersey Girl" with a lifetime passion for writing and intercultural communications. After attending the Foreign Service Language Institute for one year where she studied intensive Thai Language and Southeast Asian Area Studies, she moved to Thailand and began her consulting career. While living and working in Southeast Asia as an intercultural consultant and trainer in Bangkok, Thailand and Jakarta, Indonesia, she helped employees of major US corporations adjust to life working in remote areas of the world. Traveling to China as one of the early tourists admitted to the country, she took in the sights and sounds of a commune that would later become a foundation for writing *Really Enough: A True Story of Tyranny, Courage and Comedy* with Margaret Zhao.

At a social event in 2010, Margaret Zhao shared stories of her early childhood in rural China under the tyranny of Chairman Mao. Martens took an instant interest in her fascinating past. This chance meeting led to their collaboration on Zhao's memoir. Kathleen has a B.A. in English Literature and Sociology, and an M.A. in Educational Psychology from the University of Connecticut.

AUTHOR BIOGRAPHY

Margaret Q. Zhao

I *have so much more to share with you about my life's journey. If you would like to learn more about what happened to my family and me— and whether or not I ever found that "tree for my forest," please visit www. ReallyEnough.com to join in lively discussions on my blog and to view a fascinating gallery of family and historic photographs.*

Kathleen and I are passionate about using Really Enough *to inspire and connect with our readers. Please join our Reader's Circle on www. ReallyEnough.com and send us a message if your group would like to be considered for a Skype Book Discussion with my co-author and me.*

With gratitude,

Margaret